G000123482

BRADLEY, ROGER P.
THE STANDARD STEAM LOCOMOTIVES
OF BRITISH RAILWAYS

625

30130505134543

0715383841 2 002

THE
STANDARD STEAM
LOCOMOTIVES
OF BRITISH RAILWAYS

Rodger P. Bradley

DAVID & CHARLES
Newton Abbot London North Pomfret (VT)

Contents

Essex County Library

British Library Cataloguing in Publication Data

Bradley, Rodger P.
   The standard steam locomotives of British
Railways.
   1. Locomotives—Great Britain—History—
20th century
   I. Title
   625.2'61'0941   TJ603.4.G7

ISBN 0–7153–8384–1

© Rodger P. Bradley, 1984

All rights reserved. No part of this publication may be
reproduced, stored in a retrieval system, or transmitted,
in any form or by any means, electronic, mechanical,
photocopying, recording or otherwise, without the prior
permission of David & Charles (Publishers) Limited

Photoset by Photo-Graphics, Honiton and printed in
Great Britain by Biddles Ltd, Guildford for David &
Charles (Publishers) Limited Brunel House, Newton
Abbot, Devon

Published in the United States of America by David &
Charles Inc North Pomfret Vermont 05053 USA

625.2610941

EN24621

Introduction &
Acknowledgements

As one who grew up with British Railways and its locomotives, an interest in and enthusiasm for the Standard steam locomotives built from 1951 is quite natural. Considering that they were introduced at a time when simplicity if not austerity was a keyword in locomotive design, their replacement by diesel and electric locomotives of much more complicated and costly arrangement may seem a curious thing. By steam locomotive standards, their life span was undoubtedly brief, and for a number at least, no more than a twinkling of the eye—yet in that short time they had run the gamut from highly successful to abject failure, though perhaps this latter must be seen as tempered more by Regional and operational preferences than from any great lacking in engineering design.

The purpose of this book is to explore these locomotives in detail, both technical and constructional to operational aspects of their history. Overall, their design was soundly based on much traditional practice, differing only in application, and bringing together the ideas of all four main line railways, albeit considerably influenced by LMS thinking in the design team. In the end, a successful compromise was achieved, though the term Standard should perhaps be applied a little loosely, since there were many detail variations between classes, and between locomotives of the same class.

Initially, their reception by both railwaymen and enthusiasts alike was cool, with opinions rapidly polarised into favourable and unfavourable. Much comment in the press compared the outward appearance of the Standards to North American practice— ugly and disfiguring pipework, high running boards, exposed motion, and so on. British tradition would have all these enclosed and less accessible, for appearance sake. A few commentators ventured the opinion that three-cylinder propulsion was likely to be more economical and give better performance than two-cylinder, although this suggestion did not seem to be borne out even by the newer pre-nationalisation designs.

During the course of putting it all together I have been fortunate to have had the help of many people, for which I am grateful. I hope I have done some justice to their efforts. First I must acknowledge the assistance of the late R.A. Riddles whose name will be associated with the design of the Standards. E.S. Cox, and the many other people involved in the design, construction and operation of these locomotives provided immense help and I would particularly like to thank British Rail and Alex Murray, London Midland Region PRO; C.P. Atkins and the National Railway Museum; Messrs A.G. Powell, R. Shenton, D. Hodgson, C.J. Bacon and Jim Walker, Roger France and the Standard 4 Locomotive Preservation Society; Mr Peter Kenyon and 71000 Steam Locomotive Trust Ltd; *Railway Gazette International* and the Institution of Mechanical Engineers (Railway Division), for permission to use certain diagrams, tables and other information; Mr Sidney Weighell, former Secretary of the National Union of Railwaymen; and a number of members of the Historical Model Railway Society, including Messrs Paul Bartlett, Andrew Darby, Terry McCarthy, David Palmer, A.R. Palmer, David Larkin, Don Rowland and P.A. Wilcox.

Lastly I would like to thank my cousin, Lillian, for typing the manuscript, and most of all to my wife, Pat, for her encouragement, and putting up with a little chaos from time to time.

Rodger P. Bradley
Barrow in Furness, Cumbria

1. Standardisation: an Introductory Survey

Standardisation of both whole locomotive designs and individual components may be seen as the single most effective method of reducing the operating costs of the motive power department. In the early years of British Railways it was certainly not a new idea, and of the four main line railway companies that had existed before January 1948, all had pursued this policy to a greater or lesser degree. The variation between companies in their approach to standardisation is implicit in the fact that the nationalised British Railways inherited over 20,000 steam locomotives, of almost 500 different classes. It is interesting, in retrospect, to look at the varying attitudes of the companies up to 1947, contrasting their different approaches.

The LMS and GWR had pursued by far the most stringent standardisation policies, though these were not so effective on the former company until the arrival of W.A. Stanier in the early 1930s. It is important to remember that Stanier was trained at Swindon under the disciplines of G.J. Churchward, so perhaps the development of LMS locomotive design in the 1930s was as much influenced by GWR practice as any originality there was in Stanier's policies. These two companies handed over to British Railways almost 60% of the total locomotive stock, in 183 classes; the LNER and Southern companies amassed nearly 300 classes of locomotive for the remaining 40%. On the Great Western Railway, the trend towards fewer classes of greater numerical strength had been pursued for many years, beginning even before the 1923 Grouping. In 1948 only 73 classes represented the company's stock of over 4,000 steam locomotives, an average of 55 per class. A similar situation existed on the LMS, where nearly 8,000 locomotives were available from only 110 classes, averaging 71 per class. Such bare statistics cannot be accepted as painting an absolute picture; rather they were to illustrate the general trend towards standardisation.

By contrast, the LNER and Southern appeared content with a policy of small classes designed for particular tasks, routes or areas. The Southern Railway had the greatest variety of locomotive types per 1,000 engines, with 87 different designs covering only 2,000 locomotives. The average was only 30 to each class, almost exactly equal to the LNER, where the 6,500 locomotives were divided into no fewer than 206 classes.

Another interesting comparison of existing motive power can be made by looking at the number of new designs introduced between 1923 and 1947. Here only the LNER stands apart, with the placing in service of 80 new classes, though again the number of locomotives per class was small in comparison with other companies. On the LMS and GWR the number of locomotives per type was averaging in excess of 100, and on both railways the new designs provided well over half the operating stock. On the Southern Railway a major influence was undoubtedly the extensive and spreading network of electrified routes. By 1947 only 500 or so locomotives had been constructed, in 18 classes, leaving the majority of steam-hauled workings still in the hands of various pre-grouping designs. Intermediate and stopping passenger services, commuter and short-haul duties were in many cases worked by electric multiple-units (emu), with steam locomotives provided on main line and express passenger workings in all areas. Before the second world war the Schools 4-4-0 and King Arthur 4-6-0 classes were developed for those purposes, while on the non-electrified sections, in particular the Eastern Section, intermediate types were provided in the shape of the Class L1 4-4-0s and Classes U and U1 2-6-0s.

The LMSR on the other hand had embarked on a very ambitious standardisation programme from 1933 onwards, which in the ensuing 14 years resulted in the appearance of 4,511 new locomotives in only 29 classes. On the basis of Stanier's scrap-and-build policy for this company, the objection of discarding completely all the locomotives inherited in 1923 and replacing them with a smaller number of standard designs was almost achieved. This programme provided new designs in virtually every sphere of locomotive operation, from the most powerful Princess Royal and Coronation Class Pacifics to the much less prestigious, workaday, 0-6-0 tanks.

Modernisation on the Great Western Railway had properly begun with the appearance of the Saint Class 4-6-0 in 1902. This design was the product of G.J. Churchward's innovative ideas, despite the fact that it has been attributed to the then locomotive superintendent, William Dean. Churchward's contribution to locomotive design on the GWR and railways generally was considerable, though his most outstanding improvements were concerned with the layout of the steam circuit. The adoption of long-lap travel piston valves as standard Swindon feature was also Churchward policy. Such features as sharply tapered boilers, almost trapezoidal fireboxes, coupled with higher

Table 1 Locomotives Built 1923–1947

Railway	LMS	GWR	LNER	SR
Total classes built	29	20	80	18
Total locomotives built	4511	2286	2663	504
Average locomotives/class	155.6	114.3	33.3	28.0
% of total stock	57.5	56.4	41.3	27.9

Table 2 British Railways Locomotive Stock 1948

Railway	LMS	GWR	LNER	SR	TOTALS
Passenger types	1025	567	682	624	2898
Mixed-traffic types	802	450	777	157	2186
Freight types	3813	396	2800	360	7369
Tank types	2205	2643	2184	666	7697
Total locomotives	7844	4056	6443	1807	20150
% of total stock	38.9	20.1	32.0	9.0	100.0
Total classes	110	73	206	87	476
Pre-grouping classes	81	53	126	69	329

working pressures, were intended to improve water circulation, but came to characterise Swindon design practice, and were perpetuated by Churchward's successor, C.B. Collett. These ideas and principles were transformed into such highly successful locomotives as the Hall and Grange Class 4-6-0s for intermediate duties, with the Castle and King classes for express passenger work. Also during this period, the number of six-coupled tank locomotives for the lesser workings increased, while embodying the same basic characteristics as their larger brethren. As if to complement the staying power of Churchward's ideology, many GWR designs continued to be built after nationalisation.

An interesting comparison of locomotive types built between 1923 and 1947 is shown in Table 1.

Of the LNER's 80 classes introduced in this period, eight were Pacific types, including the original Gresley A1 design (later A10) for the former Great Northern Railway. An interesting feature of the Gresley era was the predominant use of three cylinders, and in the early years at least quite low boiler pressures. The three-cylinder arrangement was employed on almost all classes of locomotive from the express passenger Classes A4 and A3 4-6-2, through those types intended for intermediate duty, such as the V2 2-6-2 and B17 4-6-0, to the 2-6-2T passenger tank Classes V1 and V3.

The complex Gresley/Walschaerts conjugated valve gear proved less efficient in comparison with the GWR Stephenson gear of the 1920s. As a result of the trial of a GWR Castle Class 4-6-0 on the LNER in 1925, the Gresley gear was redesigned to give a longer travel and greater steam lap, along the basic Churchward guidelines. The result of this modification, together with the adoption of higher boiler pressures considerably improved the otherwise sound LNER designs.

All four companies had these basic characteristics in common, though the external appearance differed markedly from one railway to another. On all four lines, too, some of the most interesting and far reaching developments took place during and just after World War II. The trend towards simplicity and improvements in detail were common to all, with the appearance of the Ministry of Supply Austerity locomotives having a pronounced influence on the design and production of the BR Standard types.

Table 2 shows four principal locomotive types, and how they were distributed between the four companies at the time of nationalisation.

Of the four main categories of locomotive, the mixed-traffic types were perhaps the most difficult to define, since one company's 'mixed-traffic' locomotive would be another's 'intermediate passenger'. The question would be even more protracted with tank engines, since there were types intended for passenger, freight and combined passenger/freight designs. Of passenger locomotives in general, locomotives with the 4-4-0 wheel arrangement were still very much in evidence in the late 1940s on the LMS, LNER and Southern railways. This standard British passenger locomotive had its roots in the Victorian era, but was still in widespread use on all but the GWR in the mid-20th Century.

Of the three companies making greatest use of the 4-4-0 for passenger work, only the LMS did not introduce a new design between 1923 and 1947. The Class 2P 4-4-0 and Class 4P 4-4-0 compound were essentially Midland Deeley and Fowler designs. The Class 2P 4-4-0 had a great deal in common with the Southern Railway's L1 Class, with two inside cylinders operated by Stephenson valve gear, though the latter type had a slightly greater tractive effort of 18,910lb. 155 of the compound locomotives were built after the 1923 Grouping, with two outside low-pressure cylinders and the single high-pressure cylinder between the frames, and were the LMS

Table 3 Distribution of 4-4-0 Passenger Locomotives

Railway	LMSR	GWR	LNER	SR
Number of locomotives	635	72	480	353
Number of classes	15	3	24	17
Locomotives/class	42.3	24.0	20.0	20.8
% of passenger stock	62.0	13.0	70.4	56.6
% of total stock	8.1	1.8	7.5	19.5

For many years the 4-4-0 was the principal motive power on passenger duties. The LMS adopted the former Midland Railway compound type in the early years following the grouping of 1923. (*Author's Collection*)

standard express passenger type for a number of years.

Perhaps the earliest instance of standardisation BR style by a combination of various design features was seen in the construction of the Southern Railway Schools Class 4-4-0 in 1930. These locomotives besides being the most powerful 4-4-0 to run in Europe, were basically cut-down and combined versions of the same company's King Arthur and Lord Nelson Class 4-6-0s. The 16½in by 26in cylinders were the same as those fitted to the Lord Nelson Class, while the boiler was a shortened version of that fitted to the King Arthurs.

The LNER in 1927 under H.N. Gresley introduced the three-cylinder Class D49 4-4-0s, to replace older Atlantic type locomotives and prompted by the success of J.G. Robinson's Director design for the Great Central Railway. The only other LNER 4-4-0s brought into use during the inter-war period were the successful rebuilds of the former Great Eastern Railway Claud Hamilton types into the LNER D16/2 and D16/3 Classes.

The Great Western Railway's contribution to the former standard passenger type was also limited, and at nationalisation included two of William Dean's designs, and a third that had been updated by C.B. Collett in 1936. Considering the company's forward-looking design policy the construction of these locomotives at such a late stage was a curious move.

The main trend was increasingly towards the 4-6-0 and Pacific types, of multi-cylinder design with divided drive. The Pacific type found most favour initially on the LNER, with no less than 23% of its passenger stock having this wheel arrangement, while the LMS and GWR preferred the 4-6-0. The GWR was the established leader in this category, 17% of its total motive power being of this design, with the

Castle and King Class locomotives as the company's most powerful express passenger types. The Castle Class first appeared in 1923, immediately after the Grouping: with four 16in by 26in cylinders and a boiler pressure of 225lb/sq in it provided a tractive effort of 31,625lb. Collett's enlargement of the Castle design into the King Class 4-6-0, provided a locomotive that was the equal of later Pacific types for the heaviest Anglo-Scottish expresses of both the LMS and LNER. The Kings provided 40,300lb tractive effort from four 16¼in by 28in cylinders, 6ft 6in coupled wheels and a boiler pressure of 250lb/sq in. The high working pressure of GWR boilers was at that time unusual, since an average on other railways would reveal working pressures of the order of 200lb/sq in or less. Table 4 gives details of the 4-6-0 and 4-6-2 classes belonging to the four main line railways between 1923 and 1947.

On the LNER, the development of the Gresley Pacifics was an ongoing process, while the LMS had taken a large step forward with the appearance of the Stanier 4-6-2s. The LMS locomotives had four cylinders, while the A4 and A3 Classes of the LNER employed the Gresley/Walschaerts conjugated gear and three cylinders. The LMS also had the highly successful North British Locomotive Co/Henry Fowler designed Royal Scot 4-6-0, based on a combination of the design practices embodied in the GWR Castle class, and Maunsell's Lord Nelson 4-6-0 of the Southern Railway. In the intermediate category were the Jubilee and Class 5 4-6-0s, with the addition of a rebuild of the former LNWR 4-6-0 Claughton Class as the Patriots or Baby Scots. This latter involved the provision of new boilers and some structural alterations, but in some cases retained the original LNWR wheels and frames.

Table 4 Distribution of 4-6-0 and 4-6-2 Locomotives

4-6-0 Types

Railway	LMS	GWR	LNER	SR
Number of locomotives	1154	707	593	197
Number of classes	12	9	19	6
Locomotives/class	96.2	78.6	31.2	29.5
% of total stock	14.7	17.4	9.2	9.8

4-6-2 Types

Railway	LMS	GWR	LNER	SR
Number of locomotives	51	—	156	120
Number of classes	2	—	8	3
Locomotives/class	25.5	—	19.5	40.0
% of total stock	0.7	—	2.4	6.6

The King Class 4-6-0s of the GWR incorporated the successful development of Churchward's philosophy in locomotive design by his successor, C.B. Collett. During the inter-war period, Swindon practice had a pronounced influence on other railways. (*Lens of Sutton*)

The LNER during this period developed the B17 Sandringham 4-6-0 which proved very economical with rather short travel valve gear. Compensating for this were large ports and passages to the three 17½in by 26in cylinders, operated by the Gresley conjugated valve gear. With 6ft 8in coupled wheels, a tractive effort of over 25,000lb was exerted. From this, basically, Edward Thompson developed the B1 Class in 1942, as an amalgam of LNER standard components and construction techniques. The coupled wheels were the same size as those fitted to the V2 2-6-2, cylinders from the former GNR K2 2-6-0, while the boiler was very largely that of the B17 Sandringham. A major departure from previous LNER practice was the provision of two 20in diameter outside cylinders operated by conventional Walschaerts valve gear.

The Southern Railway's contribution to passenger locomotive stock of the 4-6-0 type, began in 1926 with the appearance of R.E.L. Maunsell's Lord Nelson Class. The use of four cylinders and divided drive was an undoubted GWR influence, though the front end design was rather different, permitting shorter and more direct steam passages than in the Swindon locomotives. The Lord Nelson class had four 16½in by 26in cylinders, 6ft 7in coupled wheels and a tractive effort of 35,510lb. The King Arthur Class 4-6-0 was the first to have long-lap travel valve gear fitted as standard practice. This locomotive was a direct development of R.W. Urie's N15 Class for the London & South Western Railway in 1918. Two outside cylinders 20½in diameter by 28in stroke, 6ft 7in coupled wheels and a boiler pressure of 200lb/sq in, gave a tractive effort of just over 25,000lb. Both of these classes had their mixed-traffic equivalents in the H15 and S15 Class 4-6-0s, having a reduction in

coupled wheel diameter to 6ft 0in and 5ft 7in respectively.

Freight work was handled on the LMS, LNER and GWR by 2-8-0 and 0-6-0 tender locomotives, with much goods traffic on the Southern by the 0-6-0 types alone. Some duties on the latter were worked by heavy freight tank engines. With the 2-8-0 designs, the GWR again led the way; over 52% of its goods locomotives were of that wheel arrangement. The 28XX Class with 167 examples was the largest single type, designed by Churchward and built from 1903. Two outside 18½in by 30in cylinders operated by Stephenson valve gear drove the 4ft 7½in diameter wheels and achieved a tractive effort of 35,380lb. Of the larger Class 47XX locomotives only nine were built in 1919; with 19in by 30in cylinders, 5ft 8in diameter coupled wheels, they were intended for faster rather than heavier work. Of the GWR's few 0-6-0 tender types, the Collett 2251 Class introduced in 1930 is worthy of a mention. Designed originally for light branch passenger work in Central and North Wales, it was provided with one of the smallest Swindon boilers, two 17½in by 24in inside cylinders, coupled wheels 5ft 2in diameter, and still managed a tractive effort of over 20,000lb.

As the 4-4-0 had been perhaps until the 1920s the principal passenger type, so the 0-6-0 had achieved the same status on goods workings. Even at nationalisation this design still provided over 50% of the freight locomotives on the LMS, and 75% on the LNER. The LMS standard 0-6-0 was the Fowler Class 4F, and built in huge numbers it was a development of a former Midland Railway type. The standard form from 1924 had two inside 20in by 26in cylinders, 5ft 3in coupled wheels and a 175lb/sq in boiler pressure, yielding 24,555lb tractive effort. Although the 0-6-0 was essentially a goods locomotive, it was frequently used on short-haul and stopping passenger work, and such was its overall popularity on both LMS and LNER that it came to represent over 25% of both companies' total stock. The LNER's sub divi-

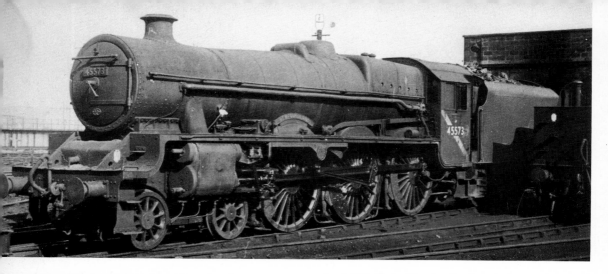

When Stanier moved from Swindon to his appointment as Chief Mechanical Engineer of the LMS, modernisation of that company's motive power included various characteristics of Churchward's design practice. The Jubilee class was typical in appearance if not in performance; they were applied with equal and greater success to all types of locomotive. (*Author's Collection*)

sions of locomotive classes provided no fewer than 29 different variations of the 0-6-0. The largest, numerically, were the 287 members of the three sub-classes of J39 built from 1926, with 20in by 26in cylinders, 5ft 2in coupled wheels and 180lb/sq in boiler pressure. Although there was dimensional similarity with

For passenger work the 4-6-0 gained much favour on all four main line railways. No 865 *Sir John Hawkins*, of R.E.L. Maunsell's famous Lord Nelson class was among the largest passenger locomotives operated by the Southern Railway, until the arrival of the Bulleid Pacifics. (*Lens of Sutton*)

the LMS Class 4F, the Gresley design was slightly more powerful. Maunsell's last designs for the Southern included the Class Q 0-6-0 of comparable proportions, illustrating at least a general trend in standardisation of approach. However the Southern Railway under O.V.S. Bulleid provided by far the most powerful 0-6-0 type, with the 40 locomotives of Class Q1, first seen in 1942. Distinctly unconventional in appearance, the Q1s had 19in by 26in inside cylinders, with 230lb/sq in in boiler pressure and 5ft 1in coupled wheels, the tractive effort being no less than 30,080lb.

The 2-8-0 however was generally accepted as the standard heavy freight locomotive, most numerous and successful being the Stanier Class 8F design for the LMS. Here the use of two outside 18½in by 28in cylinders with Walschaerts motion, 225lb/sq in boiler pressure, and 4ft 8½in coupled wheels resulted in a tractive effort of 32,440lb. These locomotives, though, were not as powerful as Gresley's O2 Class for

Table 5 Freight Locomotives
2-8-0 Types

Railway	LMS	GWR	LNER	SR
Number of locomotives	635*	208	610	—
Number of classes	2*	3	13	—
Locomotives/class	624/11*	69.33	46.92	—
% of freight stock	16.65	52.53	21.79	—
% of total stock	8.10	5.13	9.47	—

* 11 locomotives were ex-Somerset & Dorset 2-8-0s

0-6-0 Types

Railway	LMS	GWR	LNER	SR
Number of locomotives	2094	184	1666	315
Number of classes	20	3	29	9
Locomotives/class	104.70	61.33	57.45	35.00
% of freight stock	54.92	46.46	76.28	87.50
% of total stock	26.70	4.54	25.86	17.43

the LNER, or even the company's own inherited former Somerset & Dorset 2-8-0 locomotives.

As introduced in 1921, the LNER O2 Class had three 18½in by 26in cylinders, 4ft 8in coupled wheels, a boiler pressure of 180lb/sq in and a tractive effort of 36,470lb. The boiler pressure was maintained at this low figure through a number of mod-

Since H.N. Gresley took office as CME, the LNER relied on Pacific types and three-cylinder propulsion for its express passenger locomotives. The final designs in this category were produced by A.H. Peppercorn. These A2 Pacifics still retained the three-cylinder drive, and were in fact a development of Thompson's earlier rebuilding of the Gresley P2 2-8-2s. (*Author's Collection*)

ifications in 1924, 1932 and 1943, the last of which was a solitary example fitted with a B1 type boiler of 225lb/sq in working pressure. The much larger Class O4 2-8-0 was a development of the former Great Central Railway ROD design. For the Interchange Trials of 1948, a member of the Class O1 was chosen, itself rebuilt by Thompson in 1944 with the same B1 type boiler used on the O4 Class. The rebuilds, with two outside 20in by 26in cylinders, and 4ft 8in coupled wheels for the O1, and 21in diameter cylinders for the O4 were, in these dimensions at least, closer to the Stanier Class 8F 2-8-0, and proved successful modifications.

One of the most interesting developments of the inter-war period, was the LNER V2 Class 2-6-2 of 1936, designed for working fast fitted-freight trains. The V2 was an amalgam of existing standard LNER/Gresley components. It carried a foreshortened A3 Pacific boiler and the same wide firebox; the coupled wheels at 6ft 2in were identical with the Class P2 2-8-2, while the leading truck was the same as that used on the Class K3 2-6-0. The three 18½in cylinders were cast in one piece, with 9in diameter piston valves operated by the familiar conjugated valve gear. The end product was a powerful, fast-running locomotive, and although intended originally for freight duties, like the later BR Standard Class 9F 2-10-0, they were often put to work on express passenger trains.

All four of the main line railways possessed a considerable number of tank locomotive designs, from diminutive 0-4-0s through the most numerous 0-6-0, up to the largest 2-8-2 freight types. Tables 5 and 6 give details of freight tender locomotives and tank locomotives in service at the time of Nationalisation.

The GWR, in addition to providing considerable numbers of conventional side tank designs, had the further distinction of operating the 0-6-0 pannier tank. In this design, the water tanks are mounted high

Table 6 Tank Locomotives

Railway	LMS	GWR	LNER	SR
Number of locomotives	2204	2657	2184	666
Number of classes	46	52	90	47
Locomotives/class	47.91	50.83	24.27	14.17
% of total stock	48.60	65.10	33.80	36.90

up on the boiler side, rather than attached to the footplate. Over 800 of this design were eventually operated by both the GWR and BR Western Region. With two 17½in by 24in inside cylinders, driving 4ft 7½in coupled wheels, Collett's 1929 design provided a tractive effort of 22,515lb. These were however, basically a shunting and branch line type, and it was in the area of passenger and mixed-traffic designs that development was needed.

The later BR Standard tanks were of only two types, 2-6-4 and 2-6-2, and many locomotives of this arrangement were already in service on the LMS and GWR, with lesser numbers on the LNER and Southern. Maunsell's single class of 15 locomotives, the Class W 2-6-4 design, had been introduced on the Southern between 1931 and 1936, with three 16½in by 28in cylinders, boiler pressure of 200lb/sq in and 5ft 6in coupled wheels. Three-cylinder propulsion was favoured by Gresley, in his V1 and V3 tank locomotives, introduced in 1930 and 1939. Both types had 16in by 26in cylinders and 5ft 8in coupled wheels, though the V3 had the working pressure raised from 180lb/sq in to 200lb/sq in and thus was slightly more powerful.

The Great Western over the years had achieved a

Table 7 Distribution of 2-6-4 and 2-6-2 Tank Types

2-6-2 Types

Railway	LMS	GWR	LNER	SR
Number of locomotives	229	447	92	—
Number of classes	3	8	2	—
Locomotives/class	76.33	55.88	46.00	—
% of tank stock	10.39	16.91	4.21	—
% of total stock	2.92	11.02	1.43	—

2-6-4 Types

Railway	LMS	GWR	LNER	SR
Number of locomotives	548	—	51	15
Number of classes	4	—	3	1
Locomotives/class	137	—	17	15
% of tank stock	24.86	—	2.34	2.25
% of total stock	6.99	—	0.79	0.83

remarkable degree of standardisation in valve gear design and layout, opting for two cylinders and a 2-6-2 wheel arrangement. The inside Stephenson valve gear actuated the outside piston valves through a system of rockers. The cylinder sizes varied between classes from 17in by 24in to 18in and 18½in by 30in stroke. Examples of these Prairie tanks were designed by both Collett and Churchward. The LMS on the other hand had found room for both two- and three-cylinder types, the first of these appearing as the Fowler designs of 1927 and 1930. Both were two-cylinder types, those of the 1927 2-6-4T being 19in by 26in and driving 5ft 9in coupled wheels, while the later 2-6-2T were 17½in by 26in and drove 5ft 3in coupled wheels. Stanier's first offering was a three-cylinder 2-6-4 design, built in 1934, which came into the LMS power class 4, with a tractive effort of 24,600lb from the 16in by 26in cylinders and 200lb/sq in boiler pressure. Only 37 of this design were built, intended as replacements for the 4-4-2 tanks on the London, Tilbury & Southend line. Subsequently, both Stanier and Fairburn provided Class 4 tanks with two outside 19in by 26in cylinders, in 1935 and 1945 respectively.

During and immediately following World War II there was a considerably influential period in development of detail design features from the LMS and Southern companies in particular, while the work of Thompson on the LNER in rebuilding a number of the Gresley three-cylinder classes demonstrated a general trend towards the simpler two-cylinder types. Many of the characteristics of both components, and in general approach to the design of the BR Standard locomotives, can be seen to have appeared on the post-war construction initiated by H.G. Ivatt for the LMS, and by R.A. Riddles in the Austerity 2-8-0, 2-10-0 and 0-6-0 saddle tank locomotives.

Simplicity was the keynote of Riddles designs; where previously there had been extensive use of castings, with the WD types fabrications were used to save weight and cost. In the 2-8-0 and 2-10-0 tender locomotives two 19in by 26in outside cylinders were operated by Walschaerts valve gear, with 10in diameter piston valves, to drive the 4ft 8½in diameter coupled wheels. In each case, except for the additional pair of coupled wheels on the 2-10-0, the chassis was identical. The boilers although working 225lb/sq in pressure showed some differences, and the choice of parallel barrel with round top firebox was made essentially for its suitability to mass-production.

The LMS offering of the most modern practices in post-war years included characteristic features as high-degree superheat, efficient water circulation and good steaming from the Belpaire type fireboxes, waisted-in to fit between the frames on all but the largest Pacific types. Cylinders were provided with large long-lap travel valves, operated by Walschaerts motion. Other large-scale innovations brought into being during Ivatt's time included rock-

Standardisation on the GWR was equally obvious in passenger, freight or tank locomotives. The 2-8-2 design seen here passing Iver with a down freight is typical. (*Lens of Sutton*)

ing grates, self-cleaning smokeboxes, and the use of roller bearings on coupled wheels. Fitting manganese/steel liners to axlebox guides reduced susceptibility to hot boxes, and improved mileages between repairs. Modifications to draughting and valve gear, double blastpipes and chimneys, and the use of British Caprotti poppet valves, were incorporated on the later batches of the two-cylinder Class 5 4-6-0. A prominent feature of late LMS practice was the accessibility factor, and nowhere was this more apparent than in the last completely new designs built by the LMS.

The archetypal British 0-6-0 goods locomotive was nowhere more readily recognisable than in the LMS standard Class 4F, and built in considerable numbers for general freight work. (*G.W. Sharpe*)

The Class 4 2-6-0 freight locomotive, and Class 2 2-6-0 and 2-6-2T locomotives embodied most of these cost-saving features, though without recourse to the more experimental roller bearings and poppet valve gears.

The Great Western produced little that was startlingly progressive in motive power design—details remained essentially what they had been under Churchward and Collett. The company's last chief mechanical engineer, F.W. Hawksworth, produced in the County Class 4-6-0 in 1945, something that was at least controversial. This two-cylinder type was fitted with a boiler working at 280lb/sq in pressure, perhaps in some measure to justify a departure from Swindon's standard boiler construction methods. The boiler turned out to be mid-way between the Castle Class 4-6-0 and the Churchward standard No 1, using the same flangeing blocks as the LMS Class 8F 2-8-0, which had been built at Swindon during World War II. A year earlier,

in 1944, Hawksworth had successfully modified the Hall Class mixed-traffic 4-6-0, altering the main framing, providing plate-framed bogies and a higher degree of superheat. Even in the radically different County Class, standard GWR/Stephenson valve gear continued to be used, operating the outside valves through rockers.

Oil firing of steam locomotives had been tried in earlier years, particularly at times of coal shortage, but in 1946 the GWR embarked on a programme that was intended in the long term to see the conversion of many of its locomotives. Although other companies dabbled with this system, the ambitious plans of the GWR failed to materialise. Following Sir Nigel Gresley's death in 1941 and the appointment of Edward Thompson as CME, the LNER entered a further period of standardisation, marked not so much by improvements in detail design, but bringing the company's locomotive design policy into line with the new trend towards simplicity and accessibility. Boiler design continued as before, with round-topped firebox and parallel barrel, with the bulk of design rationalisation connected with the cylinders and motion. In this area, Thompson set out almost to reverse the policies of Gresley, eliminating three-cylinder propulsion for all but the heaviest express passenger types. The introduction during this period of the A1 and A2 Pacifics, provided a successful conclusion to the saga begun on that company many years earlier. The A2 and A2/3 locomotives, at 40,430lb had the highest nominal tractive effort of any British Pacific design.

By the last year of their independent existence, there seemed at least some measure of agreement between the companies as to the desirable features of steam locomotive design. In this respect, all four shared essentially the same difficulties, and tended towards similar solutions in reducing costs and improving efficiency. The Southern however, under O.V.S. Bulleid, managed to produce perhaps some of the best and worst features of detail design. The newly-built Pacific locomotives with their air-smoothed casings were undoubtedly the most dramatically different steam locomotives then seen in this country in regular service. The boilers were excellent, and incorporated within a more-or-less conventional wide-base firebox two thermic syphons to improve water circulation. Overall, the boiler may have seemed somewhat short for a Pacific type, but was proved the equal of most in steam production. Unfortunately, one major detail which led eventually to the lack of operating success was the unique oil-immersed chain-driven valve gear. Certainly this was a novel and bold experiment, and although the idea was not considered practical for subsequent BR construction, a number of details were successfully carried forward for further use. Among these was the method of attaching tyres to wheels by a shrink fit alone, and the use of an all-welded steel firebox, with its economic advantages, had for a time caused the BR designers to consider adopting this feature. One last item which was influential in the production of the BR Standard locomotives was the inclusion of the main details of the Bulleid Pacific trailing truck in the BR types.

The impending nationalisation, under an austere economic climate provided perhaps the right conditions to put together a formidable case for even greater standardisation of locomotive design. There was bound to be pressure from the newly-formed Regions for the advancement of that policy in their own particular direction. It was in consequence a logical step to examine the performance in practice of these different approaches to overall and detail design. Having regard to the need also to seek as wide a route availability as possible, the Interchange Trials were held as a prelude to developing a national rather than regional approach to steam locomotive design. That, initially at least, the products of this standard approach were seen in some measure as controversial, was an indication that partisan feelings would take some time, if ever, to dissipate.

2.   The 1948 Interchange Trials

The purpose of the trials held in 1948 was not simply a competition between locomotives belonging to the various companies, neither was it to determine which of the existing designs was the most able performer on all the Regions of BR, with a view to standardising that type for all future construction. However, where an existing Regional design satisfied all the requirements of cost of operation and route availability, then it would have been foolish indeed to embark on a new design for its own sake.

The trials were carried out on normal service trains, with locomotives that had completed 15,000 to 20,000 miles since their last general overhaul. This suggestion of taking locomotives straight from their regular links reacted unfavourably on the LNER's A4 4-6-2 60022 *Mallard*. The locomotive was chosen obviously for its prestige value, though it was in fact in rather less than average condition; on a run from Waterloo to Exeter, it failed at Salisbury and was replaced by 60033 *Seagull*.

Table 8 Locomotives used in the Interchange Trials

Passenger

Class	King	A4	Duchess	Royal Scot	Merchant Navy
Type	4-6-0	4-6-2	4-6-2	4-6-0	4-6-2
Introduced	1927	1935	1937	1943	1941
Designer	Collett	Gresley	Stanier	Stanier	Bulleid
Weight (locomotive only)	89t 0cwt	102t 19cwt	105t 5cwt	84t 1cwt	94t 15cwt
Boiler pressure (lb/sq in)	250	250	250	250	280
Cylinders	4	3	4	3	3
	16¼in × 28in	18½in × 26in	16½in × 28in	18in × 26in	18in × 24in
Coupled wheels	6ft 6in	6ft 8in	6ft 9in	6ft 9in	6ft 2in
Tractive effort (lb)	40,300	35,455	40,000	33,150	37,515
Running numbers	6018	60022	46236	46154	35017
		60033/4		46162	35018/9

Royal Scot Class locomotive was in rebuilt form.

Mixed-traffic

Class	Modified Hall	B1	5MT	West Country
Type	4-6-0	4-6-0	4-6-0	4-6-2
Introduced	1944	1942	1934	1945
Designer	Hawksworth	Thompson	Stanier	Bulleid
Weight (locomotive only)	75t 16cwt	71t 3cwt	72t 2cwt	86t 0cwt
Boiler pressure (lb/sq in)	225	225	225	280
Cylinders	2	2	2	3
	18½in × 30in	20in × 26in	18½in × 28in	16in × 24in
Coupled wheels	6ft 0in	6ft 2in	6ft 0in	6ft 2in
Tractive effort (lb)	27,275	26,880	25,455	31,050
Running numbers	6990	61163	44973	34004/5/6
		61251/92	45253	

Freight

Class	28XX	O1	8F	WD	WD
Type	2-8-0	2-8-0	2-8-0	2-10-0	2-8-0
Introduced	1903	1944	1935	1945	1943
Designer	Churchward	Thompson	Stanier	Riddles	Riddles
Weight (locomotive only)	75t 10cwt	73t 6cwt	72t 2cwt	78t 6cwt	70t 5cwt
Boiler pressure (lb/sq in)	225	225	225	225	225
Cylinders (2)	18½in × 30in	20in × 26in	18½in × 28in	19in × 28in	19in × 28in
Coupled wheels	4ft 7½in	4ft 8in	4ft 8½in	4ft 8½in	4ft 8½in
Tractive effort (lb)	35,380	35,520	32,440	34,215	34,215
Running numbers	3803	63773	48189	73774	77000
		63789	48400	73776	63169

Table 9 Testing Dates and Routes

Route	Euston–Carlisle		Kings Cross–Leeds		Paddington–Plymouth	
Week beginning	Learning route	Testing	Learning route	Testing	Learning route	Testing
19.4.48	—	Duchess	R.Scot	A4	M.Navy	King
26.4.28	—	—	Duchess	R.Scot	A4	M.Navy
3.5.48	M.Navy	R.Scot	—	Duchess	—	A4
10.5.48	—	M.Navy	King	—	Duchess	—
17.5.48	A4	—	M.Navy	King	R.Scot	Duchess
24.5.48	—	A4	—	M.Navy	—	R.Scot

Route	Waterloo–Exeter		St Pancras–Manchester		Marylebone–Manchester	
Week beginning	Learning route	Testing	Learning route	Testing	Learning route	Testing
31.5.48	A4	M.Navy	—	5MT	West C	B1
7.6.48	R.Scot	A4	B1	—	5MT	West C
14.6.48	Duchess	R.Scot	West C	B1	Hall	5MT
21.6.48	—	Duchess	—	West C	—	Hall

Route	Perth–Inverness		Bristol–Plymouth		Brent–Toton	
Week beginning	Learning route	Testing	Learning route	Testing	Learning route	Testing
28.6.48	West C	5MT	B1	Hall	—	8F
5.7.48	—	West C	5MT	B1	—	WD 2-8-0
12.7.48	B1	—	West C	5MT	O1	WD 2-10-0
19.7.48	—	B1	—	West C	—	O1

Route	London–Peterborough		London–South Wales		Bristol–Eastleigh	
Week beginning	Learning route	Testing	Learning route	Testing	Learning route	Testing
19.7.48	—	—	8F	—	—	—
26.7.48	—	O1	—	8F	—	38XX
9.8.48	8F	WD 2-10-0	—	38XX	O1	WD 2-8-0
16.8.48	38XX	8F	—	WD 2-10-0	—	O1
23.8.48	—	38XX	O1	WD 2-8-0	8F	WD 2-10-0
30.8.48	—	WD 2-8-0	—	O1	—	8F

N.B. Route-learning on down runs was Mondays and Wednesdays, Tuesdays and Thursdays for up runs. Testing was carried out on the down workings on Tuesdays and Thursdays, and for the up journeys on Wednesdays and Fridays.

The fuel used in England was of two grades, South Kirkby Grade 1A, and Blidworth Grade 2B, while in Scotland only the Grade 2B Comrie coal was used. The use of hard coals proved an unfortunate choice for the GWR locomotives, which had been designed to burn the softer Welsh coals. To prove the truth of this statement, further tests with King and Hall Class 4-6-0s using Welsh coal, showed a reduction in consumption per drawbar horsepower of 6½% in the King Class, while the Hall Class showed an improvement of no less than 18% under normal operating conditions.

All the locomotives were tender types, and were divided into three categories:

Passenger...seven 4-6-2s, three 4-6-0s
Mixed-traffic...three 4-6-2s, six 4-6-0s
Freight...two 2-10-0s, seven 2-8-0s

Curiously, no tank locomotives were represented in these trials, the omission of which added greater weight to the enthusiast's idea that a competition was taking place. With the exception of the GWR King Class 4-6-0 and 2-8-0 freight locomotive, all were recent designs, representative of current practice on their home regions. There were some restrictions to testing the locomotives under all route conditions, since a number of those on trial were prevented from operating on some lines by reason of loading gauge clearances. While it was perfectly possible to work the LMS Duchess Class locomotives on duties normally handled by GWR Kings, the reverse operation was ruled out due to these clearance restrictions. The only foreign running achieved by the Kings was on the LNER main line out of Kings Cross. Even the smaller Hall Class 4-6-0 was precluded from St Pancras to Manchester and Perth to Inverness for this reason.

The tests were conducted over a 4½-month period, between 19 April and 30 August 1948, covering the routes and workings shown in Tables 9 and 10.

During the first week of testing, locomotives of the highest passenger class were involved in trials on their home regions. The pattern established was for two up and two down runs, with the down runs being made on Tuesdays and Thursdays, and the corresponding up runs on Wednesdays and Fridays. On the LMR,

W.A. Stanier's *piece-de-résistance*, the powerful Duchess class Pacifics were among the locomotives tested during the 1948 Interchange Trials. These four-cylinder locomotives demonstrated the most consistent power outputs overall, although the highest recorded figures were achieved by Gresley's A4s of the former LNER. (*D.A. Anderson*)

Table 10 Passenger Train Test Routes and Workings

Region		Service	Locomotive types
W	1.30pm	Paddington–Plymouth	King, A4, Duchess,
	8.30am	Plymouth–Paddington	Reb Scot, M Navy
	1.45pm	Bristol–Plymouth	Hall, B1, Class 5,
	1.35pm	Plymouth–Bristol	W Country
E	1.10pm	Kings Cross–Leeds	King, A4, Duchess,
	7.50am	Leeds–Kings Cross	Reb Scot, M Navy
	10.00am	Marylebone–Manchester	Hall, B1, Class 5, W Country
LM	10.00am	Euston–Carlisle	A4, Duchess, Reb
	12.55pm	Carlisle–Euston	Scot, M Navy
	10.15am	St. Pancras–Manchester	B1, Class 5, W Country
S	10.50am	Waterloo–Exeter	A4, Duchess, Reb
	12.37pm	Exeter–Waterloo	Scot, M Navy
Sc	4.00pm	Perth–Inverness	B1, Class 5,
	8.20am	Inverness–Perth	W Country

during the week beginning 19 April 1948, the Stanier Pacific No 46236 worked the 10.00am from Euston to Carlisle, but although the same train was worked by No 46236 on 22 April, the 12.55pm from Carlisle was not worked up to London on 21 April. It seems that No 46236 failed on this working, as the train was noted passing Bletchley behind Stanier Class 5 4-6-0 No 5193, an hour late—not an auspicious beginning, but comparable perhaps with the unfortunate *Mallard*, although the A4 at least failed on foreign metals.

In the week prior to testing, locomotives away from their home region were engaged in pre-trial running and route familiarisation. The locomotives were then

The LNER A4 design, with its conjugated valve gear, three-cylinder drive, produced some of the best and worst performances for the express passenger type. The complexity of this layout was a factor which weighed against its adoption by BR in development of the Standard series. (*John Goss*)

worked back to their home depots for the weekend, returning on the following Monday.

To cover use of the selected fuel for the tests, supplies were sent to a number of depots, as follows:

LM Region:	Camden, Carlisle (Upperby), Trafford Park and Kentish Town
E & NE Region:	Leeds (Copley Hill), Kings Cross, Gorton and Neasden
S Region:	Nine Elms, Exmouth Junction
W Region:	Old Oak Common, Bristol

Passenger and Mixed-traffic Locomotives

Comparing the Pacific types on the Western Region Paddington to Plymouth run some interesting figures for coal consumption were achieved. On the down journey, with the 1.30pm, A4 No 60033 provided the lowest figures, using 2.98 and 3.24lb/drawbar hp/hr, with Stanier's Duchess Pacific No 46236 hard on its heels, using 3.22 and 3.21lb/dbhp/hr for its two runs on the same train. The figures showed the suitability of the wide firebox for burning the more plentiful Blidworth and South Kirkby hard coals. The King class 4-6-0 on its own region produced no less than 3.81 and 3.64lb/dbhp/hr, greater than even the Rebuilt Scot's 3.60 and 3.33lb. This perhaps emphasised even more the specialised nature of the GWR design, whose performance was later improved using the softer Welsh coals. The Merchant Navy's reputation was for a design that was a heavy consumer, yet on trial No 35019 burned on average only 3.59lb/dbhp/hr on the down journey, while returning on average on the up working of 3.63lb/dbhp/hr. This was a very favourable result in comparison with the other two Pacific types, and lower than either the King or Rebuilt Scot 4-6-0s. The highest average drawbar

horsepower was just under 900, from the A4 No 60033, with No 6018 *King Henry VI* as runner-up, and Merchant Navy No 35019 *French Line CGT*, in third place with 779 drawbar hp.

Mixed-traffic locomotive performance was tested on the same region, using the 1.45pm Bristol to Plymouth, and 1.35pm Plymouth to Bristol trains. Here the Stanier class 5, Thompson B1 and West Country Pacific were tested alongside the GWR Modified Hall Class 4-6-0. The poor performance of the Hall has already been outlined, and while it was not the heaviest consumer of coal, the best figures were provided by the Class 5 No 45253. The Class 5 averaged 3.32lb of coal for the down journey, and 3.46lb/dbhp/hr in the opposite direction. Train loads on this particular duty were quite high at around 490 tons, and as the B1 4-6-0 was supposedly equivalent to the Class 5, it is interesting to see that this locomotive consumed almost 20% more fuel than the former LMS design.

The five express passenger types when tested on the Eastern Region operated between Kings Cross and Leeds on the 1.10pm down, and 7.50am up. The 1.10pm was a heavily loaded train of some 512 tons, with Rebuilt Scot 4-6-0 No 46162 *Queen's Westminster Rifleman* the first to be tried. Two different A4s were selected, with a Merchant Navy Pacific, with the most economical performance again coming from the A4, although there was really very little to choose between the A4 and the Stanier locomotive No 46236 *City of Bradford*. The 4-6-0 put up a creditable performance, returning average figures of 3.31 and 3.21lb/dbhp/hr, for the down and up runs respectively. On the mixed-traffic side, B1 No 61163 was used on its home region, in company with No 6990 *Witherslack Hall* from the Western Region. The ER runs took place in May and June, working the 10.00am from Marylebone to Manchester London Road. Highest power outputs—over 800 drawbar horsepower—came from the West Country Pacific. There was again very little to choose between the Eastern and London Midland types for economy, but on the grounds of consistency the Stanier design was marginally superior. The West Country, in yielding these quite high powered runs, returned average figures of 4.00 and

3.79lb/dbhp/hr for the down and up journeys.

The Pacific types had been tested on the London Midland region Euston to Carlisle run the previous month. Between those two places, the West Coast main line provided a little under 300 miles of some of the most varied alignment in the country, in the down direction ending with the ascent of Shap Fell.

The two services concerned in these tests were the 10.00am Euston to Carlisle, and the 12.55pm Carlisle to Euston. The highest power output was achieved by No 35017 *Belgian Marine* on its second down run on 13 May, with an average drawbar horsepower of 912. Next came the A4 No 60034 *Lord Faringdon*, recording an average of 886dbhp two weeks later. The Duchess in contrast was more consistent, providing the best all-round averages for the two up and down journeys of 857 and 836.5dbhp. Coal used was also a fairly consistent figure, with only the A4 consuming less than 3lb/dbhp/hr.

Maintaining the express passenger theme, the Southern Region test route was over the former LSWR main line from Waterloo to Exeter, a distance of 171½ miles. The Bulleid locomotive was paired on its home region with its own tender, whereas on other regions the Bulleid design was fitted with a Stanier tender having water pick-up apparatus. The extra capacity of Southern Region tenders was determined by the fact that there were no water troughs on that region. Trials with four types of locomotive—Merchant Navy, Rebuilt Scot, Duchess and A4 occupied the last week of May and first three weeks of June. Train services involved the 10.50am Waterloo to Exeter and 12.37pm Exeter to Waterloo. The choice of A4 No 60022 *Mallard* proved unfortunate, since on its first up journey on 9 June the locomotive failed and

The Bulleid Pacifics were the odd ones out in the express passenger category, combining a first-class boiler with an unusual arrangement of valve gear. This Bulleid chain-driven gear produced some remarkable and unexpected results on test in the Scottish Region, from a member of the West Country class. (*Lens of Sutton*)

the test run was terminated at Salisbury. No 60033 was substituted on the remainder of the trial workings. The Stanier Pacific appeared from the results to favour the Waterloo to Exeter route, using 3.07 and 3.27lb/dbhp/hr for the down and up journeys. However, the Duchess was outshone for power output by No 60022 *Mallard*, achieving no less than 917 dbhp on the run in which that particular locomotive failed. The Rebuilt Royal Scot 4-6-0 turned in a very satisfactory performance on this train, and was more economical than the 'home-produced' Merchant Navy, with averages of 3.10 and 3.38lb/dbhp/hr. The highest power output with No 46154 was the 796 dbhp of the second up working, which for a locomotive with only a Class 6 rating, compared more than favourably with the larger Class 7 Pacifics.

No mixed-traffic trials were attempted on the Southern Region, but the despatch of a B1 4-6-0 and West Country Pacific to the Scottish Region for trials with the Stanier Class 5 4-6-0 provided some very interesting results. These tests took place on the Perth to Inverness line, during the last week of June and first three weeks of July, working out on the 4.00pm Perth to Inverness and returning with the 8.20am to Perth. The locomotives covered 118 miles of some of the most demanding alignment used for these Interchange Trials.

As if to confound its critics, some of the best performances over this steeply-graded line came from the Bulleid Pacific. Average drawbar horsepower never fell below 700 on any of its four runs, and the maximum recorded average of 825 on the first up run was far and away the highest. It may be that such consistently satisfactory work from a locomotive type that was not expected to do well was a tribute to the design of its free-steaming boiler. The most economic performance came, as might be expected, from the Stanier Class 5 4-6-0 No 44973, recording the lowest coal consumption figure of 3.63lb/dbhp/hr. The B1 4-6-0 was competing in this quarter on almost level terms, there being little difference on the whole

Edward Thompson's two cylinder B1 4-6-0s, were intended to be the LNER equivalent of Stanier's highly successful Class 5 4-6-0s for the LMS. In the mixed-traffic category, the simple layout of locomotive and valve gear was an improvement on earlier designs of 4-6-0 from the LNER, but the LMS designs still proved better performers overall. (*Author's Collection*)

between the two types, the West Country on the other hand consuming 33% more fuel—almost 5lb/dbhp/hr.

Freight Locomotives

Freight locomotives were tested during July and August 1948, and comprised four 2-8-0 designs, and one of the recently-built Austerity 2-10-0s. Only four routes were used. The shorter were between Ferme Park and New England on the Eastern Region, Bristol and Eastleigh over Southern metals, both amounting to around 75 miles. The two longer routes were between Acton and Severn Tunnel Junction on the Western Region, and Toton and Brent on the London Midland, covering 118 and 127 miles respectively. The overall picture that emerged can be demonstrated

by the closeness of the figures for coal consumption between the five types. Interestingly in this aspect, the Austerity 2-8-0 was among the heaviest consumers. In comparison with Riddles' 2-10-0, the 2-8-0 Austerity's performance was inconsistent, the coal-dbhp/hr figures on individual runs varying markedly. Most economical of the freight types overall was the Stanier Class 8F 2-8-0, yet this locomotive's lowest fuel consumption value of 2.91lb/dbhp/hr was only 5% less than the lowest obtained with the Austerity. Certainly, these figures alone provided some very difficult choices for the designers of the BR Standard classes.

Average drawbar horsepower developed was low overall, consistent with the low speeds demanded on freight turns at the time, these frequently averaging less than 20mph. The twenty test runs on the Western Region were covered at an average speed of no more

Former GWR 4-6-0 No 7909 seen near Teignmouth in July 1951, was a member of the Modified Hall class. The design was representative of GWR mixed-traffic motive power in 1948, as developed by F.W. Hawksworth. During the Interchange Trials, the type was represented by No 6990 *Witherslack Hall*. (*Derek Cross*)

Both of R.A. Riddles' Austerity designs were contenders in the 1948 trials, and in this view of 7030 (original WD numbering) at Eastleigh in August of that year, the clean, simple lines of this type are apparent. It is worth noting that the tenders, with high inset sides to the coal space, were numbered in the BR tender series as Type BR5. (*W. Gilbert*)

than 18.84mph, with the highest recorded average of 21.94mph from the 28XX 2-8-0 of Churchward design. Drawbar hp demands throughout the regions varied, between just over 300 to around 600 dbhp.

Performance of Components

Boiler designs were of two basic types, the tapered barrel with Belpaire firebox, or the simple straight barrel and round-topped firebox. Both steamed free-

The outstandingly successful, and numerous, Stanier Class 8F 2-8-0, here seen at Rowsley, was represented on the London Midland, Western and Eastern Regions, during the trials of freight locomotives. In comparison with other 2-8-0 types, there was little difference in performance, suggesting a degree of agreement between the companies in the design of freight types. (*J.A. Fleming*)

ly, and the latter was selected for Riddles' Austerity designs because of the ease with which it could be constructed. Although on the LMS the tapered barrel had been proved cheaper to maintain than the parallel boiler, no costs were available for the LNER designs, so a comparative study taking this into account was out of the question. The basic Churchward philosophy had been adopted by the LMS under Stanier, and by 1948 had been developed and improved upon to a marked degree. Similarly, Bulleid on the Southern had provided his revolutionary Pacifics with boilers similar in design to those used on the LMS, again with great success, although some additions were made with the use of thermic syphons, steel inner and outer fireboxes, and Monel metal stays in the breaking zone between the two wrappers. Viewed in this light, then the Gresley/Doncaster boiler designs may be seen as the 'odd one out' in development, there being by Nationalisation a three-to-one majority in favour of the taper boiler for new construction.

Consistency of approach in the design of the chassis/engine referred to in connection with freight types, was almost completely reversed in the express passen-

ger types, although there was some measure of agreement in the mixed-traffic category. Of the Pacific locomotive designs with more-or-less conventional valve gear, the performance of Gresley's three-cylinder propulsion left little doubt as to its success, but its complexity was a major factor against its selection as a future standard—similarly with the novel Bulleid chain-driven gear. Multiple sets of motion, inside gear, crank axles, etc had the disadvantage of increasing both construction and maintenance costs.

Notwithstanding the important variations, Walschaerts valve gear was the most common form, claimed by many to provide optimum steam distribution. The Gresley conjugated system was rapidly being removed and replaced by Thompson in the latter years of the LNER with a more conventional layout, particularly in the smaller mixed-traffic classes. On the GWR, Stephenson link motion was standard, inside the frames, with only the connecting and coupling rods outside, for both two- and four-cylinder types. Differences existed in crosshead design, with the LNER and SR favouring a three-bar arrangement, whereas the LMS and GWR carried one slidebar above and one below the crosshead.

Wheels and axles also demonstrated some diversity in approach, although there seemed a consensus to using 6ft 0in or 6ft 2in coupled wheels for mixed-traffic duties, with a variation between 6ft 2in and 6ft

9in for purely passenger types. An important fact that emerged from the running of the Bulleid Pacifics was the suitability of locomotives with the smaller mixed-traffic wheel sizes for express passenger duty. The previously-acknowledged need for small differences in wheel diameter to separate mixed-traffic from express passenger types was shown through the performance of the Bulleid Pacifics in the Interchange Trials to be an assumption not supported by fact.

All the locomotives used during the trials were fitted with plain bearing axleboxes, despite which there was a feeling that roller bearings would reduce maintenance costs in this area. Most of the work in this direction had been undertaken by H.G. Ivatt in the last years of the LMS, although Gresley had adopted roller bearings some years earlier in the small-end of the return crank on his V2 2-6-2s. Although the improved wear characteristics were a principal attribute in favour of their adoption, the plain bearing axlebox had been developed to a very high degree of reliability, notably on the LMS. Additionally, the use of manganese-steel liners for the wearing faces of the horns further contributed to the reduction of maintenance costs by increasing the mileage run between periodical repairs. Many of the detail features used on the last locomotive designs for the LMS were adapted for use in the BR Standard range with equal success.

3. Developing the Standard Designs

Taking an overall view of the 1948 trials it must be said that no single design or group of designs really stood apart from any other. They did demonstrate what was achievable with the existing level of development of steam locomotive design, and that no single approach was superior to another. The difficulty presented to those responsible for the production of the Standard locomotives was more complex than was at first thought. Selection of components and in some measure method of approach were based on the economies that might be achieved with their use or adoption, and the rather more ambiguous influence of the fact that a majority of the design personnel were of LMS extraction. So in the newly-formed Railway Executive an unintentional standardisation process had already begun, and for the locomotives an approach to standardisation British Railways style was first publicly spelled out in 1950, with R.A. Riddles' Presidential Address to the Institution of Locomotive Engineers.

However, before this statement was made, evolution of the designs was well under way, the first appearing only two months after that address was delivered in November 1950. Production of the new Standard locomotives involved an analysis of existing practices, with the results from the Interchange Trials shedding some light on performance to assist in this matter. A detailed appraisal of component design was made at the same time, by the Locomotive Standards Committee. This body was set up in January 1948 with the intention of standardising details from the best of the regional alternatives, and where no obvious advantage was gained by the use of one type over another an arbitrary choice was made for the sake of standardisation.

A fundamental question raised, particularly in view of the performance of the participants in the Interchange Trials, was why the need to standardise at all—why not let the individual regions continue with their various policies? Mr Riddles answered that

Ivatt Class 2 2-6-0 No 46401 at Upton-on-Severn 13 June 1957 with a train for Ashchurch. Precurser of the BR Standard Class 2, with only detail alterations made to bring it within the Standard family. (*A.R. Palmer*)

criticism with the reasoning that allowing the newly-formed regions to develop their own policies would mean that at the very least there would be four different types of locomotive in each traffic category. In addition, there was often little consistency of approach either to detail design or in selection of new types, and which could be altered still further with successive changes in the CME's department. Some companies had adopted a standard for virtually everything, while others preferred the variations within a

given design effected by changing traffic patterns, sub-dividing the categories to almost infinite proportions. In a national undertaking, any central headquarters might very rapidly lose its purpose if that degree of autonomy were allowed to the regions. It would naturally follow that a greater quantity of stores and spares would be needed, further increasing the operating costs.

By the end of 1948, the major factors influencing the decision to adopt a new range of Standard designs for the whole of British Railways had emerged. These can be stated as follows:

1. A wide range of fittings could be standardised, but if this were done, major alterations would be needed if they were applied to existing designs of locomotive.
2. The recently-ended trials had demonstrated that there was so little to choose between any of the latest regional designs that the Locomotive

As with the tender design, the first Standard Class 2 2-6-2 tank locomotives were almost identical with their Ivatt equivalents for the LMS. Here No 41218 at Napton & Stockton, shows the push-pull equipment fitted to the BR Standard locomotives. (*A.R. Palmer*)

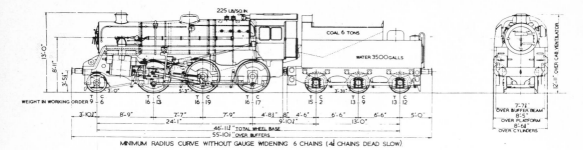

225 LB/SQ.IN.
COAL 6 TONS
WATER 3500 GALLS
13'-0"
8'-5½"
3'-5½"

WEIGHT IN WORKING ORDER 9-6   16-13   16-19   16-17   15-2   13-9   13-12

3'-10½"   8'-9"   7'-7"   7'-9"   4'-8½" 8" 4'-6"   6'-6"   6'-6"   5'-0"
24'-1"   9'-10½"   13'-0"
46'-11½" TOTAL WHEEL BASE
55'-10½" OVER BUFFERS

MINIMUM RADIUS CURVE WITHOUT GAUGE WIDENING 6 CHAINS (4½ CHAINS DEAD SLOW)

12'-11" OVER CAB VENTILATOR
7'-7½" OVER BUFFER BEAM
8'-5" OVER PLATFORM
8'-6½" OVER CYLINDERS

Class 4 2-6-0

Standards Committee was unable to recommend any one design in preference to another.

3. There was no geographical reason precluding the use of any one particular type. Most locomotive designs had been shown to be equally capable performers from the Southern to the Scottish Regions.

4. In some cases there were limitations on the wider use by reason of loading gauge and weight considerations. WR locomotives were barred from the LMR on account of their widths while, generally, locomotives of the NE Region had heavier axle loads for each category than did other types.

Having suggested that no one type of regional locomotive could be recommended above any other, it was apparent that route availability was an important factor in the new designs, which laid greater emphasis on the mixed-traffic category. Three new designs of locomotive produced by the LMS included some of the most modern detail features and construction practices, and much greater route availability than other regional types. All were built between 1945 and

A double-chimney Ivatt Class 4 2-6-0 No 3000. Again, this was a design adopted from the LMS without major alterations other than a single chimney as a BR Standard. Worthy of note in this case is the LMS-style top feed, and the regulator operating rod alongside the firebox. (L & GRP)

1947, with H.G. Ivatt as CME, and included a Class 4 and Class 2 2-6-0 tender locomotive, and Class 2 2-6-2 tank type. It was decided at a very early stage in the design process that these three locomotives came as close as any to the requirements of British Railways, so much so that they were adopted for future construction with only minor modifications.

Responsible for co-ordination of locomotive design on BR was E.S. Cox, who in 1948 was appointed Executive Officer (Design), to the Railway Executive. This position, from Riddles' interpretation, was a key post, providing a liaison with the technical, operating and commercial departments, and representatives from the various regions, who comprised the Locomotive Standards Committee. Information on design policy was channelled to both Regional and Headquarters Offices.

As early as June 1948 it was known that a number of new Standard types was to be proposed, falling into three main categories:

1. Entirely new designs:
   Class 6 4-6-2 express passenger
   Class 6 4-6-2 mixed-traffic
   Class 5 4-6-2 mixed-traffic
   Class 8 2-8-2 freight
2. Developments of existing types:
   Class 7 4-6-2 express passenger
   Class 4 4-6-0 mixed-traffic
   Class 3 2-6-2T mixed-traffic

R.A. Riddles' first essays in locomotive design were the Austerity 2-8-0 locomotives for the Ministry of Supply during World War II. No 90519 is here seen in later BR service at Selby. (*Kenneth Field*)

  3. Existing types with modified details:
     Class 4 2-6-0 mixed-traffic
     Class 4 2-6-4T mixed-traffic
     Class 2 2-6-0 mixed-traffic
     Class 2 2-6-2T mixed-traffic

An important point to remember is that the power classification system used at the time was that of the former LMS. Quite early in the life of British Railways, the Stanier Jubilee or Class 5XP locomotives were upgraded to Class 6, and correspondingly all power classes above were increased by one; the effect on the Standard locomotives was that Class 6 went to Class 7, Class 7 to 8, and the Class 8F (freight) type, to Class 9.

By 1950 there emerged twelve Standard types, with a number of modifications in conception from the original, and based around the following parameters:

  1. Maximum steam-producing capacity within weight and load gauge considerations.
  2. Minimum of working parts, all of which were visible and accessible.
  3. Reduction of disposal work on shed by use of rocking grate, self-emptying ashpan and self-cleaning smoke-box.
  4. Physical size determined by need to achieve the widest range of mixed-traffic working.
  5. Use of roller bearings where financially justified, and in other cases generously proportioned plain bearings with manganese-steel liners.
  6. Easing of shed preparation work by greater use of mechanical and grease lubrication.
  7. Adhesion factors to be as high as possible, with sensitive regulators and efficient sanding gear.
  8. High thermal efficiency, sought by use of large grate areas giving low combustion rates under average working conditions, high degree of superheat and long-lap valve gear.
  9. Both injectors to be on the fireman's side where practicable.
 10. Vacuum ejectors located outside the cab, with two-position driver's brake valve inside.

 11. Steam brakes for locomotive and tender, with graduable automatic steam brake valve.

The use of two cylinders, loading gauge dimensions and permissible hammer-blow, were critical features in the general design. All had an effect on route availability, which was to be as wide as possible. Two standard loading gauges were introduced, designated L1 and L2. The L2 gauge covered the largest types, from Class 5 upwards, while the L1 gauge imposed maximum dimensions on the smaller classes, from Class 4 4-6-0 downwards. The L1 gauge was to all intents and purposes universal, and any locomotive coming within that gauge could operate on any region of British Railways. The larger L2 gauge covered all routes where 9ft 0in wide corridor stock was operated.

The decision to use only two outside cylinders was based on the following decisions:

  1. The split inside big-end is a source of trouble at high speeds and powers, unless the highest standards of maintenance can be guaranteed.
  2. Whether built-up or cast, the crank axle is expensive to maintain, and in first cost.
  3. Four exhausts per revolution tends to provide better steaming.

The question of hammer-blow was bound up with the civil engineers' requirements for the reduction of track maintenance costs. The 1928 report of the Bridge Stress Committee recommended that at a speed of 5 revolutions per second, the axle hammer-blow should not exceed 25% of the static axle load, with a maximum value of 5 tons. The whole locomotive blow was not to exceed 12½ tons. Civil engineers preferred multi-cylindered locomotives, since no balancing of reciprocating parts was required. As it turned out, the hammer-blow values recorded by the Standard classes were well within these confines, as can be seen from Table 11.

It was finally proposed in 1950 that six of the twelve Standard types be included in the construction programme for 1951, but a comparison of Table 12 with the earliest list of Standard types proposed in 1948 reveals some interesting differences.

23

Table 11 Hammer-blow Values at 5 RPS

Locomotive type	7MT 4-6-2	6MT 4-6-2	5MT 4-6-0	4MT 4-6-0	4MT 2-6-4T	3MT 2-6-4T
Maximum axle load (tons)	20¼	18½	19½	17	18	16¼
Reciprocating mass/cyl (lb)	845.3	831.3	825.8	—	—	736.8
% of reciprocating mass balanced	40%	40%	50%	50%	40%	50%
Hammer-blow						
Per wheel (tons)	2.12	2.12	2.59	2.59	1.86	2.17
Per axle (tons)	2.55	2.55	3.11	3.11	2.20	2.58
Per rail (tons)	5.50	5.50	6.72	6.72	5.04	5.93
Whole locomotive (tons)	6.60	6.60	8.15	8.15	5.99	7.04

Table 12 The Twelve Standard Types

No	Type	Cylinders (in)	Coupled wheels ft	in	Axle load (tons)	Tractive effort (lb)
1	4-6-2	(3)18 × 28	6	2	22	39,080
2	4-6-2	20 × 28	6	2	20¼	32,150
3	4-6-2	19½ × 28	6	2	18½	27,520
4	4-6-0	19 × 28	6	2	19½	26,120
5	4-6-0	18 × 28	5	8	17	25,100
6	2-6-4T	18 × 28	5	8	18	25,100
7	2-6-0	17½ × 26	5	3	16	27,142
8	2-6-0	17½ × 26	5	3	16	21,490
9	2-6-2T	17½ × 26	5	3	16¼	21,490
10	2-6-0	16½ × 24	5	0	13½	18,500
11	2-6-2T	16½ × 24	5	0	13½	18,500
12	2-10-0	20 × 28	5	0	15½	39,670

Notes: Of these locomotives listed above, types 2–6 and 9 were due for construction 1951. The design numbered 12 was still noted in late 1950 as a 2-8-2, though it was quickly amended.

The standard layout of Walschaerts valve gear with underhung crosshead. The arrangement in this view, is on Class 4 4-6-0 No 75078, but was basically the same on all types, up to and including the Class 7 Britannia 4-6-2s and Class 9F 2-10-0 freight locomotives. The simple layout and obvious accessibility for maintenance built into the design, is clearly displayed. (*R. France/Standard 4 Locomotive Preservation Society*)

The Britannia Pacifics were the first of the Standard classes to appear. In original guise No 70031 *Byron*, is seen leaving Lichfield (Trent Valley) on 23 July 1958 with the 3.45pm Euston to Manchester London Road. (*R. Shenton*)

It was intended that all types above Class 4 would have wide fireboxes, allowing the introduction of the Class 5 Pacific, though as finalised it became a 4-6-0 with a 19 tons axle load. The Class 6 express passenger locomotive materialised as a Class 7 mixed-traffic, and the similar mixed-traffic Pacific type with 18½ tons axle load became the Clan Class 6. The two Pacifics were in the entirely new design category, and allowing for the fact that the eventual Class 5 4-6-0 was considered initially as a Pacific, then three of the first six Standard types to be built were new designs. The remaining three types consisted of Class 4 4-6-0 and Class 3 2-6-2T as developments of existing types, with the Class 4 2-6-4T based on an existing design with detail modifications.

In retrospect it may be that splitting-up design and construction functions between various works will be seen as an exercise calculated to instil some degree of unification, but it also had practical advantages. For example, giving one works responsibility for the design of boilers and fittings, including such items as flangeing plates, meant that instead of carrying a facility for their manufacture in each plant, they were supplied in sets from the works responsible for that feature, wherever the locomotives were built. In addition to carrying out design functions for certain components and assemblies, each works and drawing office was assigned responsibility for one or more complete locomotive designs. The distribution of this work was as detailed in Table 13.

Finally, Tables 14 to 16 give an indication both of the degree of standardisation and the origin of many of the components used on these locomotives.

Table 13 Distribution of Design Functions

Locomotive Types		Details/Components
Brighton		Brake and sanding equipment
Class 4	4-6-0	
Class 4	2-6-4T	
Class 9	2-10-0	
Swindon		Boilers, steam fittings and smokebox details
Class 3	2-6-2T	
Class 3	2-6-0	
Doncaster		Coupling and connecting rods, valve gear
Class 5	4-6-0	and cylinder details
Class 4	2-6-0	
Derby		Bogies and pony trucks, tenders, tyres, axles
Class 7	4-6-2	and spring gear.
Class 8	4-6-2	
Class 6	4-6-2	
Class 2	2-6-0	
Class 2	2-6-2T	

Table 14 Components Common to all Standard Locomotives

Buffers	Drawhooks
Screw couplings	Mechanical lubricators
Atomisers	Atomiser steam valves

Cylinder cocks
Air valves
Cylinder relief valves
Water gauges
Graduable steam brake
  valve

Ejector
Blower valve and nipple
Sand ejector
Blow-off cock
Washout plug
Carriage-warming valve
Tube cleaner valve
Pony trucks
Number plates
Grease nipples
Locomotive brake cylinder

Cylinder cock operating
  valves
Steam chest drain valves
Steam manifold
Pressure and vacuum gauges
Driver's brake valve

Large and small ejector
  steam valve
Vacuum relief valve
Safety-valve
Driver's sand valve
Fusible plug
Washout doors
Carriage-warming shut-off
  cock on buffer beam
Bogies
Handrails and pillars
Brake blocks
Firebar elements

Connecting rod big- and
  little-end bushes
Coupling rod bushes
Unions
Nuts, bolts, studs, rivets
Piston and valve rings
Clips
Brake hangers
Brake beams, pins and
  bushes
Smokebox door

Firedoors
Rocking grate mechanism
Roller and plain bearings
Springs (steel and rubber)
Wheels
Ashpan, damper and hopper
  door gear
Injectors
Tubes
Coal watering cock

Table 15 Standard Components with Size Variation only Between Classes

Motion pins and bushes
Tyres

Cast-iron packing
Superheater elements

This photograph shows the Standard footplate layout and controls. The Standard arrangement was maintained throughout the range, although some modifications seen in later batches of Standard types included the fitting of LMS-style reversing wheel, and safety links between locomotive and tender. (*R. France/Standard 4 Locomotive Preservation Society*)

Table 16 Components Derived from Former Companies

Great Western Railway:

Mechanical lubrication
  atomiser gear
Cylinder relief valve
Water gauge
Steam valve
Whistles for smaller
  locomotives
Smaller sizes of pipe union
Smokebox door

Brick arch
Air valve
Pressure and vacuum gauges
Live steam injector
Fusible plug
Firedoor (WR locomotives
  only)
Tender and tank water-level
  gear

London Midland & Scottish Railway

Bogies
Plain bearing axleboxes
Hornblocks and hornstays
  (except 4-6-2)
Locomotive spring
  suspension
Piston head and fastening
Valve spindle guides
Connecting rod little-end
  lubrication (double
  slidebar arrangement)
Carriage-warming valve
Water pick-up gear
Rocking grate gear

Pony trucks
Manganese liners
Two-bar crosshead and
  slidebars (locomotives
  with leading pony truck)
Valve heads
Connecting rod big-end and
  coupling rod bushes and
  lubrication
Brake cylinder
Ashpan, hopper, doors and
  operating gear
Firedoor (except WR
  locomotives)

London & North Eastern Railway

Three-bar slidebars and
  crosshead
Piston rod Packing
Whistle (for large engines)
Nameplates

Gudgeon pin and little-end
  lubrication (three-bar
  arrangement)
Brake blocks
Drawhook

Southern Railway

Frame spacing (2-10-0 and
  Pacifics)
Trailing truck (Pacifics)
Washout plugs
Tender spring suspension

Three-compartment ashpan
  (Pacifics)
Locomotive and tender
  drawgear
Top-feed valve
Tyre fastening

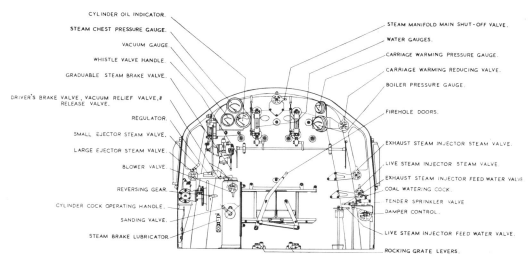

CYLINDER OIL INDICATOR.

STEAM CHEST PRESSURE GAUGE.

VACUUM GAUGE.

WHISTLE VALVE HANDLE.

GRADUABLE STEAM BRAKE VALVE.

DRIVER'S BRAKE VALVE, VACUUM RELIEF VALVE, & RELEASE VALVE.

REGULATOR.

SMALL EJECTOR STEAM VALVE.

LARGE EJECTOR STEAM VALVE.

BLOWER VALVE.

REVERSING GEAR.

CYLINDER COCK OPERATING HANDLE.

SANDING VALVE.

STEAM BRAKE LUBRICATOR.

STEAM MANIFOLD MAIN SHUT-OFF VALVE.

WATER GAUGES.

CARRIAGE WARMING PRESSURE GAUGE.

CARRIAGE WARMING REDUCING VALVE.

BOILER PRESSURE GAUGE.

FIREHOLE DOORS.

EXHAUST STEAM INJECTOR STEAM VALVE.

LIVE STEAM INJECTOR STEAM VALVE.

EXHAUST STEAM INJECTOR FEED WATER VALVE

COAL WATERING COCK.

TENDER SPRINKLER VALVE

DAMPER CONTROL.

LIVE STEAM INJECTOR FEED WATER VALVE.

ROCKING GRATE LEVERS.

Layout of cab fittings

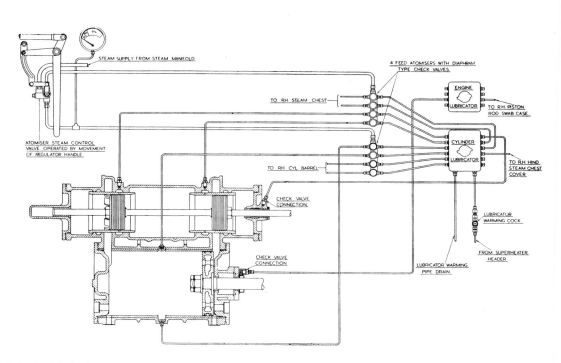

STEAM SUPPLY FROM STEAM MANIFOLD.

4 FEED ATOMISERS WITH DIAPHRAM TYPE CHECK VALVES.

ENGINE LUBRICATOR

TO R.H. PISTON ROD SWAB CASE.

TO R.H. STEAM CHEST

ATOMISER STEAM CONTROL VALVE OPERATED BY MOVEMENT OF REGULATOR HANDLE.

CYLINDER LUBRICATOR

TO R.H. HIND STEAM CHEST COVER

TO R.H. CYL BARREL

CHECK VALVE CONNECTION

LUBRICATOR WARMING COCK

FROM SUPERHEATER HEADER

CHECK VALVE CONNECTION

LUBRICATOR WARMING PIPE DRAIN

Cylinder lubrication arrangement

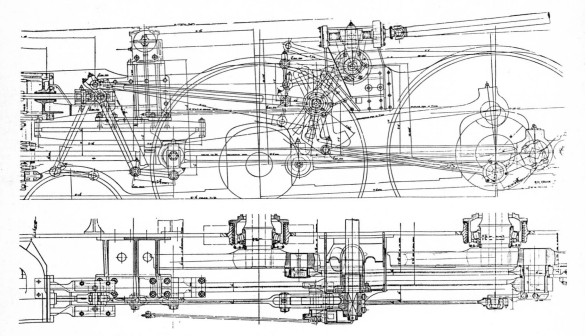

Broadside and plan view of Walschaerts valve gear on standard classes

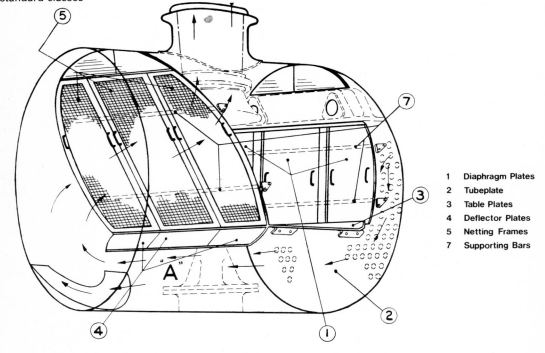

1	Diaphragm Plates
2	Tubeplate
3	Table Plates
4	Deflector Plates
5	Netting Frames
7	Supporting Bars

TYPICAL SELF CLEANING SMOKEBOX

The Standard Class 4 2-6-4 tank was one of the most attractive tank engine designs; it maintained the Standard family likeness but required some major alterations to the former LMS Fairburn type on which it was based. (*G.M. Kichenside*)

4. The Britannia Pacifics

On 3 December 1950 the first frames were laid down in the Erecting Shop at Crewe Works to order No E479, eventually to become BR Standard Class 7 Pacific No 70000 *Britannia*. The 55 locomotives of this class, if not as famous as Sir Nigel Gresley's *Flying Scotsman*, marked the beginning of the final chapter of steam locomotion on Britain's railways. One of their number, 70013 *Oliver Cromwell*, was destined to become the last main line steam locomotive in service.

It could be argued that it was not an original design, since in the Standard types was embodied the best of the former companies' practices. The end product however, drawing on all the development that had taken place in the technology of the steam locomotive, was a distinctly attractive locomotive, popular with enginemen and the lay public. There were some curious responses to the visual impact of the design at first—these varied from genuine concern at the 'distinctly American' look, to a nit-picking of the degree (or lack of it) of curvature in some visible pipework.

Originally, it was proposed that bar frames would be adopted, and two diagrams were prepared for the 1948 report from which the Britannias were developed. The Locomotive Standards Committee had

proposed a trio of entirely new designs, two Class 6 Pacifics, and a Class 5. Both Pacifics were designated Type 70, it being proposed that the express passenger type would have 6ft 6in wheels and the mixed-traffic type only 6ft 0in. The Class 5 4-6-2 Type 71 carried the same 6ft 0in diameter wheels, and the same basic characteristics as the other two. The Type 70 designs were separated only by the 6in difference in coupled wheel diameter. Results from the Interchange Trials showed that such fine steps were unnecessary, and the Class 7 came out with 6ft 2in wheels, a 21-ton axle load and 42sq ft grate. It was intended to utilise these locomotives on all duties, hence their mixed-traffic category.

Derby was chosen as the parent office for the design, with all 55 locomotives being built at Crewe Works, the first 15 of which were sent to East Anglia. An interesting feature of the pre-production phase was the production of a wooden mock-up of the footplate area. This consisted of cab, firebox back, footplate and the front half of the tender, providing the opportunity to inspect, examine and criticise the layout of controls and fittings. Representatives of the footplate crews were invited to comment on the designs. The end result was a compromise be-

Delivery of the second group of Britannias was made to the Western Region. No 70022 *Tornado* is seen in original condition, with handrails in place on the smoke deflectors, and allocated to Newton Abbot depot. (*Lens of Sutton*)

tween the driver's idea of a luxurious footplate, and the Railway Executive's most economically feasible concept. The grouping of the driver's controls met with favourable comment, since he was not required to take his eyes off the road to operate them, while in the firedoor there was room for improvement. The large door was provided so that more secondary air was admitted above the fire bed when burning hard Yorkshire coals as opposed to, say, the Welsh variety, where less air was required. Smaller doors were fitted to WR locomotives with this in mind. A point was made concerning the lack of continuity in hand rails, which on other locomotive designs had led to accidents involving footplatemen. Ironically some years later it was the design of the hand rail on the smoke deflector that was a contributory factor in the most serious accident to involve a Standard class locomotive, the derailment at Didcot. As a result of the tendency for this particular hand rail to obscure the forward vision, Britannias were modified with only handholes in the deflectors.

Mechanical Details

Firebox, Boiler, and Smokebox

The boiler fitted to the Britannia Class was an entirely new design—Type BR1. The firebox provided some 210sq ft of heating surface, with a grate of 42sq ft area, and was constructed from copper. There had been some question at an early stage of using steel, as on the Bulleid Pacifics, and some LMR Class 5 4-6-0s, but it was felt that with the variability of feed waters, copper would prove more suitable.

Including the combustion chamber, the firebox was fractionally over 9ft 0in long by 7ft 9in wide over the outer wrapper. The grate itself was wider by $4^5/_{16}$in than its length and incorporated standard cast-iron rocking sections 11in long by $2^1/_4$in wide, attached to six rocking bars spanning the full width of the grate. Air space through the grate amounted to 37% of the total area. At first the ashpan provided a problem in that the rear extension frames were narrowed-in under the grate to allow side play to the trailing truck. The use of a three-compartment hopper design successfully solved this. Based on that used on the Bulleid Pacifics which had the same trailing truck as the Britannia the total volume of the ashpan was 50 cu ft.

Class 7 4-6-2   SL/7A/1

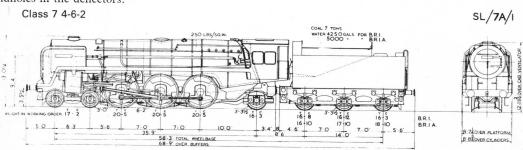

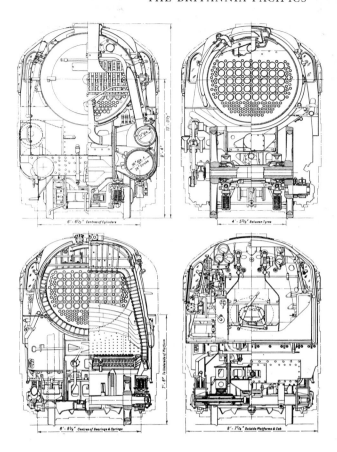

Sections through
Class 7 4-6-2:
Smokebox and cylinders,
boiler, firebox, cab

The boiler itself bore a remarkable resemblance in its main proportions to that fitted by Gresley to the V2 Class 2-6-2 locomotive. In conjunction with the desirability to provide the best steam producers, the percentage of free gas area through the tubes as a percentage of the grate area is a critical parameter in determining the difference between an indifferent boiler and a good one. With the type BR1 boiler, it was hoped to achieve a figure of over 14%. In the end 16.25% was attained, which was largely due to the increase in the rear end diameter of the barrel to 6ft 5½in.

The boiler housed 136 small tubes 2⅛in diameter and 40 superheater flues 5½in diameter. The size of the superheater tubes was a departure from traditional practice, which had settled at 5⅛in diameter for many years previously. This increase in diameter allowed for better absorption of heat with this length of flue, further increasing the efficiency of the boiler. Four 1⅜in diameter superheater elements were incorporated in each flue. Thermal efficiencies of the order of 80% were required at combustion rates of between 45 and 50 lb/sq ft grate area/hour. Under test locomotive No 70005 showed that this had been comfortably achieved—at 20lb coal/sq ft/hr 85% efficiency was

recorded, though falling to 79% at 50lb coal/sq ft/hr.

Material for the two boiler rings and smokebox was a plain carbon steel, with a tensile strength of 34–38 ton/sq in. Boiler plates were ½in thick and of rivetted construction, whilst the smokebox plates were ⅜in thick. The smokebox was of the circular drumhead pattern with a domed door and centre dart fastening. This particular method of closing the door and ensuring an airtight fit had been transported from the Great Western to the LMSR in the 1930s. Self-cleaning apparatus was fitted as standard in an effort to reduce disposal times, by requiring only a weekly instead of daily cleanout of the smokebox. It was intended to keep the front end clear over the whole boiler washout period of seven to fourteen days. As a result of research carried out at Swindon into draughting arrangements, single blastpipes and chimneys were fitted. The Superheater Company's multiple-valve regulator was positioned in the super-heater header and actuated by external rodding through a gland in the smokebox wrapper. This fitting was included to provide more sensitive control as compared with conventional slide type regulators.

Right-hand view of No 70027 showing handholds in the smoke deflectors. Western Region Britannias had handholds cut in the smoke deflectors, following removal of the handrails from the class as a result of the inquiry into the Milton (near Didcot) accident. (*R. Smithies*)

Frames, Wheels and Motion

As originally proposed, the Britannia chassis was to have been built up with bar frames. The problem with the Standards was in the weight of the castings and a lack of available workshop capacity. Eventually, the frames were constructed from 1⅛in thick mild steel plate, and stayed at various points by fabricated steel stretchers, as conventional practice. The main frames proper terminated just behind the rear coupled wheels, with slightly thicker extension frames bolted on, and narrowed-in under the wide base firebox to the locomotive drawbar. A departure from traditional

No 70028 *Royal Star*, without cab and other footplate details, undergoing a general repair at Swindon Works on 7 September 1958. The firedoors seen in this view were of the WR type, permitting less secondary air over the firebed than with the LMS type of door fitted to the majority of Standard locomotives. (*R. Shenton*)

practice here was the decision to use the frame spacing of 3ft 2¼in, where previous designs had almost always used a spacing of 4ft 1in. The narrower style was used by Bulleid on the SR Pacifics and was selected for the Standards in view of the better support it gave the axleboxes.

Welded-in horn guides were another departure, though this was not perpetuated on the rest of the Standard range. The axleboxes themselves were a source of much discussion, and although the decision was taken to equip the Britannias with roller bearings on all coupled wheels and the trailing truck, later batches Nos 70035–49 (except No 70035–39, which had roller bearings on the driving wheels only) had plain bearings on all coupled wheels. The plain bearing axlebox had been developed to a high degree of reliability, and the Swindon/Stanier design was followed on all plain bearing types. The driving axlebox was made longer than the remaining coupled wheel boxes to accommodate the considerable piston thrust of some 35 tons.

The two outside cylinders, 20in diameter by 28in stroke, were steel castings, with cast-iron liners for the 11in diameter piston valves, and the cylinders themselves were bolted onto the frames, a point which was questioned in some quarters with the suggestion that bar type frames with half-saddles cast-in with each cylinder might have given a better front end. Since these locomotives were designed to pass the larger L2 loading gauge, Walschaerts valve gear was employed with underhung crosshead arrangement. The steam circuit, designed to reduce internal friction supplied the cylinders through 2¼in wide ports. Valve travel in full gear was a fraction under 7¾in, a steam lap of 1¹¹⁄₁₆in and a lead of ¼in. The motion was designed to provide a maximum cut-offs of 77.5% in fore gear and 74.7% in reverse gear.

Cylinder clearance volume was known to have some influence on performance, the lower the figure the more pronounced the fore-and-aft movement. To

On LMR metals No 70017 *Arrow* near Duffield in Derbyshire, with the Palatine, on 18 July 1959. Again, no handrails, but with the dish and bar type handholds in the smoke deflectors, preferred by the LMR. (*Don Rowland*)

mitigate this in the Britannias the amount of clearance was 10.3% of the swept volume. This was an example of at least one area where the Interchange Trials had proved useful, demonstrating that the two-cylinder locomotives tested with low clearance volumes had produced a marked fore-and-aft effect.

To reduce the overall weight, motion parts were fluted I-section steel, though a later modification provided plain coupling rods for the driving and trailing wheels on a number of locomotives. The small-ends of the return cranks were the only motion joints to be fitted with roller bearings. Balancing of the reciprocating parts was an important consideration, especially in view of the fact that they were high-powered two-cylinder locomotives. To maintain an even, regular pull on the drawbar 40% of the mass was balanced, involving the rivetting of plates over the coupled wheel spokes, and then filling these with lead. The tubular reach rod acting on the weighshaft was a departure from previous practice, and was adapted in an attempt to eliminate the effect of vibration from the valve gear. Suspension of the expansion link was similar to the method adopted by the Southern Railway, with the trunnion carried in a fabricated hanger bolted to the mainframe.

Suspension was by underhung leaf springs made from plain carbon steel, and for coupled wheels consisted of 20 ½in thick leaves of 4ft 0in span, and a standard width of 5in. Bogie and pony trucks were 3ft 6in span, with 21 leaves for the former and 18 for the latter, from 7/16in thick plate. The original form of spring hanger bracket was of box section and a quick-release device incorporated in the assembly provided for the release of wheels, axles, springs and hangers as one unit on the removal of a safety-pin. Brake shoes were provided ahead of the wheels from single hangers, with two cross-beams. No compensation was provided in the rigging, in an attempt to simplify the layout and construction.

Two final items worthy of a mention at this point are the sanding arrangements and method of tyre

fastening. In the Britannias forward sanding was provided for all coupled wheels, including a method of ensuring dry sand from the sandboxes, which was to have been standard equipment on the entire range. In this, heating coils were provided in each box, a method devised by a running shed foreman named Downs, which following extensive trials proved initially at least successful in eliminating much of the problem of damp sand. The 3in tyres were a simple shrink fit over the cast-steel wheel centres—no other fastening arrangement was used. The method was adapted from former SR practice developed by Bulleid, and was possible due to the attainment of a high degree of accuracy during machining operations in the workshops, and considerably simplified the tyre fitting operation.

Cab, Platework and Fittings

Running boards were perhaps the most controversial feature, at least outwardly, of these locomotives. They were fixed to brackets attached to the boiler side to effect clearance and allow easy access to motion and mechanical parts. At the leading end there was a drop between levels of some 3ft, covered by a sloping plate. Smoke deflectors were fitted to all locomotives from new except Nos 70043/4 which carried Westinghouse air pumps on each side of the smokebox for a short time. Nameplates were carried on 54 locomotives, only No 70047 remaining nameless, and were cast in brass except for No 70048, which had aluminium plates. All backgrounds were red, with 4in high letters.

Some of the cab fittings were departures from previous practice, as indeed to a degree was the cab itself. The footplate was extended on a cantilever support towards the tender front, to eliminate the need for a fall plate, and provide a firmer footing for the fireman. The position of the reversing wheel, side-on to the driver was a novelty, and though it was supposed to be easier to operate was not welcomed by many. The provision of two water gauges was widely approved. The multiple-valve regulator actuated by external rodding also had its critics. In the cab two handles, one on each side of the footplate, were arranged so that to open the valve the handle was

33

The experimental fitting of Westinghouse air pumps for brake trials, to two of the Class 7s, required the removal of the deflectors. No 70044, later named *Earl Haig*, is about to leave Lichfield (Trent Valley) on 22 July 1953 with the 3.45pm Euston to Manchester London Road. (*R. Shenton*)

pulled back towards the operator. This was a considerable departure from previous practice, where the regulator arm was usually mounted centrally on the firebox back, and actuated by a sideways movement from the left-hand, or driver's side (except on GWR locomotives, which had right-hand drive). Some LNER Pacifics, though, had pull-out regulators.

Tenders

Three different types of six-wheel tender were fitted to the Britannias, each having a wheelbase of 14ft 0in equally divided. Construction of the tank and bunker was based on the design introduced by Riddles for the Austerity freight locomotives. The BR1 was the first type to be built, with high inset sides to the coal space, designed to improve visibility when running tender-first. It may seem curious to develop such a feature for inclusion in a locomotive type less likely to run tender-first than most, and a critical point to observe when setting-back to couple onto a train was the bottom back corner. The increase in coal capacity required on certain duties was dealt with by reverting to a flush-sided tender design, and the last batches of Britannias had coal pushers fitted.

Construction was a combination of rivetting and welding, with the coal space and water tanks as a single unit supported by angle brackets, bolted to the frame and buffer beams. Roller bearings were standard on all axleboxes, with 3ft 3½in wheels and overhung leaf springs. The latter was a standard feature, adopted from the form of tender suspension used by the Southern Railway. Water pick-up gear was approved as standard, and although provision was made for its fitting in every tender design, the gear itself was not always included. A last item on the tender proved to be an early source of embarrassment, and potential trouble—the drawgear. Most tenders were fitted with safety links to support the simple bar-and-spring connection. However, although the same drawgear design was used in the Standard locomotives, with the cantilever cab floor it was thought unnecessary to fit safety links. With hindsight it is easy to point out the irony of the fact that one of the earliest teething troubles of the Britannias was the tender and locomotive parting company!

Building and Numbering

All the Britannias were built at Crewe Works between January 1951 and September 1954. The total cost of construction during this period rose from £17,520 each in 1951 to £22,600 in 1954. They were programmed to be built in seven batches, as listed below:

Batch	Numbers	Year	Operating	Maintenance
1	70000–14	1951	ER	LMR
2	70015–24	1951	WR	LMR
3	70025–29	1952	WR	LMR
4	70030–34	1952	LMR	LMR
5	70035–44	1952	ER(8) {LMR(2)}	LMR
6	70045–49	1953	LMR	LMR
7	70050–54	1953	ScR	LMR

For consistency in numbering and ease of class recognition the Standard designs were allocated the block of numbers between 70000 and 99999, taking in the Austerity designs.

Treated to a special finish for display at the Festival of Britain exhibition in 1951, No 70004 *William Shakespeare* was regularly in charge of the Southern Region's most prestigious train, the Golden Arrow. The locomotive was maintained in superb condition by Stewarts Lane depot, until transferred to the LMR in 1958. (*Lens of Sutton*)

A comparison with the programme and actual construction dates reveals instances of departure from the programmed sequence. The lengthy delay evident between batches 2 and 3 is attributable to the then acute steel shortage which prompted a cutback of some 40% in the construction programmes. Although locomotives Nos 70025–34 in batches 3 and 4 appeared as planned, the cutback affected batch 5 to the extent that this was not completed until June 1953. There was then a delay of twelve months before

Although on Western Region metals, with the Red Dragon express, the locomotive carries the LMR pattern handholds in the smoke deflectors. Also worth noting in this view are the canvas draught screens fitted between locomotive and tender in an attempt to improve the draughty footplate conditions. A single red route disc is carried below the running number, as on WR Castle class 4-6-0s. (*Lens of Sutton*)

the appearance of the final two batches 6 and 7, covering Nos 70045–54.

Names did not follow any particular theme, and only No 70047 remained unnamed. Exceptions to the variety of names were found in the locomotives allocated to the Western and Scottish Regions. The Western Region ones were given names originally carried by GWR locomotives, from Gooch singles to Churchward Star Class 4-6-0s. The Scottish Britannias bore the names of some of the more well-known Scottish firths.

Operation and Performance

The adoption of a centrifugal steam drier in the dome of the BR boiler proved to be a source of trouble. The original steam intake was only 11¾in above the water level, and caused sufficient water carry-over to the cylinders to result in the breakage of several cast-iron piston heads. The first of these occurred in March 1951 soon after the Britannias had been allocated to the Great Eastern lines. Following an interim raising of the steam intake, the final solution was the complete removal of the steam drier, and a substitution of a very simple steam intake 1ft 4¾in above water level. While the investigations were proceeding into the reasons for the water carry-over, the piston heads

One of the final batch of Britannias, for the Scottish Region, and given typically Scottish names, as in this case No 70050 *Firth of Clyde*, seen on shed at Glasgow Polmadie. These final locomotives were paired with the flush-sided type BR1B tenders. (*Lens of Sutton*)

were replaced with a cast-steel variety, having ⅛in clearance with the cylinder bore. Subsequently all Britannias were fitted with the cast-steel piston head, as also were the Class 6, Clan Pacifics.

The roller bearings used on the tenders showed no signs of problems at all, though the cannon boxes originally fitted to the locomotives had a tendency to leak oil. The ingress of water prompted corrosion and rapidly increased wear. The designers were not entirely convinced at the outset of the reliability of roller bearings, and hedged their bets, so to speak, by providing some with roller bearings on the driving axle only, and some with plain bearings for all coupled wheels. Main frame cracks which showed up in the early running were demonstrated to be caused by the lack of support given by the spring hanger bracket at a point where considerable flexing occurred. The original design was modified to provide greater strength in the area of the bottom front edge, where perhaps a more traditional design of horn guide and fastening could have prevented this.

By far the most serious of the teething troubles were the seven instances of wheels shifting on axles. On the first occasion in July 1951 No 70014 failed with all coupled wheels shifted on the axles. Bent coupling rods occurring at the same time were themselves subject to a modification. All 25 locomotives were withdrawn temporarily from service for a full investigation. Fortunately it was discovered that seven of the LMR Class 5 4-6-0s built with roller bearings on the coupled wheels between 1947 and 1950 had also failed in the same way, yet 23 locomotives similarly fitted had been trouble-free. Similar experience from the continent demonstrated that the assembly of coupled wheels with roller bearings was an operation demanding special treatment, which may

seem an obvious point, though no problems were expected with the techniques used initially.

Two major differences that presented themselves centred around the facts that since the roller bearing had to pass over the wheel seat, the diameter of the latter was smaller than the journal, with a reduction in the gripping surface of the wheel seat. Also, by comparison with the plain bearing, the roller variety presents a hard, unyielding surface to impact forces, whereas the clearances in plain bearings offer some cushioning. There was also the question that workshop techniques developed in the fabrication of plain bearings were not wholly suited to that needed in the fitting of roller bearings. A further possible influence was the boring of a 4½in diameter hole through the axle to counter the increased weight of the bearings. This was not an unknown practice but the hollowing-out was larger than previously known, and there was a possible loss in pressure between wheel boss and axle as a result of the "squashing" effect on the hollow cylinder when pressing the wheels on.

The use of a technique involving the pressing of wheels onto a dummy axle for quartering, tyre-fitting and balancing also contributed to the multiplication of marginal errors when the wheels were pressed off again and fitted to the axles with the roller bearing axleboxes. Curiously No 70005, which had been subjected to a series of intensive operating trials, covering hundreds of miles under conditions of maximum power output, experienced no trouble. The indications were that there was nothing materially wrong with the basic design, but the dividing line between success and failure was very narrow.

The wheel-shifting incidents also highlighted a weakness in the leading coupling rods. As originally fitted they were deeply fluted, fine-grain steel with a tensile strength of 40 tons, though the web thickness was only ⅜in. The shock loading of the rods caused by the wheel movement provided a lateral deflection much greater than that which they were designed to withstand. In the event, the leading coupled rods were replaced by plain-section steel of the same quality as before, but with a uniform thickness of 1⅝in and varying in depth from 4½in to 5½in along the length.

Lubrication had received some detailed attention at the design stage, the layout of which is illustrated in the diagram. Mechanical pumps were incorporated with various features to ensure an adequate supply, particularly at the cylinders and valves. Some difficulties arose in the Britannias which in fact varied between the regions, from such problems as shortage of oil brought on by incorrect pump settings, insufficient oil being delivered from a particular setting, and difficulties with check valves. The automatic shut-off of atomiser steam was held to be a problem under shortage conditions, and to counter this its control was linked with the cylinder cock operation, so that under no-power conditions the atomiser steam supply was not turned off easily. Curiously, the Eastern Region Britannias showed little signs of cylinder and valve wear, but those allocated in the early days to the Western Region experienced pronounced difficulties in removal of valves at examinations, due to carbon deposits in the boxes.

For the most part the performance in service of components stood up well, excepting odd items such as the failure of the 'Downs' sanding system. Steam sanding was standardised as replacement for the 'Downs' arrangement, it would seem solely on the argument that the arrangement would not work with sand available in the South of England. Later modifications were made to the cab side-sheets to reduce draughts, and tender fall-plates were fitted.

Some interesting comments were passed, both technical and general, when the Britannias and the rest of the Standard range took to the rails. Many people questioned the feasibility of a Pacific type for general-purpose work, suggesting that the narrow-firebox 4-6-0 was sufficient for all such duties. While applauding the use of plate frames of 1¼in thickness, bar frames were considered for possible future use. The tyre fastening adopted was a new idea, and according to one commentator insufficient experience had been gained, so that large sections of the tyre could be thrown off in the event of a double fracture. Two water gauges were considered unnecessary too, surprisingly perhaps, since knowledge of the boiler water level is vitally important. This comment was based possibly on rarity of water gauge failures, though the same commentator added that the Western Region had always managed with one gauge and one test cock.

The reversing gear was welcomed by most.

Although it was felt that steel fireboxes fitted with thermic syphons would offer improvements, most recognised the difficulty of providing suitable water supplies. Against the cost savings made in the use of steel, it was necessary to add the cost of water treatment.

The Britannias allocated to the Eastern Region, and used on the former GER main line from Liverpool Street to Ipswich and Norwich, were an immediate success. In July 1951 the operating authorities introduced a regular-interval service between London and Norwich with the four fastest down runs booked to reach Ipswich in 76 minutes. The eleven diagrams worked from Stratford and Norwich were covered by twelve Britannias, with three West Country Class locomotives held in reserve. So intensively were they worked in the first week of operation that No 70013 logged almost 3,000 miles. This success continued with the Eastern Region claiming the down Broadsman as the fastest train in Britain. In addition to GE line workings, Britannias were employed on passenger turns from Sheffield to Harwich (Parkestone Quay), and to speed up the services to Clacton. By the end of the 1950s and early 1960s, the Britannias had been drafted on to the GNR main line, on expresses from Kings Cross to Immingham among others. Displaced from the GE line by diesels, the class was noted regularly from April 1961 on expresses between Colchester and York. The early 1960s saw diesels beginning to make their presence felt on duties that would normally have been given to Britannias, and by December 1963 all were transferred to the Midland Region.

The Southern Region acquired three in the early 1950s in exchange for Bulleid Pacifics transferred to the ER, and these were set to work initially on the Western Section. Workings to Bournemouth out of Waterloo were relatively short-lived, and it was some time before the class was authorised to work the SR lines in Devon and Cornwall. Transfer to the Eastern Section and Stewarts Lane found the most popular workings for the Britannias on that region, with regular appearances for a long time on the Golden Arrow. Ironically, it was while working that train at speed near Headcorn, that one of the first instances of wheels shifting was noted with No 70004. The Britannias were popular with footplate crews, and turned in some very creditable performances.

On the West of England main line from Paddington the Britannias were least successful, yet by contrast those stationed at Cardiff Canton depot were well-liked and appeared on such prestigious services as the Red Dragon and Capitals United expresses. At first it seemed that WR men did not like them since they were not Swindon products. From those allocated to Old Oak Common, Laira and Newton Abbot there were comments of much slipping and hard riding, and ultimately Nos 70017–24 were exchanged for Castle Class locomotives from Cardiff Canton.

Near Didcot in 1955 the worst accident to befall a member of the class occurred when No 70032 *Tennyson* became derailed while working an up excursion from South Wales. The driver claimed the smoke deflector handrails obscured his view of the signals, in

Technical Data—Britannia Class 7MT 4-6-2s Nos 70000–70054

Note: The information relates to locomotives in original or 'as built' condition

Cylinders and valve gear

Cylinders—diameter × stroke	20in × 28in
Piston swept volume (one cylinder)	8796cu in
Clearance volume as % of piston swept volume	10.3%
Maximum piston thrust	78540lb
Steam chests	
—volume between valve heads	4558cu in
—volume as % of piston swept volume	51.8%
Piston valves	
—diameter	11in
—steam lap	$1^{11}/_{16}$in
—lead	¼in
—exhaust clearance	NIL
Maximum travel of valves	7.73in
Maximum cut-off %	78%
Travel at 20% cut-off	4.05in

Balancing data

Revolving masses, weight per cylinder	1500lb
Reciprocating masses,	
—total weight per cylinder	846lb
—percentage balanced	40%
—unbalanced	508lb
Ratio of unbalanced reciprocating weight per cylinder to total weight of locomotive	1/414
Hammer-blow at 5 revolutions per second	
—per wheel	2.12 tons
—per axle	2.55 tons
—per rail	5.50 tons
—whole locomotive	6.60 tons

Boiler proportions

Free area through tubes	
—large	4.13sq ft
—small	2.66sq ft
—total	6.79sq ft
Area through large tubes as % of total	60.9%
Total free area as % of grate area	16.2%
A/S ratio	
—large tubes	1/420
—small tubes	1/435
Steam pipe in boiler	
—bore	7in
—cross-sectional area	38.5sq in
Regulator fully open—area	48.8sq in (multiple-valve regulator)
Superheater elements—total area	39.3sq in
Steam pipes to cylinders—total area	56.5sq in
Blast pipe cap—diameter	5⅜in
—area	22.7sq in
Chimney throat—diameter	1ft 3⅝in
—area	1.29sqft
Throat area as % of grate area	3.09%
Height—blastpipe cap to chimney throat	2ft 10¾in
Taper of chimney	1 in 14

any case sited for right-hand drive locomotives. As a result of investigating this accident, the handrails were removed from the smoke deflectors to improve the drivers' forward view, but No 70032 retained its handrails from new until withdrawal. By 1961, all the WR Britannias had been transferred to the LMR, but not before No 70016 became the first and only member of the class to visit Caerphilly Works for repair.

The first official allocation to the LMR was to have been Nos 70030–4, though a number of others were already in service on that region, including Nos 70005/15/16. Those stationed at Holyhead were used regularly on the Irish Mail, though they were not over-popular with the crews, and some difficulties were experienced with the welds of the tender seams coming open. Repairs and overhauls were carried out at Crewe for the whole class, though in 1956 it was decided that the ER locomotives would be maintained by Doncaster. A curious incident to involve a Britannia was that of the locomotive and tender parting company. On the LMR, this befell No 70014 whilst working on the down Palatine near Hazel Grove, while a similar event took place on the ER on Ilford flyover involving No 70012. By the mid-1960s all the Britannias were in service on LMR metals and based largely at Carlisle Kingmoor. Most workings by that time were excursions and specials to other regions and some of the rather less prestigious passenger duties, fitted freight and parcels turns. By 1966, surviving Britannias were seldom seen far from the North-West, though at least one ventured as far south as Bournemouth.

Although withdrawals began in 1965, almost all were taken out of service in 1967, leaving only No 70013 as the last main line steam type in service in August 1968. The majority of the class was cut-up in Scotland, by various concerns in 1967 and 1968, with Nos 70000 and 70013 to be preserved. No 70013 ran light from Carnforth to Norwich after working its last steam special, where it was transported by road to the Bressingham Steam Museum. No 70000 *Britannia* was recently restored to working order on the Severn Valley Railway, being renamed by its designer, R.A. Riddles, 30 years after its very first appearance.

Summary Table—Britannia Class 7MT 4-6-2s Nos 70000–70054

No	Name	Built	Withdrawn	Final MPD	Disposal
70000	*Britannia*	1/51	5/66	Newton Heath	Preserved on Severn Valley Railway
70001	*Lord Hurcomb*	2/51	8/66	Carlisle Kingmoor	Motherwell Machinery Co.
70002	*Geoffrey Chaucer*	3/51	1/67	Carlisle Kingmoor	G.H. Campbell, Airdrie
70003	*John Bunyan*	3/51	3/67	Carlisle Kingmoor	G.H. Campbell, Airdrie
70004	*William Shakespeare*	3/51	12/67	Carlisle Kingmoor	T.W. Ward, Inverkeithing
70005	*John Milton*	4/51	7/67	Carlisle Kingmoor	G.H. Campbell, Airdrie
70006	*Robert Burns*	4/51	5/67	Carlisle Kingmoor	J. McWilliam, Shettleston
70007	*Coeur de Lion*	4/51	6/65	Carlisle Kingmoor	Crewe Works
70008	*Black Prince*	4/51	1/67	Carlisle Kingmoor	G.H. Campbell, Airdrie
70009	*Alfred the Great*	5/51	1/67	Carlisle Kingmoor	J. McWilliam, Shettleston
70010	*Owen Glendower*	5/51	9/67	Carlisle Kingmoor	J. McWilliam, Shettleston
70011	*Hotspur*	5/51	12/67	Carlisle Kingmoor	J. McWilliam, Shettleston
70012	*John of Gaunt*	5/51	12/67	Carlisle Kingmoor	T.W. Ward, Sheffield
70013	*Oliver Cromwell*	5/51	8/68	Carnforth	Preserved at Bressingham Steam Museum
70014	*Iron Duke*	6/51	12/67	Carlisle Kingmoor	T.W. Ward, Inverkeithing
70015	*Apollo*	6/51	8/67	Carlisle Kingmoor	J. McWilliam, Shettleston
70016	*Ariel*	6/51	8/67	Carlisle Kingmoor	J. McWilliam, Shettleston
70017	*Arrow*	6/51	9/66	Carlisle Kingmoor	J. Cashmore, Newport
70018	*Flying Dutchman*	6/51	12/66	Carlisle Kingmoor	Motherwell Machinery Co.
70019	*Lightning*	6/51	3/66	Carlisle Upperby	West of Scotland Shipbreaking Co.
70020	*Mercury*	7/51	1/67	Carlisle Kingmoor	J. McWilliam, Shettleston
70021	*Morning Star*	8/51	12/67	Carlisle Kingmoor	T.W. Ward, Inverkeithing
70022	*Tornado*	8/51	12/67	Carlisle Kingmoor	T.W. Ward, Inverkeithing
70023	*Venus*	8/51	12/67	Carlisle Kingmoor	T.W. Ward, Sheffield
70024	*Vulcan*	10/51	12/67	Carlisle Kingmoor	T.W. Ward, Sheffield
70025	*Western Star*	9/52	12/67	Carlisle Kingmoor	G.H. Campbell, Airdrie
70026	*Polar Star*	10/52	1/67	Stockport Edgeley	J. Cashmore, Newport
70027	*Rising Star*	10/52	6/67	Carlisle Kingmoor	Motherwell Machinery Co.
70028	*Royal Star*	10/52	9/67	Carlisle Kingmoor	J. McWilliam, Shettleston
70029	*Shooting Star*	11/52	10/67	Carlisle Kingmoor	J. McWilliam, Shettleston
70030	*William Wordsworth*	11/52	6/66	Carlisle Upperby	T.W. Ward, Sheffield
70031	*Byron*	11/52	11/67	Carlisle Kingmoor	J. McWilliam, Shettleston
70032	*Tennyson*	12/52	9/67	Carlisle Kingmoor	J. McWilliam, Shettleston
70033	*Charles Dickens*	12/52	7/67	Carlisle Kingmoor	G.H. Campbell, Airdrie
70034	*Thomas Hardy*	12/52	5/67	Carlisle Kingmoor	J. McWilliam, Shettleston
70035	*Rudyard Kipling*	12/52	12/67	Carlisle Kingmoor	T.W. Ward, Inverkeithing
70036	*Boadicea*	12/52	10/66	Carlisle Kingmoor	Motherwell Machinery Co.
70037	*Hereward the Wake*	12/52	11/66	Carlisle Kingmoor	J. McWilliam, Shettleston
70038	*Robin Hood*	1/53	8/67	Carlisle Kingmoor	J. McWilliam, Shettleston
70039	*Sir Christopher Wren*	2/53	9/67	Carlisle Kingmoor	J. McWilliam, Shettleston
70040	*Clive of India*	3/53	4/67	Carlisle Kingmoor	J. McWilliam, Shettleston
70041	*Sir John Moore*	3/53	4/67	Carlisle Kingmoor	J. McWilliam, Shettleston
70042	*Lord Roberts*	4/53	5/67	Carlisle Kingmoor	J. McWilliam, Shettleston
70043	*Earl Kitchener*	6/53	8/65	Crewe South	T.W. Ward, Sheffield
70044	*Earl Haig*	6/53	10/67	Stockport Edgeley	T.W. Ward, Sheffield
70045	*Lord Rowallan*	6/54	12/67	Carlisle Kingmoor	T.W. Ward, Sheffield
70046	*Anzac*	6/54	7/67	Carlisle Kingmoor	G.H. Campbell, Airdrie
70047	★	6/54	7/67	Carlisle Kingmoor	G.H. Campbell, Airdrie
70048	*Territorial Army 1908–1958*	7/54	5/67	Carlisle Kingmoor	J. McWilliam, Shettleston
70049	*Solway Firth*	7/54	12/67	Carlisle Kingmoor	J. McWilliam, Shettleston
70050	*Firth of Clyde*	8/54	8/66	Carlisle Kingmoor	G.H. Campbell, Airdrie
70051	*Firth of Forth*	8/54	12/67	Carlisle Kingmoor	J. McWilliam, Shettleston
70052	*Firth of Tay*	8/54	4/67	Carlisle Kingmoor	G.H. Campbell, Airdrie
70053	*Moray Firth*	9/54	4/67	Carlisle Kingmoor	J. McWilliam, Shettleston
70054	*Dornoch Firth*	9/54	11/66	Carlisle Kingmoor	Motherwell Machinery Co.

All were built at Crewe Works.

★No 70047 was never named

5. Class 9F 2-10-0s

The 251 locomotives constructed to this design were the most numerous of the Standards. They were also the most non-standard of the twelve designs, incorporating some major departures from the original layout. Amongst these were Franco-Crosti boilers, Berkeley mechanical stoker and Giesl ejector, with no fewer than six weight diagrams covering the basic Class 9F 2-10-0.

In 1948, when Messrs Riddles, Cox and colleagues were formulating their proposals for future locomotive construction, included in the first category of entirely new designs was a 2-8-2 freight type. Designated Type 90, it was to have utilised the same boiler as the Britannias, but working at 225lb/sq in, and with a grate area of 36sq ft. The 1948 proposal of course, as with all the others, was for a bar-frame construction, with same 19½in × 28in cylinders as the Pacifics. The wheel size of 5ft 3in was adopted to improve the speed characteristics as compared with existing 2-8-0 freight types which had coupled wheels of around 4ft 8in diameter. Another interesting feature of the Type 90 proposal was that both leading and trailing pony trucks were to have outside roller-bearing axleboxes, with overhung leaf springs. The coupled wheel axleload was to have been 16½ tons for Class 2-8-2 compared with 15½ tons of the eventual Class 9.

Comparing the diagrams for the Type 90 2-8-2, a considerable degree of standardisation appears to have been decided. The boiler, firebox, grate, smokebox and double blastpipe/chimney were identical with the proposed Class 5 Pacific, while the cylinders were of the same proportions as the larger Class 7 4-6-2. The tender design was the same as for the three Pacific types, carrying seven tons of coal and 4,000 gallons of water on a six-wheel tender of 14ft 0in wheelbase.

The 2-8-2 design was adopted as a Standard type for a time, since a full detail weight diagram appeared in common with others in the Standard range. This diagram, produced as the details of the Class 7 Britannia had been finalised, was to include as many features of the Pacific as possible. In fact, the only departure from the Britannia design was in the wheel arrangement and locomotive details. The boiler was the BR1 type, with 2474sq ft of evaporative heating surface, a 42sq ft grate and working pressure of 250lb/sq in. The tender was the BR1 type with 4250 gallons water capacity and seven tons of coal on a six-wheeled chassis.

The two outside cylinders were 19½in × 28in as in the Type 90 proposal, driving the third coupled axle through standard Walschaerts valve gear. The 5ft 3in diameter wheels were also maintained, with an axle load of just under 17 tons. A curious feature which was to have been adopted had the 2-8-2 been built was the braking of the trailing truck, which had become a carbon copy of the truck fitted to the Class 7 Pacifics. Of the total weight 141 tons 16 cwt for this type of locomotive 92.85 tons was the brake load, including the brake force applied to the trailing truck. The calculated tractive effort of the Class 8F 2-8-2 was just below 36,000lb, while that of the 2-10-0 was marginally under 40,000lb.

There were two main reasons for the non-production of the 2-8-2s. First, a heavy freight type was not an immediate priority of the operating department because it already had literally hundreds of eight-coupled locomotives for this work. Second, Riddles had noted that as freight locomotive performance was largely dependent on adhesion, and as a 2-8-2 design would have little additional characteristics to offer in this area, a ten-coupled arrangement

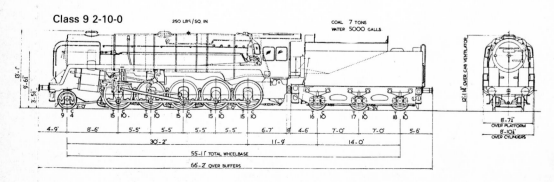

The basic Class 9F 2-10-0 is seen here; No 92122 newly built, and standing outside the Paint Shop at Crewe Works. (R. Shenton)

was preferable. The successful performance of the Austerity 2-10-0s had some influence on this decision, so a re-design was undertaken, to fit a wide firebox over 5ft 0in coupled wheels, within the L2 loading gauge.

The parent office for this design was Brighton, with the first 178 locomotives built at Crewe, and the remaining 73 at Swindon. The first order was for 20 locomotives, shared between the Western, London Midland and Eastern Regions.

Mechanical Details

Firebox, Boiler and Smokebox

Four entirely new boiler designs were prepared for the Standard range, the BR1, BR2 and BR13 covering the Pacific types, while the 2-10-0 sported the type BR9 boiler. Constructed at high-tensile steel plate in

Among the many detail modifications to the Class 9Fs was the fitting of double chimneys. This broadside of No 92220 shows the copper capped version on this locomotive. A plaque noting that this was the last steam locomotive built for BR read:

> No 92220 Built at Swindon
> March 1960
> The Last Steam Locomotive For British
> Railways
> Named at Swindon on March 18th 1960 By
> K.W.C. Grand Esq
> Member of the British Transport Commission

two rings, the second of which was tapered, and using the Britannia flangeing blocks for the front tubeplate and the Class 6 blocks for the rear, it was something of a compromise. The whole assembly tapered only slightly from 5ft 9in diameter at the front to 6ft 1in at the firebox end. 138 small tubes of 2in outside diameter were fitted, and 35 superheater flues 5¼in outside diameter, with a length between tubeplates of 15ft 3in. For a locomotive of this size the total heating surface of the tubes, at 1836sq ft may have seemed small, though it was 77sq ft greater than that of the highly satisfactory MD 2-10-0. The superheater, providing 535sq ft of heating surface used standard 1⅜in elements, with ball joints, and conventional cast-iron header. The free area through the tubes was 5.49sq ft, representing only 13.6% of the grate area. This was the lowest value attained by any of the Standard boilers, but was acceptable considering that a freight type was intended to operate at only moderate steam rates. The fibreglass lagging applied to other Standard types was also used on the Class 9Fs, though some examples were fitted with lightweight asbestos mattresses.

The firebox, like the boiler, was a compromise design, and developed from the need to carry the grate over the axle of the trailing coupled wheel. The

EVENING STAR

use of a wide firegate, with 5ft 1in coupled wheels necessitated the use of a much shallower assembly, which was sloping for only part of its length. It measured 7ft 5½in long with a maximum width of 7ft ⅛in. The steel outer wrapper was ½in thick plate, while the copper inner firebox had a ⅝in thick wrapper. At the front end a 1in thick copper tubeplate was fitted, and a combustion chamber with inclined throatplate. Water space stays were of Monel metal, except for a number of rows nearest the back throat- and tube-plates, with steel nuts fitted on the inside. The use of Monel metal was a procedure adopted from late LMSR practice because of the increased resistance it offered both to corrosion and electrolytic action. Roof longitudinal and transverse stays were steel. Standard rocking grate firebars were used, 12 of which were fitted to each of the 12 rocking sections, arranged as six on either side of the centre line. Each half of the grate could be rocked independently, in either full- or short-travel positions of the cab operating lever. The triple hopper ashpan used on the Pacific locomotives was not practicable with the 2-10-0, hence a conventional arrangement was settled on, with twin hopper doors fitted in the base. Front and rear dampers were fitted, controlled by a handwheel and screw from the cab. The self-emptying ashpan could be operated from ground level, using the key provided for working the rocking grate.

The cylindrical-pattern smokebox was constructed from ⅜in steel plate as standard practice, though in this case of slightly smaller outside diameter than the boiler front tubeplate. It was attached to a fabricated saddle, which also served as a frame stay, and incorporated the full standard self-cleaning apparatus, with deflector and table plates and a wire gauze screen. The blastpipe in the original Standard design had a single nozzle of 5⅜in diameter and included the four-jet Cardew pattern blower. Later locomotives had double blastpipes, and at least one of these first batches was modified in this way. No 92250 was fitted with a Giesl oblong ejector, and ten locomotives were for a time fitted with Franco-Crosti boilers.

Frames, Wheels and Motion

The Class 9Fs were provided with one of the most rigid and substantial mainframe assemblies, using the established pattern of 1¼in thick plate stayed apart at a distance coinciding with the axlebox centres lines. Horizontal fabricated plate stretchers were fitted just above the hornways, forming an almost continuous "decking" from saddle to the leading end of the ashpan. At the bottom of the frame rigid cross-stretchers were constructed integrally with the vertical stays. In addition, stiffening the bottom edges was accomplished with steel castings of inverted 'T-shape', which also provided a location for the hornstays and included the spring hanger brackets.

A problem occurred with the wide firebox design,

in that since its width caried over and outside the frames there was a need to cut away the upper portion of the mainframe between the fourth and fifth coupled axles. To retain adequate strength at this point it was then necessary to rivet stiffening plates on either side of the frame plates. The fabricated dragbox also acted as a frame stay under the cab, and included the drawbar with a plain eye at both ends. Boiler mountings on the frame consisted of a saddle fixed to a cross-stretcher at the front end, close to the front tubeplate. At the rear, extensions of the firebox foundation ring were fitted with shoes at the four corners, which allowed for the relative movement of the boiler on the frame stretchers, where the expansion blocks were positioned.

The coupled axleboxes of all the Class 9Fs were plain bearing type, cast in steel, with pressed in brasses, and the standard manganese steel liners for the hornguides. Pony truck axleboxes were bronze castings. The coupled wheels themselves were 5ft 0in diameter with tyres shrunk onto the cast-steel centres. The standard practice of balancing 40% of the weight of the reciprocating masses was employed, with the lead weights being carried between plates rivetted to the coupled wheel spokes. The "Downs" sanding system first seen on the Britannias was dispensed with, and more conventional steam sanding used, ahead of the leading and driving wheels, with back sanding only used with the driving wheels.

Construction of the pony truck was an established standard pattern, with 3ft 0in wheels. The main suspension was of two nests of helical springs on each side of the axlebox, with the load transmitted through a yoke and shoe. Side control was also effected through coil springs, with front and rear dampers, to reduce oscillation. The main coupled axles' suspension was through underhung leaf springs, with the cotter assembly as adopted for the Britannia Pacifics. The laminated spring plates were 5in by ½in in section, and of 4ft 0in span.

Cylinders were almost identical with the Britannia class, though with a slightly increased valve travel of 7.87in. Interestingly, the first Class 9Fs were turned out with the standard box-type piston head, with two rings and spring-loaded slipper, but subsequent locomotives were fitted with a forged-steel head butt welded to the piston rod. Both cylinders and steamchests were fitted with cast-iron liners. Valve gear was of conventional Walschaerts pattern, with three slidebars and underhung crosshead, of the same type as the Class 7 Pacific. The drive was to the middle pair of coupled wheels, which were flangeless, resulting in the ability to negotiate curves of as little as 4½ chains (297 ft) radius.

Lubrication of the cylinders of the BR Standard locomotives, and the arrangement of mechanical lubrication through atomisers was as first introduced, in the form shown in the diagram. By the time the Class 9Fs appeared the linkage of the regulator to the

No 92085 under construction at Crewe Works on 6 May 1956. The firebox and boiler lagging bands can be seen already in position, though the fibreglass and asbestos insulation mats have still to be fitted. (*R. Shenton*)

atomiser steam control valve had been abandoned. Instead, the working of the atomisers was connected to the cylinder cock operating handle. The first standard arrangement was such that whatever the position of the regulator, the atomiser steam valve was fully open and atomised lubricating oil was dispensed to the cylinders and valves. Although it was customary on most regions to coast with the regulator fractionally open, on the WR it was common practice to close it completely, with the result that the atomiser steam valve was also closed. Since it was impractical to guarantee the adaption of a new driving practice which in fact only applied to the Standard types it was decided to link the operation of the atomiser steam valve to the cylinder cocks. In this, the only occasions when the steam supply to the former was closed was when the locomotive was standing with the cylinder cocks open.

The main axleboxes had underkeeps provided with an oil tray containing a worsted pad to distribute the lubricant. Oil was fed to the trays through a mechanical lubricator, to the coupled wheels only. The various joints and bearing surfaces in the valve gear were grease lubricated.

The rods and motion were fine-grain steel, with only the connecting, eccentric and smaller rods being fluted. Coupling rods were plain section, jointed at the second and fourth axles.

Cab, Platework and Details

Although the basic layout of the cab and footplate was of the standard pattern, the sides, roof and other panels were a welded structure, and bolted to the cantilevered platform support. Also included in the support frame were pedestals carrying the brake, blower and sanding valves. Another non-standard feature introduced from new with the 2-10-0 was the provision of fallplates between locomotive and tender, together with gangway doors. The attention given to providing some comfort for the footplate crews was evident in the provision of seats with backrests. Oddly, only the driver's seat was padded and fitted with a vertical screen behind it to protect his back from draughts.

As had become standard practice the injectors, one live steam and one exhaust steam, were mounted on brackets fixed to the firebox foundation ring. In this case both were mounted on the right-hand side, with all the controls grouped for ease of access by the fireman. The regulator of the standard pull-and-push operation actuated the regulator valve through external rodding along the left-hand side of the boiler. The valve itself was carried in the dome, and of the horizontal grid type, so arranged because for clearance within the loading gauge the dome was quite squat in appearance and the valves needed to be placed as high as possible. The operating rod passed through a stuffing box in the boiler side, connecting with the linkage from the cab. A central rocking lever was used to split the rod into two lengths, allowing for thermal expansion.

The arrangement of running boards, carried on brackets fixed to the boiler side, with a sloping fall plate at the smokebox end joining the upper and lower levels, were standard features. Smoke deflectors were a standard fitting on the first members of the Class, although the Crosti-boilered locomotives appeared

One of the most dramatic modifications to the Class 9Fs was the fitting of Crosti boilers to ten of their number. Here No 92028 is seen from the fireman's side, in steam at Wellingborough MPD. (*D. Larkin Collection*)

without them. Safety-valves set to 250lb/sq in were of the Ross Pop pattern, mounted on the second boiler ring immediately behind the dome.

The brake gear was a relatively simple uncompensated rigging, providing shoes from single hangers ahead of all coupled and tender wheels. On both locomotive and tender the brakes could be applied either by the gradual steam brake valve, or in conjunction with the vacuum brakes of the train.

Tenders

Although the first members of this class were built with tenders of the original standard pattern with the high inset side to the coal space, there were a number of varieties. Of the 251 locomotives only 58 were paired with this type of tender, the remainder having flush-sided tenders of varying capacities. Three locomotives, Nos 92165–7 were provided with tenders having the Berkeley mechanical stoker.

The BR1G tender was first paired with locomotives of this class, and carried seven tons of coal and 5,000 gallons of water. The fitting of fallplate and gangway doors was the only difference between the BR1A and BR1G types. The final 48 members of the class, Nos 92203–92250, built at Swindon for the Western Region, were all paired with BR1G tenders.

The smaller BR1B tender had flush sides and carried seven tons coal and 4,725 gallons of water and was fitted to Nos 92020–9 for the LM Region and Nos 92060–6, 92097–9 for the North Eastern Region. The additional coal capacity, required by the LM Region was provided on the 85 2-10-0s intended for service there, in the flush-sided type BR1C tender. Although carrying an extra two tons of coal, this had the same

water capacity as the type 1B. The reverse occurred with the 85 locomotives allocated to the Eastern Region, where an additional 900 gallons capacity was required in the tank, with seven tons of coal, providing the BR1F tender, the largest of the five types. The majority of the Class 9Fs, covering 170 locomotives, were paired with flush-sided tenders of either BR1C or BR1F design.

The fifth design of tender was fitted to only three locomotives, for service on the LM Region, and designated type BR1K. The locomotives were Nos 92165–7, which had originally been paired with BR1G tenders Nos 1375–7, but from new until 1961 had BR1K tenders and mechanical stokers. The equipment comprised four main components: the stoker engine, tender conveyor and intermediate and riser conduits. Mounted on the tender-front dragbox, the engine powered the conveyor screw fitted into a trough under the bunker, including a crusher and gearbox. The trough was provided with rollers to allow for any movement between locomotive and tender, with power transmitted to the gearbox through a slip shaft and universal joints.

The intermediate and riser conduits enclosed seven conveyors connected to one another through special ball joints. The riser conduit was carried up through the cab floor to the firebox backplate, and at the extreme end of the riser screw, a reverse flight was included to break down and spread out the coal over the distribution plate. This was fixed above the jet plate and just below the firehole. The jet plate was provided with four compartments in the lower portion of the risen conduit mouth, to allow controlled distribution of coal delivery with separate operating valves to each jet. Pressure gauges in the cab indicated the jet pressures for each of the four jets, using black heads for the front corners and red heads for the back corners.

It would seem by all accounts that the stoker-fitted

Another of the Crosti-fitted Class 9Fs No 92022 at Wellingborough on 10 April 1960, in company with the other nine of this type, awaiting conversion to a conventional boiler arrangement. The fitting of the final chimney and smoke deflector on the right side, considerably impaired the fireman's forward vision. Noteworthy, too, is the fitting of both main boiler feed clacks on this side, and the fastening of both upper and lower smokebox doors, using a number of screwed-down clamping dogs. (*R. Shenton*)

locomotives were best suited to long journeys, since shorter trips would not allow sufficient time to obtain correct settings for coal feed and jet pressures. In any event it was still possible to fire the locomotives by hand in the case of stoker failure or to clear the firebed. The idea was to provide for better utilisation of poor quality coal. The official reason for its abandonment in 1961 was the increasing use of diesel locomotives and the size of coal.

Construction and Operation

The first 30 9F 2-10-0s were planned for construction in the 1953 programme, but the difficulties posed by the acute steel shortage of a year or so earlier had had repercussions. It was well into 1954 before the latest heavy freight type was operating in any quantities, with the first seven being despatched to the South Wales coalfields.

The LMR was allocated the lion's share of these locomotives, 100 in all, with 56 going to the WR, 85 to the ER, and the remaining 10 to the North Eastern Region. Virtually all the LMR stock was distributed throughout the region, remaining there from building to withdrawal, though a couple of examples were withdrawn from Wakefield in the NER. A number were centred around Birkenhead and Warrington, with over 140 in service on LMR metals by the 1960s.

The North Eastern Region, although operating only ten Class 9Fs, maintained all 98 locomotives allocated to the Eastern and NE Regions, at Darling-

ton. Of the 56 allotted to the Western Region, the rapid progress of dieselisation soon rendered the steam types superfluous and by the mid-1960s, only 29 remained. Of these, No 92220 *Evening Star* was withdrawn for official preservation in March 1965, having enjoyed a useful working life of only five years!

The locomotives proved very able performers on heavy freight and mineral workings, but surprisingly proved equally at home on express passenger duties. Such incidents became increasingly frequent, on relief and excursion trains particularly, and the first reported occurrence took place not long after their introduction. Oddly it appeared, perhaps unwittingly, in a report in *The Motor* magazine, describing a demonstration run from Coventry to Glasgow in an

Planned Construction of Class 9F 2-10-0s

Batch	Nos	Built	Date	Maintaining region	Operating region
1	92000–7	Crewe	1953	W	W
2	92008–9	Crewe	1953	LM	LM
3	92010–4	Crewe	1953	ENE	E
4	92015–29	Crewe	1953	LM	LM
5	92030–44	Crewe	1954	ENE	E
6	92045–59	Crewe	1954	LM	LM
7	92060–66	Crewe	1954	ENE	NE
8	92067–76	Crewe	1954	ENE	E
9	92077–86	Crewe	1954	LM	LM
10	92087–96	Crewe	1954	ENE	E
11	92097–99	Crewe	1956	EVE	NE
12	92100–39	Crewe	1956	LM	LM
13	92140–9	Crewe	1956	ENE	E
14	92150–67	Crewe	1956	LM	LM
15	92168–77	Crewe	1956	ENE	E
16	92178–202	Swindon	1956	ENE	E
17	92203–20	Swindon	1957	W	W
18	92221–50	Swindon	1958	W	W

Not strictly a modification to the locomotives themselves, a number were fitted with Westinghouse pumps, for operating the hopper doors on the wagons of Tyne Dock to Consett iron-ore trains. No 92064 shows clearly the mounting of the air pumps on the fireman's side. (*Don Rowland*)

Alvis car! Running alongside a 14-coach express at 80mph through Nithsdale, a photograph taken by the passenger revealed none other than No 92023, a Crosti-boilered Class 9F 2-10-0. This event took place in 1955 and a number of other recorded incidents of high-speed running were reported in the press, including a maximum of 90mph descending from Stoke summit on the ER by No 92184 in July 1958. The saga of the speedy Class 9Fs, although exciting, was frowned upon, and instructions were despatched that it should cease. The climax was the running on five occasions during June and July 1960 of No 92220 *Evening Star* on the principal South Wales expresses, the Red Dragon and the Capitals United between Paddington and Cardiff. This locomotive, apart from enjoying its fame as the last steam locomotive built for BR, was allocated to Cardiff Canton, and almost became the depot's mascot. The first occasion that a Paddington and return working was made with No 92220 was on 27 June when the Britannia scheduled to perform the duty was failed. The load was some 13 coaches, 450 tons, and by all accounts the results were excellent—coal consumption was less than average with Britannias and Castles worked at 16% to 17% cut-off in level sections, and with estimated maximum speeds of 80mph to 85mph. The driver was one of Canton's senior men, and perhaps due to his glowing report of the first run four more were worked before the hand of authority put a stop to the practice.

Excursion and relief train workings of the Class 9Fs included the Somerset & Dorset route with the Pines Express, and provided admirable examples of the power and potential of these locomotives.

Overall, the Class 9Fs were distributed far and wide, though none found their way to the Southern or Scottish Regions. Four examples are preserved, including *Evening Star*. At Sheffield Park on the Bluebell Railway is No 92240, and No 92272 is on Great Central metals at Loughborough. The artist David Shepherd owns No 92203, now named *Black Prince*, which is preserved by the Shepherd Locomotive Trust on the East Somerset Railway at Cranmore.

Class 9F Modifications

The Class 9Fs were the subject of a number of major modifications—the fitting of Berkeley mechanical stokers to three locomotives had already been outlined—and others are discussed below. There were in fact a number of major non-standard details fitted to some locomotives. These ranged from the ten with Franco-Crosti boilers and the Giesl ejector fitted to the last of the class, to the basically cosmetic alterations to 92220 *Evening Star*. The double blastpipe and chimney of this latter was a feature of a number of other 2-10-0s, while examples were fitted with Westinghouse air pumps for operating the doors on Tyne Dock—Consett iron-ore trains.

The most dramatic of the Class 9F modifications was undoubtedly the Crosti boilers applied to Nos 92020–9, built at Crewe Works. The main frames, cylinders and motion remained essentially as they were on the standard locomotives, but some alteration was necessary to the frame stays to accommodate the pre-heater drum. These locomotives were not double boilered; the arrangement of preheater and boiler was so designed as to increase the overall efficiency of the steam locomotive. The basic principle of operation was that the products of combustion passing through the main boiler were re-directed at the front smokebox to pass through a bank of tubes in a secondary drum. These gases instead of escaping to

An impressive view of another of the Westinghouse-fitted Class 9Fs, No 92097, from the left side. An air reservoir for operating the hopper door gear can be seen behind the motion bracket, under the running boards. (*Don Rowland*)

atmosphere through the chimney served to raise the temperature of the boiler feed water contained in the secondary drum. In addition, exhaust steam was circulated through a jacket surrounding the pre-heater drum, further adding to the heat savings of this system. In theory it should also have been possible to demonstrate an improvement in combustion efficiency for the firebox, since less fuel was required.

In the arrangement provided on the Class 9Fs due to the restrictions of loading gauge, it was possible to

Last of the BR Standards, No 92250, fitted with Giesl ejector, at Southall on 10 June 1964. (*G.W. Sharpe*)

use only one preheater drum, slung under the main boiler. The boiler was built in two rings, as standard practice, from ½in and ¾in high-tensile steel plate and tapered from 4ft 11⅝in at the front to 5ft 7½in at the firebox end. The length between tubeplates was 16ft 6in, and accommodated twenty-eight 5½in diameter large flues, and 60 2⅜in diameter small tubes, providing a heating surface oif 1274sq ft. The preheater drum was a welded tube, with an inside diameter of 2ft 7in and housing 90 steel tubes of 2¼in diameter. The distance between tubeplates was 19ft 3in. A large manhole for inspection purposes was fitted to the preheater at one end, and a safety-valve attached to the cover plate prevented the build-up of excessive pressure. The safety-valve was set to blow-off at 275lb/sq in.

The front smokebox was a welded assembly, attached to the main boiler, with supports under the front barrel ring. Forward mounting of the smokebox

was allowed for, with expansion brackets attached to the frame plates. Two deflector plates were positioned inside the chamber to direct the gas flow through the preheater tube bank and trap any char, which could be removed later. The chimney, in the traditional position, was only required for lighting. The main smokebox, blast chamber and final exhaust were located at the rear of the preheater drum. The smokebox was of welded construction, with a hinged door secured by clamping dogs. A tubular extension to the smokebox was led off to the right-hand side of the footplate, where the elbow-shaped blast chamber housed the four 2½in diameter blast nozzles. The chimney extended above this and inclined inwards following the contour of the boiler, and was made as high as possible within the limits of the loading gauge. The boiler and preheater drum lagging used asbestos mattresses.

The performance of the Crosti boiler was not as successful as had been anticipated originally, nor did it come close to making the savings that were claimed for it by the designer, *Dott Ing* Piero Crosti of Milan. The royalties agreed between BR and Dr Crosti were based on the savings made as compared with a conventional Class 9F. It appears though that the conventional locomotives operated by BR, Class 9F 2-10-0s included, were far more efficient thermally than a great many foreign designs, hence the disappointing results of the experiment. A very few years after their introduction, the preheater drums were blanked-off and normal blastpipes and chimneys

fitted, so that for the remainder of their lives the locomotives were operated conventionally.

The installation of the Giesl ejector on No 92250 was successful, as tests in 1961 showed. The equipment consisted of a blastpipe casting which was fixed at its lower end to the same seating used in the double-chimney locomotives, tapering upwards to a narrow slot 1ft 9in long, whose width was variable to suit the type of coal used. The nozzle area under test was varied from 30.2sq in for Blidworth coals, to 26.2sq in for Whitwick and Cossall coals. This compared with the free nozzle area of 25.13sq in of the double-chimney Class 9Fs. The design of the chimney petticoat arrangement differed considerably between the double-chimneyed and Giesl-fitted locomotive. The distance from blastpipe cap to chimney choke and from choke to tap was 2ft 2in and 2ft 2¾in in the double-chimney locomotives, with an area at the choke of 198.8sq in. On No 92250 these same dimensions were 12in, 3ft 5½in and 150.5sq in respectively.

With this ejector it was claimed that the reduction in back-pressure would result in an increased power output from the cylinders at a given steam rate, and a lower fuel consumption. In comparison with the control locomotive used on the tests the Giesl-fitted locomotive showed a superior performance with the poorest quality slack used as fuel. One of the conditions agreed in using Dr Giesl's ejector was that in two years it would have saved its installation cost of £500. A 7½% saving in fuel costs was demanded using cheaper, poorer quality coals.

Standard Class 9F 2-10-0 Nos 92000–92250

No	Built	Withdrawn	Disposal	No	Built	Withdrawn	Disposal
92000	1/54	7/65	Birds', Long Marston	92024	6/55	11/67	G.H. Campbell, Airdrie
92001	1/54	1/67		92025	6/55	11/67	G.H. Campbell, Airdrie
92002	1/54	11/67	G.H. Campbell, Airdrie	92026	6/55	11/67	G.H. Campbell, Airdrie
92003	1/54	3/65	J. Cashmore, Newport	92027	7/55	8/67	J. Buttigieg, Newport
92004	1/54	3/68	J. Cashmore, Newport	92028	7/55	11/66	J. Buttigieg, Newport
92005	2/54	8/65	T.W. Ward, Beighton	92029	7/55	11/67	G.H. Campbell, Airdrie
92006	2/54	4/67	A. Draper, Hull	92030	10/54	2/67	Arnott Young, Rawmarsh
92007	2/54	12/65	J. Cashmore, Newport	92031	11/54	1/67	T.W. Ward, Killamarsh
92008	3/54	10/67	J. Buttigieg, Newport	92032	11/54	4/67	
92009	3/54	3/68	J. Cashmore, Newport	92033	11/54	9/65	T.W. Ward, Beighton
92010	5/54	4/66	J. Cashmore, Newport	92034	11/54	5/64	T.W. Ward, Killamarsh
92011	5/54	11/67	G.H. Campbell, Airdrie	92035	11/54	2/66	T.W. Ward, Killamarsh
92012	5/54	10/67	J. McWilliam, Shettleston	92036	11/54	12/64	G. Cohen, Kettering
92013	4/54	9/66	G. Cohen, Kettering	92037	12/54	2/65	A. Draper, Hull
92014	5/54	10/67	J. Buttigieg, Newport	92038	12/54	4/65	J. Cashmore, Great Bridge
92015	10/54	5/67	J. McWilliam, Shettleston	92039	12/54	10/65	
92016	10/54	10/67		92040	12/54	8/65	A. Draper, Hull
92017	10/54	12/67	Arnott Young, Carmyle	92041	12/54	8/65	
92018	10/54	4/67	Motherwell Machinery Co.	92042	1/55	12/65	T.W. Ward, Beighton
92019	10/54	6/67	Motherwell Machinery Co.	92043	1/55	8/66	G.H. Campbell, Airdrie
92020	6/55	10/67	J. Buttigieg, Newport	92044	1/55	4/65	J. Cashmore, Great Bridge
92021	6/55	11/67	G.H. Campbell, Airdrie	92045	2/55	9/67	Woodham Bros., Barry
92022	6/55	11/67	G.H. Campbell, Airdrie	92046	2/55	10/67	J. Buttigieg, Newport
92023	6/55	11/67	G.H. Campbell, Airdrie	92047	2/55	11/67	G.H. Campbell, Airdrie

No	Built	Withdrawn	Disposal	No	Built	Withdrawn	Disposal
92048	2/55	9/67	T.W. Ward, Beighton	92108	10/56	11/67	G.H. Campbell, Airdrie
92049	3/55	11/67	G.H. Campbell, Airdrie	92109	10/56	12/67	G.H. Campbell, Airdrie
92050	8/55	9/67	J. Buttigieg, Newport	92110	10/56	12/67	
92051	8/55	10/67	Motherwell Machinery Co.	92111	11/56	10/67	T.W. Ward, Beighton
92052	8/55	8/67	J. McWilliam, Shettleston	92112	11/56	11/67	G.H. Campbell, Airdrie
92053	9/55	2/66	J. Cashmore, Great Bridge	92113	11/56	10/67	J. Buttigieg, Newport
92054	9/55	5/68	Arnott Young, Parkgate	92114	11/56	7/67	G.H. Campbell, Airdrie
92055	9/55	12/67	T.W. Ward, Killamarsh	92115	12/56	2/66	T.W. Ward, Killamarsh
92056	10/55	1/67	Motherwell Machinery Co	92116	12/56	11/66	A. Draper, Hull
92057	10/55	9/65	T.W. Ward, Beighton	92117	12/56	12/67	T.W. Ward, Killamarsh
92058	10/55	10/66	J. McWilliam, Shettleston	92118	12/56	5/68	T.W. Ward, Beighton
92059	10/55	9/66	A. Draper, Hull	92119	1/57	9/67	Motherwell Machinery Co
92060	10/55	10/66	A. Draper, Hull	92120	2/57	7/67	Birds, Long Marston
92061	11/55	9/66	A. Draper, Hull	92121	2/57	7/67	T.J. Thompson, Stockton
92062	11/55	6/66	H. Bolckow, Blyth	92122	2/57	11/67	Woodham Bros, Barry
92063	11/55	11/66	T.J. Thompson, Stockton	92123	3/57	10/67	T.W. Ward, Beighton
92064	11/55	11/66	T.J. Thompson, Stockton	92124	3/57	12/66	T.W. Ward, Killamarsh
92065	12/55	4/67	Arnott Young, Parkgate	92125	3/57	12/67	Arnott Young, Carmyle
92066	12/55	5/65		92126	3/57	8/67	J. McWilliam, Shettleston
92067	12/55	11/66	J. McWilliam, Shettleston	92127	4/57	8/67	J. Buttigieg, Newport
92068	12/55	1/66	W. of Scotland Shipbreaking Co	92128	4/57	11/67	
92069	12/55	6/68	Arnott Young, Parkgate	92129	4/57	6/67	Motherwell Machinery Co
92070	1/56	11/67	G.H. Campbell, Airdrie	92130	4/57	5/66	Motherwell Machinery Co
92071	1/56	11/67	Motherwell Machinery Co	92131	5/57	9/67	T.W. Ward, Beighton
92072	2/56	1/66	T.W. Ward, Beighton	92132	5/57	10/67	Motherwell Machinery Co
92073	2/56	11/67	G.H. Campbell, Airdrie	92133	5/57	7/67	T.J. Thompson, Stockton
92074	2/56	4/67	Motherwell Machinery Co	92134	6/57	12/66	Woodham Bros, Barry
92075	3/56	9/66	A. Draper, Hull	92135	6/57	6/67	A. Draper, Hull
92076	3/56	2/67	J. McWilliam, Shettleston	92136	6/57	11/66	
92077	3/56	6/68		92137	6/57	9/67	Motherwell Machinery Co
92078	3/56	5/67	T.J. Thompson, Stockton	92138	6/57	7/67	Birds, Long Marston
92079	4/56	11/67	G.H. Campbell, Airdrie	92139	7/57	9/67	Motherwell Machinery Co
92080	4/56	5/67	J. McWilliam, Shettleston	92140	7/57	4/65	J. Cashmore, Great Bridge
92081	5/56	2/66	T.W. Ward, Killamarsh	92141	7/57	12/65	T.W. Ward, Beighton
92082	5/56	11/67	G.H. Campbell, Airdrie	92142	7/57	2/65	G. Cohen, Kettering
92083	5/56	2/67	A. Draper, Hull	92143	8/57	2/65	G. Cohen, Kettering
92084	5/56	11/67	G.H. Campbell, Airdrie	92144	8/57	12/65	T.W. Ward, Beighton
92085	6/65	12/66	Woodham Bros, Barry	92145	8/57	2/66	
92086	6/65	11/67	G.H. Campbell, Airdrie	92146	9/57	4/66	
92087	6/65	2/67	J. McWilliam, Shettleston	92147	9/57	4/65	J. Cashmore, Great Bridge
92088	10/56	6/68	Arnott Young, Dinsdale	92148	9/57	12/65	T.W. Ward, Beighton
92089	10/56	2/67	A. Draper, Hull	92149	9/57	6/65	T.W. Ward, Beighton
92090	10/56	5/67	G. Cohen, Kettering	92150	9/57	4/67	A. Draper, Hull
92091	11/56	6/68	T.W. Ward, Beighton	92151	11/57	4/67	A. Draper, Hull
92092	1/57	11/66	A. Draper, Hull	92152	11/57	11/67	G.H. Campbell, Airdrie
92093	1/57	8/67	Motherwell Machinery Co	92153	11/57	1/68	J. Cashmore, Newport
92094	2/57	6/68	Arnott Young, Parkgate	92154	11/57	7/67	T.J. Thompson, Stockton
92095	2/57	9/66	A. Draper, Hull	92155	11/57	11/66	A. Draper, Hull
92096	4/57	2/67	J. McWilliam, Shettleston	92156	11/57	7/67	T.J. Thompson, Stockton
92097	7/56	10/66	A. Draper, Hull	92157	12/57	8/67	J. Buttigieg, Newport
92098	7/56	7/66	A. Draper, Hull	92158	12/57	8/66	A. Draper, Hull
92099	8/56	9/66	A. Draper, Hull	92159	12/57	7/67	T.J. Thompson, Stockton
92100	8/56	5/67	G. Cohen, Kettering	92160	12/57	6/68	
92101	8/56	10/67	J. Buttigieg, Newport	92161	12/57	12/66	Motherwell Machinery Co
92102	9/56	11/67	G.H. Campbell, Airdrie	92162	12/57	11/67	G.H. Campbell, Airdrie
92103	9/56	6/67	G. Cohen, Kettering	92163	4/58	11/67	G.H. Campbell, Airdrie
92104	9/56	2/67	A. Draper, Hull	92164	4/58	8/66	A. Draper, Hull
92105	9/56	1/67	T.W. Ward, Killamarsh	92165	4/58	3-68	J. Cashmore, Newport
92106	10/56	7/67	T.J. Thompson, Stockton	92166	6/58	11/67	G.H. Campbell, Airdrie
92107	10/56	2/67	A. Draper, Hull	92167	5/58	6/68	

No	Built	Withdrawn	Disposal	No	Built	Withdrawn	Disposal
92168	12/57	6/65	T.W. Ward, Beighton	92209	6/59	12/65	J. Cashmore, Newport
92169	12/57	5/64	T.W. Ward, Killamarsh	92210	8/59	11/64	J. Buttigieg, Newport
92170	12/57	5/64		92211	9/59	5/67	A. Draper, Hull
92171	2/58	5/64	T.W. Ward, Killamarsh	92212	9/59	1/68	Woodham Bros, Barry
92172	1/58	4/66	Station Steel, Wath	92213	10/59	11/66	J. McWilliam, Shettleston
92173	2/58	2/66		92214	10/59	9/65	Woodham Bros, Barry
92174	2/58	12/65		92215	11/59	6/67	A. Draper, Hull
92175	2/58	5/64		92216	12/59	10/65	J. Cashmore, Newport
92176	3/58	5/64	T.W. Ward, Killamarsh	92217	12/59	8/66	A. Draper, Hull
92177	3/58	5/64	Crewe Works	92218	1/60	6/68	Arnott Young, Parkgate
92178	9/57	10/65	T.W. Ward, Killamarsh	92219	1/60	9/65	Woodham Bros, Barry
92179	11/57	11/65	H. Bolckow, Blyth	92220	2/60	3/65	Preserved—National Collection
92180	10/57	4/65	J. Cashmore, Great Bridge	92221	5/58	5/65	H. Bolckow, Blyth
92181	11/57	2/65	G. Cohen, Kettering	92222	6/58	3/65	J. Cashmore, Newport
92182	12/57	4/66		92223	6/58	4/68	Arnott Young, Dinsdale
92183	12/57	4/66		92224	6/58	9/67	J. McWilliam, Shettleston
92184	1/58	2/65	A. Draper, Hull	92225	6/58	7/65	J. Cashmore, Newport
92185	1/58	2/65	A. Draper, Hull	92226	6/58	9/65	J. Cashmore, Newport
92186	1/58	8/65		92227	7/58	10/67	T.W. Ward, Beighton
92187	2/58	2/65	A. Draper, Hull	92228	7/58	1/67	T.W. Ward, Beighton
92188	2/58	2/65	A. Draper, Hull	92229	7/58	11/64	Cox & Danks, Park Royal
92189	3/58	12/65	T.W. Ward, Beighton	92230	8/58	12/65	J. Cashmore, Newport
92190	3/58	10/65	T.W. Ward, Beighton	92231	8/58	11/66	A. Draper, Hull
92191	4/58	12/65	T.W. Ward, Beighton	92232	8/58	12/64	Woodham Bros, Barry
92192	5/58	2/65		92233	8/58	2/68	T.W. Ward, Beighton
92193	5/58	6/65	A. Draper, Hull	92234	8/58	11/67	G.H. Campbell, Airdrie
92194	6/58	12/65		92235	8/58	11/65	J. Cashmore, Newport
92195	6/58	4/65	A. Draper, Hull	92236	9/58	4/65	R.S. Hayes, Bridgend
92196	8/58	12/64	T.W. Ward, Beighton	92237	9/58	9/65	J. Cashmore, Newport
92197	9/58	9/65	T.W. Ward, Beighton	92238	9/58	9/65	J. Cashmore, Newport
92198	10/58	8/64	T.W. Ward, Beighton	92239	9/58	11/66	A. Draper, Hull
92199	10/58	8/64	T.W. Ward, Beighton	92240	10/58	9/65	Preserved—Bluebell Railway
92200	11/58	10/65	T.W. Ward, Killamarsh	92241	10/58	7/65	J. Cashmore, Newport
92201	12/58	3/66		92242	10/58	5/65	J. Cashmore, Newport
92202	12/58	12/65	T.W. Ward, Beighton	92243	10/58	12/65	J. Cashmore, Newport
92203	4/59	12/67	Preserved—W. Somerset Rly, Cranmore	92244	10/58	12/65	J. Cashmore, Newport
				92245	11/58	12/64	Woodham Bros, Barry
92204	4/59	12/67	T.W. Ward, Beighton	92246	11/58	12/65	J. Cashmore, Newport
92205	5/59	6/67	A. Draper, Hull	92247	12/58	10/66	A. Draper, Hull
92206	5/59	5/67	Arnott Young, Parkgate	92248	12/58	5/65	J. Cashmore, Newport
92207	6/59	12/64	Woodham Bros, Barry	92249	12/58	6/68	Arnott Young, Parkgate
92208	6/59	10/67	J. McWilliam, Shettleston	92250	12/58	12/65	J. Cashmore, Newport

Notes: (a) Nos 92000–92177 were built at Crewe, Nos 92178 to 92250 at Swindon
(b) No 92200 *Evening Star* was the only one named by BR. No 92203 has been named *Black Prince* by its owner, David Shepherd.

Technical Data—Class 9F 2-10-0s Nos 92000 to 92250

Note: The information refers to locomotives in original or "as built" condition

Cylinders and valve gear

Cylinders—diameter × stroke	....	20in × 28in
Piston swept volume—one cylinder	....	8796cu in
Clearance volume as % of piston swept volume	....	10.3%
Maximum piston thrust	....	78540lb
Steam chests—volume between valve heads	....	4558cu in
—volume as % of piston swept volume	....	51.8%

Piston valves—diameter	....	11in
—steam lap	....	$1^{11}/_{16}$in
—lead	....	¼in
—exhaust clearance	....	NIL
Maximum travel of valves	....	7.87in
Maximum cut-off %	....	78%
Travel at 20% cut-off	....	4.06in

Balancing data

Revolving masses—weight per cylinder	....	2040lb
Reciprocating masses—total weight per cylinder	....	865lb
—percentage balanced	....	40%
—unbalanced weight per cylinder	....	519lb
Ratio—unbalanced reciprocating weight per cylinder to total weight of locomotive	....	1/374
Hammer-blow at 5 revolutions per second—per wheel	....	0.78 tons
—per axle	....	1.56 tons
—per rail	....	3.38 tons
—whole locomotive	...	6.77 tons

Boiler proportions

Free area through tubes—large	....	3.10sq ft
—small	....	2.35sq ft
—total	....	5.45sq ft
Area through large tubes as % of total	....	56.9%
Total free area as % of grate area	....	13.6%
A/S ratio—bore	....	7in
—cross sectional area	....	38.5sq in
Regulator fully open—area	....	22.2sq in
Superheater elements—total area	....	32.6sq in
Steampipes to cylinders—total area	....	56.5sq in
Blastpipe cap—diameter	....	5⅜in
—area	....	22.7sq in
Chimney throat—diameter	....	1ft 3¼in
—area	....	1.27sq ft
Throat area as % of grate area	....	3.16%
Height—blastpipe cap to chimney throat	....	2ft 4⅞in
Taper of chimney	....	1 in 14

Crosti-boilered Class 9 2-10-0

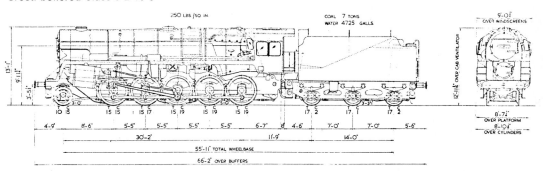

6. The Other Pacifics:
Class 6MT and Class 8P

Both of these designs were in their way oddities in the Standard series, and even now it is hard to see any justification for the building of the Clan Pacifics in particular. The solitary Class 8P *Duke of Gloucester* was built as a prototype, and notwithstanding the steaming troubles was a successful experiment. Had the dieselisation of BR to have been deferred for a few years, it is quite probable that a class of 8P locomotives based on this design would have represented the ultimate in development of the express passenger type. The one example built in 1954 was in existence as a replacement for the Stanier Pacific 46202 destroyed in the Harrow disaster two years earlier.

Class 6MT 4–6–2s

The Clan Pacific first took to the rails in 1952 and came to number ten locomotives in all, allocated to the Scottish Region. Interestingly the first conception of this design was as a Class 5 Pacific locomotive with an 18½-ton axleload, for the duties already worked by a number of Regional designs. There seemed at this point in the design stage a certain amount of confusion brought about by the already successful performance of Class 5 duties by 4-6-0 types with narrow fireboxes. Was the provision of additional potential capacity really necessary in this category? The decision was influenced by R.C. Bond's suggestion that lower combustion rates from the wide firegrate of the Pacific would cover the costs of including and operating the trailing truck. By this means it then compared favourably with the Class 5 4-6-0s. However, to secure the potential extra power, it was more logical to develop a Class 6 design. This choice was made more certain with the performance results from Bulleid's West Country Pacific in the Interchange Trials. The initial Type 72 design with 6ft 0in coupled wheels, 18in × 28in cylinders and a grate area of 36sq ft was rejected in favour of the Class 6MT development. This utilised the same chassis as the Britannia, but with smaller cylinders and boiler. The single frame pattern used for both Class 7 and Class 6 Pacifics would have been a great advantage, had the manufacture of bar frames proceeded. It is interesting to record that early in the life of this design it was proposed that the locomotives would take over duties such as were performed by ex LMSR Class 5X 4-6-0s. The first ten Clans were allocated to the Scottish Region, and of the two batches scheduled for 1952

construction five were allotted to the Southern, and another ten to the Scottish Region. These 15 were quickly cancelled, as circumstances proved their building to be unnecessary.

Mechanical Details

Firebox, Boiler, and Smokebox

The boilers fitted to the Class 6 Pacifics were a new design designated type BR2, and pitched at 9ft 2in, were 2in lower than the Britannia boilers. However, the overall height at both chimney and cab was identical. The boilers were made in two rings, and tapered from 5ft 4in diameter at the smokebox end to 6ft 1in diameter at the combustion chamber tubeplate. All the joints used in the construction were rivetted, and designed to withstand a working pressure of 225lb/sq in. As with the Britannia design, the use of two outside cylinders permitted the increase in boiler diameter at the firebox end from the 5ft 9in originally planned to 6ft 1in, while still maintaining clearance within the L2 loading gauge. The total heating surface of 1878sq ft came from 108 2in diameter small tubes, with the 35 5½in diameter large tubes also housing 1⅜in diameter superheater flues to provide 592sq ft of superheater heating surface. The length between tubeplates of 17ft 0in was the same as the Britannia BR1 boiler, with the free area through the tubes at 15.9% of the grate area, being only marginally lower.

A standard rocking grate of 36sq ft area was provided in a firebox 6ft 9in long and varying in width from 7ft 0in at the forward end to 6ft 8in at the back. The copper inner firebox provided 195sq ft of evaporative heating surface. The grate was built up from standard cast-iron firebars, twelve of which were incorporated in the ten rocking sections. The mechanism was linked to a pair of operating levers in the cab, with catches to limit the stroke. In the short stroke, the firebars were tilted through a few degrees only, while in the larger stroke a full 90° turn was possible, to permit easier disposal of the fire. The short stroke was intended to assist the fireman to remove ash and clinker when the locomotive was running. The ash pan was the three-compartment hopper type, so fitted because of the narrowing in of the rear frame extensions over the trailing truck. A major departure in the boiler and firebox designs was the use of fibreglass

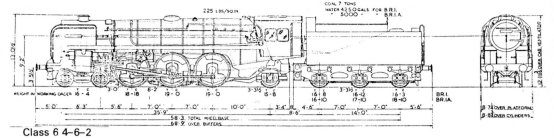

Class 6 4–6–2

mats as lagging, rather than the traditional asbestos. The idea was previously used by Bulleid, though it had been introduced at Doncaster by Gresley some years earlier. Its use in the Standard types was not uniform, and there were on most, a mixture of asbestos and fibreglass.

At the opposite end of the boiler, a cylindrical drumhead smokebox was fitted, including the standard self-cleaning equipment. This apparatus was essentially an American idea imported to this country and adopted on the LMS in post-war days. As referred to in an earlier chapter, it was tried out in principle on the LNER before World War II. In the Standard form, it consisted of a set of plates which were so arranged to re-direct the path followed by the exhaust gases under the blastpipe and through a grille set across the front of the box and then out of the chimney with the steam exhausted from the cylinders. The effect of this construction in redirecting the gas flow also increased its velocity, carrying ash particles out through the chimney that would ordinarily have accummulated on the floor of the smokebox. The wire mesh had the effect of a spark arrestor, causing the larger incandescent particles to be trapped and fully burned before escaping as fine black ash through the chimney.

As a result of the experimental work carried out by S.O. Ell at Swindon into draughting methods, a simple single blastpipe of 5¼in diameter was settled upon for the Clans. In fact, the first six of the Standard designs incorporated this feature, and it was not until the mid to late 1950s that any alterations were made. It was felt initially at least that the single blastpipe was the most economic in operation over the range of outputs which it was required to work the Standards. The four-jet Cardew design blower was fitted around the blastpipe cap.

Frames, Wheels and Motion

The chassis was identical with the Britannias, the only departure being the size of the cylinders. These were 19½in × 28in stroke, with a swept volume of 8,362cu in, and operated by Walschaerts valve gear with underhung crossheads. Cylinders and valves were fitted with cast-iron liners, and a spring-loaded bronze slipper was attached to the underside of the piston to maintain a clearance between the piston head and cylinder liner. The head was attached to the piston rod in the LMS manner, with a nut and

locknut at the outer end. The 11in diameter piston valves were standard with the Britannias, Class 9Fs and Class 5MT 4-6-0s with the same lap and lead, the travel being 7.73in.

Curiously, since the 6ft 2in diameter driving wheels, hollowed-out coupled axles and roller bearing ashboxes were identical with the Britannias, there were no instances of wheels shifting. The narrower than usual frame spacing possible with the two-cylinder layout meant that the frame centre line being over the axlebox centres removed some of the effects of offset loading through the spring hangers.

To take account of boiler expansion, a forward extension of the dragbox provided a bearing surface for a sliding shoe attached to the two rear corners of the foundation ring, and two at the front two corners. Again, this was a former LMS practice of fairly recent introduction being seen first on the Ivatt Class 4 2-6-0 locomotives.

Both bogie and trailing truck were interchangeable with the Britannias, having the standard 3ft 3½in wheels for the latter and nine-spoke 3ft 0in wheels in the former. The locomotive weight was carried on side bolsters and laminated springs attached to compensating beams. For the trailing truck, the weight was supported at three points using Ferrobestos pads, one at the pivot centre, the other two on the truck frame behind the axle. Side control of bogies and trailing trucks was effected through coil springs.

Cab, Platework and Fittings

The standard arrangement was adopted with the cab attached to the boiler rather than the chassis, by cantilever supports. The layout as first evolved was the only arrangement used on this small class of locomotive. One advantage in carrying the cab higher than normal was that the washout holes at the rear corners of the firebox were readily accessible.

A perennial problem in all pipework associated with steam locomotives was that of differential expansion. To obviate this problem—at least in so far as the injectors were concerned—was the attachment of these fittings to the firebox, with the controls grouped on the fireman's side of the cab. Other boiler fittings were standard features, including the main steam manifold, safety-valve, steam pressure and vacuum gauges, water gauges, and between the Pacific types, the multiple-valve regulator. The fact that the boiler was smaller in size than the Britannia, but in overall

No 71000 *Duke of Gloucester* passing Rugby with the down Mid-Day Scot in September 1958. Normally in its short career the locomotive was rostered to work this train north from Crewe. (*T.E. Williams*)

height from rail the locomotives were the same, meant that such features as the chimney and dome were taller fittings.

To maintain the family likeness, the same high running boards were carried along the boiler sides, with the different levels joined by the sloping plate in front of the smokebox. Smoke deflectors were carried, with brass nameplates attached below the handrails. Here again, a departure from the Britannia arrangement was that these locomotives always carried the handrails, and were not later fitted with either of the later Britannia handhole arrangements.

Tenders

All ten Clans were paired with BR1 type tenders with high inset sides to the coal space, carrying seven tons of coal and 4,250 gallons of water. Pick-up gear was fitted in all cases. Between the first and second axles on each side was a feedwater sieve. These were attached to the frames in the line connecting the tender tank with the injector and were intended to filter water drawn from the tender. The sieve was a renewable element and could be removed, cleaned and replaced. Home comforts for the crew were provided on the tender in the shape of a food locker with a stainless steel tray.

Construction and Operation

The first locomotive, No. 72000, was named *Clan Buchanan* at Glasgow Central Station on 15 January 1952. They were built in a single batch at Crewe Works between December 1951 and March 1952; the parent office for design was Derby. Nos 72000–4 were allocated to Polmadie in the Scottish Region, while Nos 72005–9 were sent to Carlisle Kingmoor. The latter depot was actually a Scottish Region base in

early BR days, but following several attempts at regional boundary shuffling, found itself in the LMR stable. From the original planned building dates, with Crewe being responsible for construction, it seemed to follow that the LMR should also be responsible for maintenance.

The Clan design suffered from being overshadowed by its larger compatriot; as a consequence, little recorded data is available of the day-to-day performance. No critical tests were made to establish the principal characteristics, and although they appeared adequate, there was the suggestion that a degree of improvement could be made at the front end. Alteration of the chimney/blastpipe proportions could have provided some improvement, as with the Class 5 4-6-0s.

Although there were no recorded instances of wheels shifting on axles, referred to earlier, there were one or two frame fractures in the area of the leading horns. These were understandable in view of the reasons mentioned in reference to the Britannia Class, and the fact that the same frame and spring hanger bracket was used in the Clan design.

Following construction, most Clans used running-in turns between Shrewsbury and Crewe, while in February 1952 a series of trials was made in the Birmingham area on local and main line turns, including a run to Euston, before delivery to the Scottish Region. Running-in turns to Birmingham continued to be used by Clans, following repairs and overhauls at Crewe Works. The five locomotives allocated to Polmadie were put to work on such passenger turns as the 1.45pm and the 4.05pm Glasgow (Central) to Manchester, returning from Manchester the following day with the 9.30am and 2.00pm. A spare locomotive was maintained for relief purposes.

Although the locomotives featured prominently on the Manchester and Liverpool workings, they were reportedly not popular with crews. The Kingmoor locomotives worked as far north as Perth, Dundee and Aberdeen, while a regular turn included the Stranraer boat expresses. On this working, a three- to

five-coach load was usual and the Clans performed better than the Class 5 4-6-0s over the hilly Stranraer to Girvan line. The reverse was the case with the heavier loads on the main line between Stranraer and Carlisle, where the locomotives tended to steam badly and were prone to slipping.

The extensive use of Clan Pacifics throughout southern Scotland was curtailed in late 1954, with the influx of both Britannias and Standard Class 5 4-6-0s to Polmadie shed. Both types took over Clan workings to Manchester and Liverpool to the relief of some crews, and subsequent forays south of the Border were rare. Relegation to scondary work was inevitable, including freight, excursion and intermediate and stopping passenger duties.

Their withdrawal was in two batches, with the Polmadie locomotives first to go in September 1963, when Nos 72000–4 were despatched to Darlington Works for cutting-up. The Kingmoor locomotives survived almost three more years before being sold to various breaker's yards in Scotland.

Class 8P 4-6-2 No 71000 *Duke of Gloucester*
Mechanical Details

Boiler Type BR13

The original proposal of 1948 for this locomotive, designated Type 75, had a boiler some 19ft 3in between tubeplates. However, since the largest dia-

meter permitted under the L2 loading gauge was 6ft 5½in, it was decided to use again the BR1 barrel fitted to the Britannias. It was perhaps in this decision to use an existing boiler design that the Class 8's steaming problems lay. The two rings housed the 136 2⅛in diameter small tubes, and 40 5½in diameter superheater flues, between the tubeplates, measuring 17ft 0in overall as before. There is a curious anomaly in that the superheater elements, numbering 40 of 1⅜in outside diameter for both BR1 and BR13 boilers provided no fewer than three different heating surface areas! However 677sq ft was quoted for the Britannias on the first diagrams, 691sq ft for No 71000 on diagram SL/8A/1 and 677sq ft on SL/8A/2. It may be that an alternative method of calculation of heating surface was used during the period between the building of the Britannias and *Duke of Gloucester*, but with the same boiler at the time of the performance tests on the Class 8 locomotive, at least one source quotes a figure of 718sq ft for the Britannias by comparison!

The problems of steam collection with the BR1 design having been overcome by the time No 71000 was in building, the final, simple collector without the centrifugal steam drier was fitted. The boiler working pressure was 250lb/sq in. Water was supplied through two clacks mounted on each side of the boiler on the front ring, incoming feedwater was deflected away from the tube bank and down the sides of the barrel. Ross 'Pop' safety-valves were supplied as standard

Class 8 4-6-2

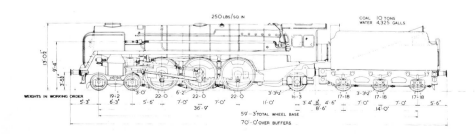

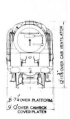

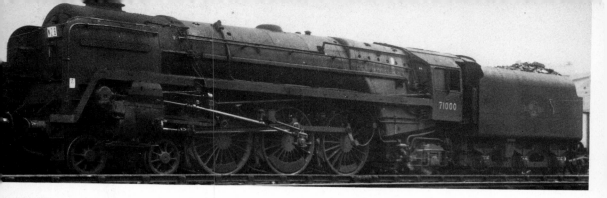

Still on LMR metals No 71000 is seen at Derby on 15 August 1960. The trailing truck shows the modified springing adopted, in comparison with the Britannias, and the layout of the cardan shaft drive to the cambox from the return crank. No 71000 is also shown with the second type of tender, BR1J. (*G.W. Sharpe*)

and fitted to the rear boiler ring.

An unfortunate result of increasing the size of the firebox to 8ft 0in in length and varying in width from 7ft 9in at the front to 7ft 4in at the back, was a reduction in the ratio of free gas area to grate area. The free gas area of 6.79sq ft remained the same as for the Britannias but the 48.6sq ft of grate provided a total free area of only 14% of grate area. Construction of the grate was from the standard cast-iron replaceable bars, in this case 196 arranged in 14 rocking sections. The two halves of the grate were rocked independently on either full or short travel of the operating handles in the cab and the standard through compartment hopper ashpan was fitted. Air flow through the front damper doors was controlled by handwheel and screw.

The smokebox was the conventional cylindrical rivetted type, carried on a cast-steel saddle, and with full self-cleaning apparatus. A double blastpipe was fitted, having two plain circular caps of 4in diameter, each of which was fitted into the superheater header, actuated with the cardan pattern blower ring. A multiple valve regulator was fitted through a gland in the smokebox wrapper, via external mechanical link-up. An interesting feature of the double blastpipe arrangement was that during tests it enabled the boiler to be steamed up to the grate limit. Using the same boiler, and a single blastpipe, the grate limit of the Britannia was not approached. With the Class 8 at higher rates of firing, not necessarily approaching the grate limit, much unburnt fuel was thrown out of the chimney.

Cylinders, Wheels and Motion

The chassis was arranged on a 36ft 9in wheelbase, with the standard bogie and pony trucks and 6ft 2in coupled wheels. Here again there was a marked difference between the Class 8 as built and the Type 75 concept. The wheelbase as proposed in 1948 for the express passenger type with a 22½-ton axle load

was 38ft 0in, with 6ft 9in coupled wheels. The bogie wheelbase was much longer at 7ft 6in in the original plan, though the distance between the leading coupled axle and the trailing truck was the same. The lengthening of the front end was necessary to accommodate the four 16½in × 28in cylinders in this proposal. These were to have been operated by conventional Walschaerts valve gear, but in No 71000 as it eventually entered service only three cylinders 18in × 28in were provided, operated by British Caprotti valve gear. The application of poppet valve gear on this design proved to be the most successful and efficient form ever provided on a British steam locomotive.

As with the other Standard designs, bar frames were considered but quickly over-ruled in favour of mild-steel plate. By 1954 the arrangement had become standard, using 1¼in thick material stayed with fabricated and cast stretchers at 3ft 2½in apart, coinciding with the axlebox centre lines. Welded-in hornguides were fitted with manganese-steel liners, a feature which had already-proven wear characteristics in the earlier Standards. The front of the boiler and firebox throat plate was supported on brass liners attached to the vertical stretchers, with the firebox rear carried on brackets fixed to the rear frame extensions. The method of allowing for expansion of the boiler was as described for the Clan Class locomotives. Roller bearing axleboxes of the non-split type were fitted to bogie, trailing truck and leading and trailing coupled axles. The split boxes were fitted to the driving axle.

The three cylinders were steel castings with cast-iron liners, with the middle cylinder incorporating the smokebox saddle inside slide bar carriers. Separate valves for inlet and exhaust were located at each end of the cylinders, operated by rotating cams. The drive was taken to the two outside cam boxes from worm gearboxes mounted on the return crank, though a main driving shaft (hind), intermediate driving shaft and main driving shaft (front). All three shafts were of tubular construction and connected with universal joints. The middle cylinder cam box drive was taken from the left-hand outside cylinder, through a right-angle bevel gearbox mounted in front of the LH cam box. The inside cam box was positioned in front of the smokebox saddle and arranged to slide forward for ease of access in dismantling and repair. There were also three reversing gearboxes directly in line with one another across the locomotive frames, each being connected to the other by two cross-shafts and flexible couplings. A tubular shaft connected with each of the three camboxes through a splined coupling, and a flange coupling to the reverse gearboxes. Only the gearbox on the left-hand side of the locomotive was directly connected to the reversing shaft and driver's handwheel in the cab. The actual process of reversing the locomotive was done by advancing or retarding the angular position of the cams relative to the camshafts. Regulation or cut-off was achieved through a change in the angular adjustment of the inlet cams in relation to one another.

One last interesting departure from standard practice in cylinder design was the method of attachment of the piston head to the rod. The previous practice adopted from the LMS was to fit the head over a plain seat on the rod, and then a nut and locknut to secure the assembly. This resulted in a fairly complicated assembly of some 17 separate parts, and soon after the first details were published in 1951 it was suggested that in order to comply with the simplicity dictum, a one-piece forged rod and head might be better. In the case of No 71000, this was a resurrection of a technique introduced by Gresley on the LNER, whereby the piston head was butt-welded to the rod.

The inside connecting rod came in for much attention, being a source of potential trouble at the big-end. The design of this feature on No 71000 was a

The Clan class Pacifics numbered only ten in all, and were confined largely to working between Glasgow, Carlisle, Liverpool and Manchester. No 72006 *Clan Mackenzie* was based at Carlisle Kingmoor, and is shown here without nameplates, AWS battery box on running boards in front of cab, and with the yellow diagonal stripe on the cab side, prohibiting the locomotive from working south of Crewe after electrification. (*Don Rowland*)

particular interest of J.T. Harrison, who had succeeded H.G. Ivatt as chief mechanical engineer in the LMR. Absolute rigidity of the split brass bearing was an essential ingredient to reliable performance, together with the means of attachment being sufficiently resistant to vibration. In this design, the jaws of the forked end of the rod were fastened by a substantial clip. The locking device for the cotter allowed precisely the right degree of tightness and consisted of a special locking plate with serrations on both sides. These serrations were arranged such that four different positions were possible relative to the serrations on the big-end cotter. This permitted adjustment to a very fine degree, to as little as 0.002in when necessary. The success of this design of inside connecting rod big-end may be judged by the fact that there were no reported failures directly attributable to it.

Cab, Platework and Details

The cab layout and structure was Standard practice, with the normal cantilevered floor. The hinged supports were so designed, working in conjunction with a diaphragm plate connected to the drag box, to allow the entire cab to move as necessary with expansion of the boiler and firebox. With the fitting of an inside cylinder the sloping fall plate at the smokebox end was provided with a removable hatch for access to the cylinder and cam box.

An interesting feature with all the Standard tender locomotives was the provision on the locomotive of only the front footsteps, all cab or rear footsteps being attached to the leading end of the tender. Unusually, on No 71000 the buffer heads were oval, although these seemed a common feature of the heaviest regional express passenger types. Conventional screw coupling drawgear was provided, with vacuum brake and steam heating connections on locomotive front and tender rear buffer beams. The use of speedometers on

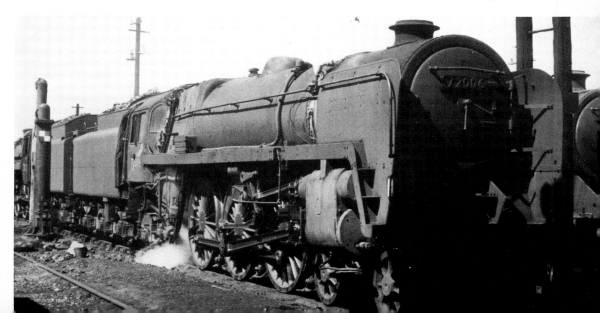

Last of the Clans No 72009 *Clan Stewart* receives rear end assistance with an excursion near Greskine on 1 August 1964.

steam locomotives had been a rare feature of previous designs, but a number of the Standards, including No 71000, had this fitting. A small generator attached to a light return crank on the trailing coupled wheel provided the drive, with a flexible connection to a gauge mounted in the cab.

A bracket fastened to the firebox foundation ring provided the standard mounting for injectors, with the live steam injector on the driver's side, and an exhaust steam injector on the fireman's side. Delivery was through the twin-feed clacks mounted on the front ring of the boilers. Pipework and handrailing were prominent features of these designs, though

No 72003 *Clan Fraser* heads a Liverpool–Glasgow train on the climb to Shap with banking assistance. Oddly the Clans retained handrails on the smoke deflectors throughout their life. (*Derek Cross*)

some of the smaller pipes, such as connections to the ejector at the smokebox end on the right-hand side were covered by a sheet-steel guard. The multiple-valve regulator was a standard fitting in the Pacifics, though with the Class 8, a connection was made to supply steam to return the Caprotti valves to their seats, the operation being controlled by the regulator pilot valve.

Tenders

Two types of tender were used with *Duke of Gloucester*, the first being designated type BR1E and used from 1954 to 1958, while the second type BR1J was used after that date until No 71000's withdrawal from service in 1962. The BR1J type had a capacity of ten tons of coal and 4,725 gallons of water, and was fitted with a coal pusher. To allow for the increased coal capacity, the previously standard layout of tender with high inset sides, was replaced by a flush-sided arrangement. This tender was one of the largest of the fourteen variations, although the underframe was the

standard 14ft 0in wheelbase for the BR1 series. Oddly, the diagram SL/8A/2 shows the BR1J tender to carry only 4,325 gallons of water, yet the list of 4,725-gallon tenders includes BR1J No 1528 built at Crewe under Lot 246. The BR1E tender was built to Lot 234 and numbered 1271. It was of identical size and capacity, and paired with No 71000 from 1954 until 1958.

Construction and Operation

Duke of Gloucester was designed as a prototype, the opportunity to press ahead with its construction being taken in the wake of the decision to write off the LMS Pacific No 46202, involved in the 1952 Harrow disaster. Built to Crewe Works Order No E486, the frames were laid down on 21 March 1954, No 71000 was noted on display at the International Railway Congress exhibition at Willesden during May 1954. By 13 June it was returned to Crewe North to begin working on the West Coast Main line, with the first regular turns being on the Mid-Day Scot from July 1954.

The name was adopted by permission of the late Prince Henry, HRH Duke of Gloucester, who at the time was President of the International Railway Congress.

A curious feature of No 71000 was the front end arrangement, which up to the early construction period had been settled as single blastpipe and chimney with a cross-sectional area of 33sq in. However, in some haste it seems, only two months before No 71000 was completed, this idea was discarded and a double blastpipe and chimney designed and fitted. Responsibility for this rests with S.O. Ell, who substituted twin-blast nozzles with a total area of 25sq in, each nozzle having the same proportions as the GWR Dean Goods 0-6-0. The design was not a good one, and in later results from trials prompted one commentator to remark that the evaporation rate sustained was not what would have been expected from this nozzle area, particularly in comparison with results obtained with the Britannia Pacifics. Yet a satisfactorily sharp blast was attained, since 8in of smokebox vacuum was measured with a blastpipe pressure of 5.6lb/sq in.

By all accounts there was no consistency of performance with this locomotive, on test and under normal service conditions. Taken to Swindon test plant for an extensive series of stationary and controlled road trials, these tended to indicate that the locomotive proper—cylinders and valve gear—did achieve its designers' expectations, but that the boiler was if anything inferior to the Britannias. On the Swindon test plant, the grate limit was reached at an evaporation rate of only 34,000lb of steam per hour delivered to the cylinders. At firing rates of between 2,000 and 4,000lb coal per hour, the BR13 boiler was

always producing less steam than the BR1 of the Class 7 locomotives. The reasons for the poor performance of the boiler fitted to the Class 8 Pacific were never fully investigated, since by the end of its testing period, BR had already decided on a course of dieselisation. It has been suggested that much of the problem may have been connected with the grate and the transmission of an excessive amount of vibration from undamped suspension on the trailing truck, the vibration tending to cause the break-up of the firebed in a manner associated with proximity to the grate limit on combustion long before that point should have been reached.

The cylinder performance was quite a different story, and the diagram showing the IHP characteristics illustrate this point. Short cut-offs were a characteristic of British Caprotti valve gear, and unlike the Class 7 locomotives *Duke of Gloucester* showed no signs of a fall in IHP at constant steam rates, at road speeds approaching 90mph. A comparison of cylinder efficiency with other Class 8 locomotives shows a very marked improvement in No 71000, and approaches 86% of the theoretical maximum possible with steam locomotives of this type. The drawbar horsepower characteristics show No 71000 as a very free-running locomotive and at a firing rate of 3000lb/hr produced 1000dbhp continuously at 80mph, with a maximum under test at this rate of 1260dbhp, with grade 1A coal.

The road tests were carried out over the West of England main line, and the Berks & Hants line on the Western Region. The test route was from Marston Yard, near Swindon, to Reading, then through Reading West and Southcote Jct, over the gently-graded line, through Newbury to Westbury. The only major speed restrictions were at the Western approaches to Reading, negotiating a series of junctions, and the rather severe curve at Midgham. Both road and stationary tests were conducted between December 1954 and June 1955. Out on the road, No 71000 did indeed prove a very free-running locomotive under a controlled output of 30,000lb steam per hour. On one occasion almost 80mph was maintained for 12 miles up to the 15mph slowing to negotiate Reading West Junction; the coal consumption rate was 4850lb/hr. The same steam rate produced an almost unbroken average of 60mph all the way from Southcote Jct to beyond Newbury, with similarly constant drawbar tractive effort of 9000lb, and actual horsepower values of 1542 at milepost 40 to 1540 at just west of Newbury. Train loads were in the order of 600 tons gross.

An interesting feature discussed in the reports was the application of a cost and energy diagram covering theoretical values thought achievable with this locomotive between Euston and Rugby. The diagram was prepared using test data from the WR trials, and a later comparison with point to point time on this route with LMR Class 8 Pacifics showed some superiority with the standard locomotive and loads of 450 tons. It has been suggested that at the start of this particular line, footplate crews were reluctant to work the Duchess Class hard up the initial 1 in 77 of Camden Bank, hence *Duke of Gloucester*'s time to Willesden Jct was always around two minutes quicker. But overall the Duchess class was more economical on fuel, on both the theoretical values calculated in the BTC bulletin, and the actual 80-minute schedule from Euston to Rugby.

One of the hardest sections of route regularly worked by No 71000 was between Carnforth and Carlisle, involving the ascent of Shap. As with the Euston-Rugby road, a predicted performance diagram was prepared for this section. The schedule for the 69 miles was 73 minutes, an average speed of just over 56mph. Two of the Duchess Class Pacifics succeeded in getting inside this timing with 500-ton loads, but No 71000 managed to gain almost seven minutes with 437 tons and an average speed of just less than 58mph. Though again the LMR Class 8s were more economical in operation, *Duke of Gloucester*'s coal consumption rose quite sharply at evapora-

tion rates of more than 24,000lb per hour.

Despite its steaming curiosities, No 71000 was regarded as an excellent design by many, including such insular operating authorities as the WR, where the locomotive was used on the Cornish Riviera Express for a time. Finally, returning to the LMR on the Mid Day Scot amongst other Anglo-Scottish services, *Duke of Gloucester*'s fate was sealed by the decision to go ahead with dieselisation and electrification, and it was withdrawn from service on 1 December 1962. It was scheduled for preservation by BR, but for some reason the plans were changed, and the left-hand cylinder was removed, sectioned and put on display in the Science Museum, the rest of the locomotive being transported to South Wales for scrapping in September 1967. However, the hulk was purchased in 1973 for private preservation, and is currently nearing completion of an almost complete rebuilding. In this, the decision has been taken to substitute the original plain double blastpipe and chimney with the Kylchap pattern, a decision which R.A. Riddles wished had been made much earlier.

Summary Table—Standard Class 8P 4-6-2

No	Name	Built	Works	Withdrawn	Final MPD	Sold to*
71000	*Duke of Gloucester*	4/54	Crewe	12/62	Crewe North	Woodham Bros/preserved

*The locomotive was sold in November 1967, and taken to Woodham Bros site at Barry, from where it was purchased in 1973 by the Duke of Gloucester Steam Locomotive Trust.

Summary Table—Class 6MT Nos 72000–72009

No	Name	Built	Withdrawn	Final MPD	Sold to/BR Scrapyard
72000	*Clan Buchanan*	12/51	12/62	Polmadie	Darlington Works
72001	*Clan Cameron*	12/51	12/62	Polmadie	Darlington Works
72002	*Clan Campbell*	1/52	12/62	Polmadie	Darlington Works
72003	*Clan Fraser*	1/52	12/62	Polmadie	Darlington Works
72004	*Clan MacDonald*	2/52	12/62	Polmadie	Darlington Works
72005	*Clan MacGregor*	2/52	5/65	Carlisle Kingmoor	West of Scotland Shipbreaking Co
72006	*Clan MacKenzie*	2/52	5/65	Carlisle Kingmoor	J. McWilliam, Shettleston
72007	*Clan MacKintosh*	3/52	12/65	Carlisle Kingmoor	G.H. Campbell, Airdrie
72008	*Clan MacLeod*	3/52	4/66	Carlisle Kingmoor	J. McWilliam, Shettleston
72009	*Clan Stewart*	3/52	8/65	Carlisle Kingmoor	Motherwell Machinery Co

Notes: 1 Nos 72000–72009 all built at Crewe
2 The names proposed for Nos 72010–72024, which were not built, were:

72010	*Hengist*	72015	*Clan Colquhoun*	72020	*Clan Gordon*
72011	*Horsa*	72016	*Clan Graham*	72021	*Clan Hamilton*
72012	*Canute*	72017	*Clan MacDougall*	72022	*Clan Kennedy*
72013	*Wildfire*	72018	*Clan MacLean*	72023	*Clan Lindsay*
72014	*Firebrand*	72019	*Clan Douglas*	72024	*Clan Scott*

Technical Data—Class 6MT Nos 72000–72009

Note: The information relates to locomotives in new or 'as built' condition

Cylinders and valve gear

Cylinders—diameter × stroke	19½in × 28in
Piston swept volume (one cylinder)	8362cu in
Clearance volume as % of piston swept volume	10.8%
Maximum piston thrust	67196lb
Steam chests—volume between valve heads	4558cu in
—volume as % of piston swept volume	54.5%
Piston valves—diameter	11in
—steam lap	1¹¹⁄₁₆in
—lead	¼in
—exhaust clearance	NIL
Maximum travel of valves	7.73in
Maximum cut-off %	78.0%
Travel at 20% cut-off	4.05in

Balancing data

Revolving masses, weight per cylinder	1500lb
Reciprocating masses—total weight per cylinder	846lb
—percentage balanced	40%
—unbalanced weight per cylinder	508lb
Ratio—unbalanced reciprocating weight per cylinder to total weight of locomotive	1/390
Hammer-blow at 5 revolutions per second—per wheel	2.12 tons
—per axle	2.55 tons
—per rail	5.50 tons
—whole locomotive	6.60 tons

Boiler proportions

Free area through tubes—large	3.62sq ft
—small	2.11sq ft
—total	5.73sq ft
Area through large tubes as % of total	63.2%
Total free area as % of grate area	15.9%
A/S ratio—large tubes	1/420
—small tubes	1/435
Steampipe in boiler—bore	7in
—cross-sectional area	38.5sq in
Regulator fully open—area	37.0sq in (multiple-valve regulator)
Superheater elements—total area	34.4sq in
Steampipes to cylinders—total area	56.5sq in
Blastpipe cap—diameter	5¼in
—area	21.6sq in
Chimney throat—diameter	1ft 3⅝in
—area	1.29sq ft
Throat area as % of grate area	3.57%
Height—blastpipe cap to chimney throat	3ft 0½in
Taper of chimney	1 in 14

7. The 4-6-0s

The 4-6-0 wheel arrangement was a popular British type. Two new classes were introduced in the Standard series: a Class 5 with 18 tons axle load, and 17 tons axle load, Class 4. The Class 5 design had started life in 1948 as the type 72 Pacific, from which was developed both the design under discussion and the Clan Class described earlier. It was conceived as an entirely new design along with the Britannia, Clan and Class 9F 2-10-0. Although the cylinders, wheels and motion were similar to the Class 6, the boiler design was basically that of the LMS Class 5 4-6-0s of Stanier and Ivatt. The Standard Class 5, numbered from 73000, was designed at Doncaster, and first built in 1951. Various contemporary press reports indicate that it was intended that the Standard Class 5s would work similar duties to the LMR Class 5, E & NER B1 4-6-0, and WR Hall class, which had a combined total of some 1441 locomotives.

In the 17 tons axle load category, it was felt that there was a need for a tender locomotive design which could provide a larger working range than a tank type. Routes in Central Wales were a case where this additional capacity was required, and although the GWR Manor Class was prominent, the dimensions of these locomotives precluded them from working further afield. Not so with the Standard Class 4 4-6-0, which satisfied the L1 loading gauge and had virtually universal route availability. It was developed from the LMR's Class 4 2-6-4 tank engine design, which had already gained a good reputation for its performance. Although the Class 4 4-6-0s were to have the same power characteristics as the LMS 2-6-4T, the boilers were 9in longer, with the same design of firebox.

Mechanical Details

Boilers, Smokeboxes, Fireboxes

In the Class 5 locomotive, a major departure from the original concept was the decision to adopt a narrow firebox. In both types of 4-6-0, the use of former LMS designs of boiler was decided upon, with the Class 5 taking that of the 44800 series of Ivatt version. This had a barrel rolled from two rings of steel plate, the second of which was tapered. Plate thickness was $^{17}/_{32}$in and $^{19}/_{32}$in, with the diameter varying from 4ft 11$^{11}/_{16}$in at the front tubeplate to 5ft 8½in at the firebox end. Length between tubeplates was 13ft 2⅞in and housed 151 small tubes of 1⅞in outside diameter, 28 large flues of 5⅛in od, with the latter

housing the Superheater Company's standard 1⅜in diameter elements. The Class 4 boiler, also made in two rings, tapered from 4ft 9in at the front to 5ft 3in at the rear. The increase in the number of small tubes to 157 was permissible at the reduced diameter of 1¾in with a small superheating surface, contained in only 21 5⅛in diameter large flues. When fitted to the Standard Class 4 tank the boiler arrangement was unaltered save for an increased working pressure, and modified staying arrangement. Both types of boiler were pressed to work at 225lb/sq in, and were known as types BR3 and BR4, for the Class 5 and Class 4 4-6-0 respectively.

Total heating surfaces were 1,444sq ft in the Class 4, and 1,650sq ft in the Class 5, this latter identical with the LMSR 4-6-0s built from No 45472 onwards. Considering that both boiler designs were successful, as their forerunners had been, details of the characteristics are worth noting. In one critical parameter, that of the free gas area through the tubes, there was some disparity between the two boilers, with the BR3 reaching 15.9% of grate area and the BR4 only 14.2% of the grate area. In another critical area, that of the A/S ratio, both types came close to the desirable ideal figure of 1/400. The A/S ratio is the relationship between the free cross-sectional area of the tubes and the total swept surface. (The internal surface area.) When this value is approximately 1/400, then the resistance to gas flow through the tubes is such that the heat absorption capacity reaches an optimum value. With 5⅛in diameter flues, this is reached when the tube length is 14ft 0in; shorter tubes provide lower A/S ratios, reduced resistance to gas flow, and a loss of boiler efficiency. Larger tubes restrict the gas flow and tend towards lower superheat temperatures, reducing cylinder efficiency.

The firebox in both cases was of the Belpaire type and fitted between the frames. The Class 5 design was 9ft 2$^{13}/_{16}$in long by 3ft 11⅞in wide, and provided an evaporative heating surface of 171sq ft. The Class 4 was of course smaller, only 8ft 6in long, but at 4ft 0½in was slightly wider than the 73XXX design and provided 143sq ft of heating surface. Only the Class 5 was fitted with a sloping throat plate and had a larger level section at the rear of the grate, though both types were fitted with Standard rocking grates. In the Class 5, there were eight rocking sections, each carrying fourteen firebar units, and providing an area of 28.7sq ft. The Class 4 had only seven rocking sections.

All firebox stays were of steel, except those in the

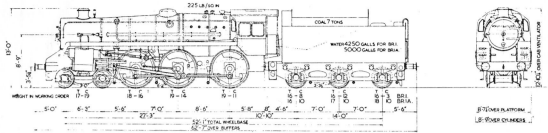

Class 5 4-6-0

water space area which were Monel metal, with steel nuts inside the firebox. This was the standard practice on all BR designs, and adopted from procedures developed by H.G. Ivatt in the latter years of the LMS. The ashpans were of the self-emptying hopper type with three compartments on the Class 5 design. In both cases the bottom flap doors could be operated from ground level by the same hand lever used to work the rocking levers for the firegrate. The standard practice of operating front and rear damper doors by means of a handwheel and screw was also used.

At the front end, the smokebox design and layout was virtually identical in both classes, save for obvious dimensional differences. The cylindrical drumhead pattern smokebox attached to a fabricated saddle incorporated standard self-cleaning equipment. In the original design, both classes were fitted with a single blastpipe with plain circular cap. Later members of the Class 4 were fitted with double blastpipe, but were again provided with the plain circular cap. The nozzle diameter of the Class 5 was 5⅛in while that of the

single-blastpipe Class 4 was 4¾in.

Boiler fittings were all standard items of equipment, many of which were first seen on the Britannia Pacifics. Water supply was taken from the injectors, one live steam, one exhaust, and both mounted on the right-hand side of the firebox, to the top-feed clacks fitted on the front boiler ring 30° on either side of centre. Through the feed clacks, a design adapted from one developed on the Southern Railway by Bulleid, water was delivered to two inclined trays deflecting around the inside of the barrel clear of the tube bank. Also mounted at the front end of the locomotive was the standard 'Tri-Tone' whistle, positioned immediately behind the chimney and the type SSJ vacuum ejector fitted on the left-hand side of the smokebox. The regulator was in both classes on the vertical grid design mounted in the dome. In this, the regulator head attached to the main steampipe had four ports, two small for starting and two large for normal running. The main valve was provided with four ports and was fitted to slides on the regulator head; the pilot valve, seated on the back of the main valve, was held in place by a flat spring. The function of this was to allow for easier and more accurate adjustment of the regulator position. Movement of the regulator arm in the cab actuated the valve through external rodding and a transverse shaft entering the boiler through a stuffing box in the barrel, on the left-hand side.

No 73088 built at Derby in June 1955, and seen here passing Luton on 9 June of that year on its way to the Southern Region. Note the Tri-Tone whistle, carried just behind the chimney, and the plain rectangular-section coupling rods, compared with the earlier fluted style. (*D. Larkin Collection*)

A rather begrimed No 73100, with high-sided BR1B tender, on a Class K pick-up freight at Shields Junction in the Scottish Region. The whistle on later Standard Class 5s, including No 73100, was placed in the more conventional position on the firebox roof, just in front of the cab. (*Don Rowland*)

On top of the firebox were mounted the twin pop safety-valves and the main steam manifold. The latter supplied steam to various components, and each steam supply pipe was provided with its own cut-off valve, with the main shut-off valve operated from inside the cab.

Frames, Wheels and Motion

The standard 1¼in thick mild-steel plate was used for the main frames, though because of the use of narrow fireboxes, these were stayed apart at a distance of 4ft 1½in. Fabricated horizontal and vertical stretchers were provided, with pin-jointed cross-stays attached to lugs on the coupled wheel axlebox guides. The main hornguides were cast-steel, with manganese-steel liners fitted as standard to the wearing faces. Unlike the Pacific types, the horns were bolted in place rather than welded.

On the Class 5 locomotives it had been decided to fit roller-bearing axleboxes of Timken manufacture, with both coupled wheel and bogie types of the non-split cannon type.

The Class 4 locomotives, and all the Standard designs from that category down, were provided with plain bearing axleboxes of traditional design. They were steel castings with pressed in whitemetal horseshoe brasses. The arrangement of this particular design was taken from the GWR to the LMS by Sir William Stanier in the 1930s. Lubrication of the plain bearings was effected through a worsted pad fitted into a sliding underkeep, and supplied with oil from a mechanical lubricator. The bogie axleboxes on the

Class 4 design were also plain bearing, but with the axlebox cast in bronze.

Underhung leaf springs were used in both designs, which in common with the Class 7 and Class 6 Pacifics, Class 4 and Class 3 tank locomotives, were 4ft 0in span when loaded. All plates were 5in × ½in section on coupled wheels, with 18 leaves for the Class 5, and 16 for the Class 4. The standard cotter-pin fastening and adjustment was used, with rubber damping pads.

There were only four sizes of driving wheel covering all twelve Standard designs, and the decision to use 5ft 8in and 6ft 2in in the larger classes was arbitrary. For the Class 5MT 4-6-0 the 6ft 2in size was adopted, and 5ft 8in for the Class 4. Cast-steel centres were standard, with tyres shrunk on. Lips were provided on the inner faces of the tyres for securing, but were small enough so that when the tyres were expanded during fitting, the lip passed easily over the wheel centre.

The cylinders were arranged for inside admission, and operated by Walschaerts valve gear, with the crosshead underhung from the slidebars. This arrangement was derived from late LNER practice, and Doncaster was the drawing office responsible for the design of the valve gears for all twelve Standard classes. The three slidebar design was fitted to all locomotives which had to pass the larger L2 loading gauge, whereas the smaller L1 gauge required the one of LMS-style double slidebars, one above and one below the crosshead. Traditional British practice had been to use cast-iron for the cylinder castings, but the cast-steel used in the larger Standard designs was also adapted for the Class 5 4-6-0s, cast-iron being employed from the Class 4 4-6-0 down. Both types were fitted with cast-iron liners.

The Class 5 design was fitted with 11in diameter piston valves, and had the same valve events as the Britannia Pacifics. Maximum valve travel of almost

7¾in was the largest of any British Class 5 locomotive, with a maximum cut-off of 78% in forward gear. In the Class 4 design, 10in diameter piston valves were employed, having the same 1¹¹⁄₁₆in steam lap and ¼in lead as the larger types, but with a travel of just over 7¼in and a maximum cut-off of 75%. The valve heads themselves carried six narrow rings on each, and as had been developed as a standard practice the front head was made ⅛in smaller in diameter than the rear, for easier withdrawal and assembly. The standard piston head was fitted in both designs, secured to a parallel seat by a collared nut, locking plate and lock nut. Two piston rings were used, with the head held clear of the cylinder barrel on its spring-loaded carrier. Lubrication of the cylinders was the standard arrangement using atomised oil, fed from a mechanical lubricator. All motion joints were grease-lubricated, with the exception of the return crank small-end, this being provided with a Skefco single-row self-aligning ball bearing. Reversing rods were tubular and with the screw inserted at the forward end, acting directly on the weighshaft, it was hoped to reduce the effects of vibration and wear.

In basic layout, the four-wheel bogie was identical in both designs, except for the use of roller-bearing axleboxes in the Class 5. The locomotive weight at the front end was supported on side bolsters and trans-

mitted this load through leaf springs carried in compensating beams. Side movement was controlled through double coil springs. In earlier work on the designs, it had been planned to standardise on an interchangeable 3ft 0in diameter wheelset that could be used for all carrying wheels, and fitted with outside roller bearing axleboxes. Due to clearance limitations within the loading gauge it was possible to use outside axleboxes with larger diameter wheels only, hence 3ft 3½in was standardised for all tender wheels and the trailing truck wheels of the Pacifics, with outside bearings, with 3ft 0in diameter wheels retained on leading trucks and bogies, with inside bearing axleboxes.

Superstructure and details

Uniformity of appearance or family likeness was assumed, with the running boards attached to brackets on the boiler side and the cab on its cantilevered mounting. The cab itself was the established standard arrangement and referred to in some quarters as a limousine cab. All platework was a mixture of welding and rivetting, with the profile following an essentially LMS style. To meet the restrictions of the loading gauge, the cabsides tapered inwards from just below the window level to the gutter. The near-side windows were sliding, and a spring loaded windshield was fitted to the pillar between the two side windows. A sliding roof ventilator was also provided over which the maximum height was 12ft 10¼in on the Class 5 and 12ft 11¹³⁄₁₆in on the Class 4.

The Class 5 locomotives numbered 73125 to 73167 built at Derby in 1956, in addition to the rather dramatic change by the fitting of Caprotti valve gear, incorporated one or two other minor alterations. In the cab, the previously standard provision of fixed

One of the Caprotti valve gear Class 5s, 73135 at Patricroft shed in Manchester. This view clearly shows the drive from the return crank mounted gearbox, and reversing gearbox driven by a cross-shaft from the left side of the locomotive. Boiler feed and auxiliary steam supplies, pipework and injectors, are visible alongside the firebox, and under the running boards and cab. (*D. Larkin Collection*)

Bird's-eye view of No 73059 climbing past the photographer at Murrayfield on 5 February 1955. (*Don Rowland*)

front windows were replaced by hinged versions, and the gangway doors (themselves an earlier alteration to the Standard layout) were fixed to the tender. The alteration to the front cab windows was made in response to a number of complaints from footplate crews on other Standard designs, and the modifications were carried out on new construction after 1954.

The design of coupling rods had come in for scrutiny following the problems with the Britannia Pacifics. Although all the Class 4 4-6-0s and the majority of the Class 5 were fitted with the fluted type, later batches of Class 5, including the Caprotti-fitted examples, had plain-section rods. It was recognised that there was a need to examine the design and performance of these components further, particularly following a survey of stresses in coupling rods produced in 1952. BR for its part laid down a uniform procedure to be followed in design, and while most later Standard locomotives were turned-out with slab-sided rods, simply increasing the size of the section was not the most satisfactory approach to this particular design problem.

Tenders

Covering both classes of 4-6-0, there were no fewer than eight separate tender designs, from the BR1 type first seen on the Britannias, to the BR2 newly-introduced with the Class 4. Of these, the Class 5 locomotive was paired with five different types, all on the standard 14ft 0in wheelbase underframe. The majority had the large flush-sided BR1B tender while

three were paired with the 2-10-0s BR1G design. The BR2 type was the smallest Standard tender available at the time of its introduction with the Class 4 4-6-0s, and while retaining the high inset sides to the coal space, accommodated six tons of fuel and 3,500 gallons of water on a 13ft 0in wheelbase. There were in fact only two types of underframe used with all the Standard tenders, the smaller being used on BR2, BR2A and BR3 designs. For both classes, the tender pairings were originally as given below:

Locomotive type	No	Tender type
Class 5 4-6-0	73000–49	BR1
	73080-9/100-9/20–34/45/71	BR1B
	73065–79/90–9/135–44	BR1C
	73110-9	BR1F
	73050-2	BR1G
	73053–64	BR1H
Class 4 4-6-0	75065–79	BR1B
	75000–49	BR2
	75050–64	BR2A

Class 5 locomotives fitted with BR1F and BR1G tenders were allocated to the Southern Region, where the increased water supply of 5,625 and 5,000 gallons respectively was needed. On the LMR, locomotives fitted with BR1C tenders had the coal supply increased from seven to nine tons. Water pick-up gear was not fitted to SR locomotives, though the fittings were provided as standard.

The two types of BR2 tender were different only by

virtue of the fact that the 2A design was provided with fallplate and gangway doors. In these smaller designs, the only departure from the main BR1 range was the use of shorter frames and wheelbase, outside roller-bearing axleboxes with standard overhung leaf springs of the same size as their larger brethren, and the 3ft 3½in diameter wheel sets.

Construction and Operation

The early production difficulties caused by the post war recession and affecting availability of steel had its effect on the construction programmes for virtually all the Standard classes. Both types of 4-6-0 were programmed for introduction in 1951 with the Class 5s coming from Derby and the Class 4s from Swindon. Later batches of Class 5, from 1955/6 were built at Doncaster in the programmes, since Derby was then in the throes of the early dieselisation phase. Table 17 lists the originally programmed building dates for both classes, together with Regional allocations:

Table 17   Programmed Construction of Class 5 and Class 4 4-6-0

Class 5

Batch	Nos	Built	Year	Operated	Maintained
1	73000–4	Derby	1951	LMR	LMR
2	73005–9	Derby	1951	ScR	LMR
3	73010–29	Derby	1951	LMR	LMR
4	73030–39	Derby	1952	ScR	ScR
5	73040–49	Derby	1952	LMR	LMR
6	73050–52	Derby	1953	SR	SR
7	73053–54	Derby	1953	LMR	LMR
8	73055–64	Derby	1953	ScR	ScR
9	73065–74	Derby	1953	LMR	LMR
10	73075–79	Derby	1954	ScR	ScR
11	73080–89	Derby	1954	SR	SR
12	73090–99	Derby	1955	LMR	LMR
13	73100–109	Doncaster	1955	ScR	ScR
14	73110–119	Doncaster	1955	SR	SR
15	73120–124	Doncaster	1955	ScR	ScR
16	73125–134	Derby	1956	WR	WR
17	73135–144	Derby	1956	LMR	LMR
18	73145–154	Derby	1956	ScR	ScR
19	73135–159	Doncaster	1956	ER	NER
20	73160–171	Doncaster	1956	NER	NER

Class 4

Batch	Nos	Built	Year	Operated	Maintained
1	75000–9	Swindon	1951	WR	WR
2	75010–19	Swindon	1951	LMR	WR
3	75020–29	Swindon	1952	WR	WR
4	75030–49	Swindon	1952	LMR	LMR
5	75050–64	Swindon	1953	LMR	LMR
6	75065–79	Swindon	1953	SR	WR
7	75080–89★	Swindon	1954	ER	NER

★This batch although authorised was cancelled; the locomotives were never built.

A comparison with the Table showing actual building and withdrawal dates reveals some bunching of production caused by the steel shortage and cutbacks in the various programmes, although overall the delivery of both classes achieved a close following of the original schedules.

The successful application of Caprotti poppet-valve gear to the Class 8 Pacific No 71000 *Duke of Gloucester* promoted the construction two years later of thirty similarly-fitted Class 5s. These were numbered 73125–73154, and ten were allocated to each of the London Midland, Scottish and Western Regions. These thirty locomotives were identical in all other respects with the remainder of the class, with the

Footplate arrangements of Standard Class 4 4-6-0 No 75078. The edge-on reversing wheel can be seen on the left, while the two screw-down handwheels, just to the right and below the firedoors, were for adjusting the front and rear dampers on the ashpan. (*R. France/Standard 4 Locomotive Preservation Society*)

layout of the valve gear following that of the Class 8 Pacific. The 19in × 28in cylinders were retained, with separate inlet and exhaust valves contained within a cambox mounted on top of each cylinder. The valves were pushed open into cages by cams driven from a worm gearbox mounted on the return crank of the centre pair of coupled wheels. The drive was taken as on the Pacific designs through three tubular shafts and universal joints to the cambox. The two worm reversing gearboxes were connected by a transverse shaft and Layrub flexible couplings, with the self-locking gearbox on the left-hand side of the locomotive being connected to the reversing wheel in the cab. An auxiliary steam supply from the regulator allowed saturated steam through a special valve to lift the bottom of the valves into their working position before the main steam supply was admitted. The main principles of operation were as described for *Duke of Gloucester*.

Distribution of the Class 5 was varied, though numerically they were strongest on the London Midland and Scottish Regions. Only five went to the North Eastern and twelve to the Eastern Region, with the Western's only allocation being the ten Caprotti-fitted locomotives. On the Southern Region, twenty of the twenty-three received names, which were previously carried by Southern Railway N15 King Arthur Class locomotives. Names and dates of naming are given in Table 18.

The first of the Standard 5s was on view at Marylebone Station on 26 April 1951, and followed on 23 May by Swindon's first Class 4, No. 75000. The LMR's allocation of Class 5s were seen on many parts of the system, including cross-country work between Derby and Bristol, and along the North Wales coast from Chester to Bangor and Llandudno Junction. In Scotland, the first went to Perth, while amongst the first workings there was the 10.00am Glasgow–

Table 18 Named Standard Class 5 4-6-0s

No	Name	Date named	Former N15 Class No
73080	*Merlin*	2/61	30740
73081	*Excalibur*	2/61	30736
73082	*Camelot*	8/59	30742
73083	*Pendragon*	10/59	30746
73084	*Tintagel*	11/59	30745
73085	*Melisande*	8/59	30753
73086	*The Green Knight*	12/59	30754
73087	*Linette*	5/61	30752
73088	*Joyous Gard*	5/61	30741
73089	*Maid of Astolat*	5/59	30744
73110	*The Red Knight*	1/60	30755
73111	*King Uther*	2/61	30737
73112	*Morgan le Fay*	4/60	30750
73113	*Lyonnesse*	12/59	30743
73114	*Etarre*	3/60	30751
73115	*King Pellinore*	2/60	30738
73116	*Iseult*	9/62	30749
73117	*Vivien*	4/61	30748
73118	*King Leodegrance*	2/60	30739
73119	*Elaine*	6/59	30747

Aberdeen. Oddly, perhaps, the Standard Class 5s were rostered to work over the Highland line between Perth and Inverness, and since none was fitted with tablet-exchange apparatus, this required the use of a Stanier Class 5 4-6-0 as pilot. The spread of the Class 5s was quite rapid throughout the Region with Manchester-based locomotives working into Leeds over the L&YR routes, and early in 1952 two were sent on loan to Stratford on the Eastern Region. Their use on that Region was very limited, and although officially Nos 73155–71 were to be allocated to both Eastern and North Eastern Regions, none was actually in use at the time of the withdrawals in the mid-1960s.

Soon after their introduction, one of the class was selected to undergo trials at Rugby and the results of the testing of No 73008 gave rise to some modifications to the front end design. Performance of these locomotives with the original 5⅛in diameter blastpipe produced on occasions a shortfall in evaporation rates with lower grades of coal, particularly when worked hard. With a reduction in blast nozzle diameter to 4⅞in, the front end limit on evaporation was raised by no less than 26%, much improving the Class 5s performance.

The Caprotti-fitted locomotives, although having what may be classed as one of the most efficient steam distribution systems devised, had their share of problems in operation. The ten locomotives operated by the LMR were allocated to Holyhead for a trial period on Manchester–Holyhead workings, but footplate staff felt that they were not quick enough on starting away, with the result that the locomotives were not rostered for stopping trains, and were soon transferred away. In fact they spent most of their lives allocated to Patricroft (Manchester), from where they were withdrawn in 1967/8. This kind of reaction to

Standard Class 4 4-6-0s were allocated to the LMR for banking and piloting over Shap; here No 75032 pilots a Stanier Class 5 on a Morecambe–Glasgow train on 15 January 1967. (*John Goss*)

these locomotives was neither typical or unique, but may have been produced through unfamiliarity in handling non-traditional designs.

Elsewhere the Walschaerts-fitted Class 5s, particularly following the modifications to the blast nozzle, were relatively popular. This was especially so on the Southern, where perhaps due previously to lack of a Class 5 of such power, they were greeted with some enthusiasm. On the Eastern Section for instance the performance of Standard Class 5s was unsurpassed. Their free running and hill-climbing ability were widely acclaimed, with recorded instances of speeds well into the 90s, with quite heavy trains.

The first withdrawals took place in 1964, with No 73027 the first to go, and followed that same year by 20 more. In 1965, area dieselisation of the Western Region was proceeding rapidly such that of the 42 Class 5s withdrawn the majority came from WR depots. Of the remainder, most came from the London Midland and Scottish Regions, with complete withdrawal of the class achieved with the exception of No 73069, by June 1968. No 73069 saw out steam on BR to the last, being finally removed from Carnforth in August 1968. Three members of this class were purchased for preservation, including No 73050, now restored and running on the Nene Valley Railway. No 73082 was purchased by the Camelot Railway Society in 1979—this particular example was one of those eminently successful Class 5s allocated to the Southern's South Eastern Section, being withdrawn from Guildford in 1966. The third and final preserved is Caprotti-fitted No 73129, at the Midland Railway Centre in Derbyshire.

The Class 4 4-6-0s were shared firstly and in the main between the London Midland and Western Regions, with the final double-chimneyed fifteen going to the Southern. The cut-back in locomotive construction programmes had a curious effect on the building of the Class 4s. One of the middle batches, Nos 75020–9, although scheduled for 1952 construction was delayed by almost two years. The first WR

No 75076 is seen here at Eastleigh, shortly before withdrawal in July 1967. The final fifteen Class 4 4-6-0s were fitted with double blastpipe and chimney, and type BR1B tenders. (*G.W. Sharpe*)

locomotives were allocated work in the West Midlands, shortly after their introduction, on duties as far north as Wolverhampton and Shrewsbury. The LMR's allocation at Patricroft were rostered to work local services on the former L&YR routes, while those sent new to Southport were initially used on some Stanier Class 5 turns.

Late in 1953 a number of Class 4s was allocated to Oswestry for working the Central Wales line, and in consequence ex-GWR Manor Class 4-6-0s used formerly were transferred away. One of the principal turns for locomotives of this class was the Cambrian Coast Express, a duty which they held for many years, and shared for a time with the Manor class. A number of the WR locomotives ventured into the West Country, and even at the time of their withdrawal two were stationed at Yeovil, and two at Templecombe. Much of their work involved piloting duties over the South Devon main line west of Newton Abbot.

On the London Midland, some were allocated to the Home Counties, and regularly worked stopping trains into St Pancras. To the north, the ten Class 4s allocated to Accrington did for a time in the mid-1950s cause some public outcry due to a propensity they developed for groaning brake blocks. This escalated to the extent that a formal complaint was made through the Police regarding the offending locomotives' disturbance of the peace. What the mechanical reasons for this were may never be known, but for certain duties a Hughes/Fowler Crab 2-6-0 was borrowed from nearby Rose Grove depot.

The Southern's allocation of fifteen, Nos 75065–79, were fitted with double-chimneys and blastpipes as a result of tests carried out on No 75006 at Swindon in 1953. In addition Nos 75003/6/20/9 were also modified to this arrangement. The original single-chimney design produced a maximum evaporation rate on test of 19,600lb/h, with the front end limit reached at a maximum firing rate of 3250lb of coal. The improved performance with the double-chimney version was sought, since it was required to have the additional capacity available on certain duties, from which Class 5 locomotives with their higher axleloads were precluded. The eventual maximum evaporation capacity with the double blastpipe was found on checking the locomotive so fitted to have been raised to 22,400lb/h, with coal of similar quality. Externally, there were two different designs of double chimney, the Swindon design, fitted to Nos 75003/6/20/9, and the shorter Brighton type carried by Nos 76065–79.

First withdrawals were made in 1964, starting in October of that year with No 75067, one of the Southern's batch stationed at Eastleigh. In the main the fifteen locomotives allocated to the SR remained there throughout their working lives with the LMR acquiring ten from the WR. Though the Croes Newydd locomotives were on LMR stock, the depot had been presented to the LMR by the WR during the boundary changes of the 1950s—similarly for the Machynlleth residents. The LMR had concentrated its Class 4s in the North-West, mainly at Carnforth, Skipton and Tebay, with odd examples at Bank Hall and Aintree.

Four of the class were saved for preservation and include No 75027 on the Bluebell Railway East Sussex and No 75029 at the East Somerset Railway, Cranmore, Somerset. Two double chimneyed 4s, Nos 75069 and 75078, are also safe. The former is working on the Severn Valley Railway at Bridgnorth, while the latter is preserved by the Standard Class 4 Preservation Society at Keighley in West Yorkshire. Of the preserved locomotive No 75029 was purchased by the artist David Shepherd, repainted in BR green livery and named *The Green Knight* before moving to the East Somerset Railway in 1973.

One final claim to fame that a member of the Class 4 can make is that No 75042 was the very last steam type to be overhauled at Derby Works, leaving the erecting shop there on 20 September 1963.

Summary Table—Standard Class 5MT 4-6-0s Nos 73000–73171

No	Built	Withdrawn	Disposal	No	Built	Withdrawn	Disposal
73000	4/51	3/68	J. Cashmore, Great Bridge	73060	8/54	5/67	G.H. Campbell, Airdrie
73001	4/51	12/65	J. Cashmore, Newport	73061	9/54	12/64	Motherwell Machinery Co
73002	5/51	3/67	J. Cashmore, Newport	73062	10/54	6/65	
73003	6/51	12/65	J. Cashmore, Newport	73063	10/54	6/65	Motherwell Machinery Co
73004	6/51	10/67	J. Cashmore, Newport	73064	10/54	5/67	G.H. Campbell, Airdrie
73005	6/51	6/66	Motherwell Machinery Co	73065	10/54	7/67	J. Cashmore, Newport
73006	6/51	3/67	J. Cashmore, Great Bridge	73066	10/54	4/67	
73007	7/51	3/66	Motherwell Machinery Co	73067	10/54	3/68	J. Cashmore, Great Bridge
73008	7/51	9/65		73068	10/54	12/65	J. Cashmore, Newport
73009	7/51	7/66	Corkerhill MPD	73069	10/54	6/68	J. Cashmore, Newport
73010	9/51	6/68	J. Cashmore, Great Bridge	73070	11/54	4/67	J. Cashmore, Great Bridge
73011	9/51	11/67	J. Cashmore, Great Bridge	73071	11/54	9/67	J. Cashmore, Newport
73012	9/51	11/64	J. Buttigieg, Newport	73072	1/55	10/66	
73013	9/51	5/66	J. Cashmore, Great Bridge	73073	1/55	11/67	J. Cashmore, Newport
73014	9/51	7/67	J. Cashmore, Newport	73074	1/55	9/64	J. Cashmore, Newport
73015	10/51	8/65	J. Cashmore, Newport	73075	4/55	12/65	J. McWilliam, Shettleston
73016	10/51	12/66	J. Cashmore, Newport	73076	4/55	8/64	Cowlairs Works, Glasgow
73017	10/51	10/64	J. Cashmore, Newport	73077	5/55	1/65	
73018	10/51	7/67	J. Cashmore, Newport	73078	5/55	7/66	
73019	11/51	1/67	J. Cashmore, Newport	73079	5/55	5/67	G.H. Campbell, Airdrie
73020	11/51	7/67	J. Cashmore, Newport	73080*	5/55	12/66	J. Cashmore, Newport
73021	11/51	8/65	J. Cashmore, Newport	73081*	6/55	7/66	Preserved—Camelot Rly Society
73022	11/51	4/67	J. Cashmore, Newport	73082*	6/55	6/66	Woodham Bros
73023	12/51	8/65	J. Cashmore, Newport				Preserved—Camelot Rly Society
73024	12/51	11/64	J. Buttigieg, Newport	73083*	6/55	9/66	J. Cashmore, Newport
73025	12/51	10/67	J. Cashmore, Newport	73084*	6/55	12/65	J. Buttigieg, Newport
73026	12/51	3/67	J. Cashmore, Great Bridge	73085*	6/55	7/67	J. Cashmore, Newport
73027	12/51	2/64		73086*	6/55	10/66	J. Cashmore, Newport
73028	12/51	12/66	J. Cashmore, Newport	73087*	6/55	10/66	J. Cashmore, Newport
73029	1/52	7/67	J. Cashmore, Newport	73088*	6/55	10/66	J. Cashmore, Newport
73030	7/53	8/65	J. Cashmore, Newport	73089*	6/55	9/66	J. Cashmore, Newport
73031	7/53	9/65	J. Cashmore, Newport	73090	10/55	10/65	
73032	7/53	8/65	J. Cashmore, Newport	73091	10/55	5/65	Birds, Risca
73033	8/53	1/68	J. Cashmore, Newport	73092	10/55	5/67	J. Cashmore, Newport
73034	8/53	3/68	J. Cashmore, Newport	73093	11/55	7/67	J. Cashmore, Newport
73035	8/53	1/68	J. Cashmore, Newport	73094	12/55	5/67	J. Cashmore, Great Bridge
73036	9/53	9/65	T.W. Ward, Beighton	73095	12/55	8/66	Arnott Young, Carmyle
73037	10/53	7/67	J. Cashmore, Newport	73096	12/55	11/67	Woodham Bros, Barry
73038	10/53	10/65	J. Cashmore, Great Bridge	73097	12/55	5/67	
73039	10/53	9/67	J. Buttigieg, Newport	73098	12/55	3/66	Motherwell Machinery Co
73040	10/53	6/68	J. Cashmore, Great Bridge	73099	12/55	10/66	Motherwell Machinery Co
73041	10/53	6/65	Eastleigh Works	73100	8/55	1/67	Motherwell Machinery Co
73042	10/53	8/65	J. Cashmore, Newport	73101	8/55	8/66	Motherwell Machinery Co
73043	10/53	7/67	J. Cashmore, Newport	73102	9/55	12/66	G.H. Campbell, Airdrie
73044	11/53	3/65	Birds, Long Marston	73103	9/55	10/65	Arnott Young, Carmyle
73045	11/53	8/67		73104	9/55	10/65	Arnott Young, Carmyle
73046	11/53	9/64	J. Cashmore, Newport	73105	12/55	9/66	Motherwell Machinery Co
73047	12/53	12/64		73106	12/55	6/65	P & W McLellan, Langloan
73048	12/53	10/67	J. Cashmore, Newport	73107	12/55	9/66	Arnott Young, Carmyle
73049	12/53	3/65	Birds, Long Marston	73108	1/56	12/66	G.H. Campbell, Airdrie
73050	4/54	6/68	Preserved—Nene Valley Railway	73109	1/56	10/64	Cowlairs Works, Glasgow
73051	5/54	8/65	J. Cashmore, Newport	73110*	10/55	1/67	J. Cashmore, Newport
73052	5/54	12/64	J. Buttigieg, Newport	73111*	10/55	9/65	J. Cashmore, Newport
73053	6/54	3/68		73112*	10/55	6/65	T.W. Ward, Beighton
73054	6/54	8/65	J. Cashmore, Newport	73113*	10/55	1/67	J. Cashmore, Newport
73055	6/54	5/66	P. & W. McLellan, Langloan	73114*	11/55	6/66	J. Cashmore, Newport
73056	7/54	6/65	Arnott Young, Old Kilpatrick	73115*	11/55	3/67	J. Cashmore, Newport
73057	7/54	3/66	P. & W. McLellan, Langloan	73116*	11/55	11/64	
73058	7/54	11/64		73117*	11/55	3/67	J. Cashmore, Newport
73059	8/54	5/67	G.H. Campbell, Airdrie	73118*	12/55	7/67	J. Cashmore, Newport

No	Built	Withdrawn	Disposal	No	Built	Withdrawn	Disposal
73119★	12/55	3/67	J. Cashmore, Newport	73146	2/57	5/67	J. Cashmore, Newport
73120	1/56	12/66	J. Cashmore, Newport	73147	2/57	8/65	G.H. Campbell, Airdrie
73121	1/56	2/66	J. Cashmore, Great Bridge	73148	3/57	9/65	
73122	1/56	9/65		73149	3/57	12/66	Motherwell Machinery Co
73123	2/56	5/65	J. Cashmore, Newport	73150	4/57	12/66	Motherwell Machinery Co
73124	3/56	12/65	W. of Scotland Shipbreaking Co	73151	4/57	8/66	J. McWilliam, Shettleston
73125	7/56	6/68	G.H. Campbell, Airdrie	73152	5/57	12/65	J. Cashmore, Great Bridge
73126	7/56	4/68	Motherwell Machinery Co	73153	5/57	12/66	A. Draper, Hull
73127	8/56	11/67	Motherwell Machinery Co	73154	6/57	12/66	J. Cashmore, Newport
73128	8/56	5/68	Shipbreaking Industries, Faslane	73155	12/56	7/67	J. Cashmore, Great Bridge
73129	8/56	12/67	Shipbreaking Industries, Faslane	73156	12/56	11/67	Woodham Bros
			Motherwell Machinery Co	73157	12/56	5/68	Preserved—Midland Rly Centre
73130	10/56	1/67	J. McWilliam, Shettleston	73158	12/56	10/67	J. Cashmore, Newport
73131	10/56	1/68	Shipbreaking Industries, Faslane	73159	1/57	10/67	J. Cashmore, Great Bridge
73132	10/56	3/68	G.H. Campbell, Airdrie	73160	1/57	11/67	J. Cashmore, Great Bridge
73133	10/56	6/68	J. Cashmore, Newport	73161	1/57	12/64	J. Cashmore, Great Bridge
73134	10/56	6/68	Woodham Bros, Barry	73162	1/57	5/65	J. Cashmore, Great Bridge
73135	10/56	3/68	J. Cashmore, Great Bridge	73163	2/57	11/65	J. Cashmore, Great Bridge
73136	10/56	3/68	J. Cashmore, Newport	73164	2/57	12/64	J. Cashmore, Newport
73137	11/56	6/67	J. Cashmore, Newport	73165	2/57	9/65	J. Cashmore, Great Bridge
73138	11/56	4/68	J. Cashmore, Newport	73166	3/57	12/65	
73139	11/56	5/67	J. Buttigieg, Newport	73167	4/57	8/65	J. Cashmore, Newport
73140	11/56	10/67	J. Cashmore, Newport	73168	4/57	12/65	Birds Motors, Bridgend
73141	12/56	7/67	T.W. Ward, Beighton	73169	4/57	10/66	J. Cashmore, Newport
73142	12/56	4/68	J. Friswell, Banbury	73170	4/57	6/66	
73143	12/56	6/68	J. Cashmore, Great Bridge	73171	5/57	10/66	J. Cashmore, Newport
73144	12/56	8-67	J. Cashmore, Newport				
73145	1/57	9/66	J. Cashmore, Newport				

Notes: Locomotives built at Derby: Nos 73000–73099; 73125–73154
Locomotives built at Doncaster: Nos 73100–73124; 73155–73171
Locomotives marked ★ were named—see Table 18

Summary Table—Standard Class 4 4-6-0s Nos 75000–75079

No	Built	Withdrawn	Disposal	No	Built	Withdrawn	Disposal
75000	5/51	12/65	T.W. Ward, Killamarsh	75021	11/53	2/68	T.W. Ward, Inverkeithing
75001	8/51	12/64	J. Cashmore, Newport	75022	12/53	12/65	T.W. Ward, Killamarsh
75002	8/51	8/67	Birds, Long Marston	75023	12/53	1/66	T.W. Ward, Killamarsh
75003	8/51	10/65	Birds, Bridgend	75024	12/53	11/67	Birds, Long Marston
75004	8/51	3/67	J. Cashmore, Newport	75025	4/54	12/65	T.W. Ward, Killamarsh
75005	9/51	11/65	Birds, Morriston	75026	5/54	12/67	Arnott Young, Carmyle
74006	9/51	8/67	Birds, Long Marston	75027	5/54	8/68	Preserved on Bluebell Rly, Sussex
75007	9/51	4/65	Birds, Bynea	75028	5/54	12/65	T.W. Ward, Beighton
75008	10/51	12/65	T.W. Ward, Killamarsh	75029	5/54	8/67	Preserved on East Somerset Rly
75009	10/51	8/68	G.H. Campbell, Airdrie	75030	6/53	12/67	Arnott Young, Carmyle
75010	11/51	10/67	Motherwell Machinery Co	75031	6/53	2/66	T.W. Ward, Beighton
75011	11/51	11/66	T.W. Ward, Beighton	75032	6/53	2/68	
75012	11/51	1/67		75033	7/53	12/67	
75013	12/51	8/67	Birds, Long Marston	75034	7/53	2/68	T.W. Ward, Inverkeithing
75014	12/51	12/66	Woodham Bros, Barry	75035	8/53	7/67	G.H. Campbell, Airdrie
75015	12/51	12/67	Arnott Young, Carmyle	75036	8/53	6/66	Birds, Long Marston
75016	1/52	7/67	T.W. Ward, Killamarsh	75037	8/53	12/67	Arnott Young, Carmyle
75017	1/52	1/67	T.W. Ward, Beighton	75038	8/53	12/65	T.W. Ward, Beighton
75018	3/52	6/67	J. Buttigieg, Newport	75039	8/53	9/67	Motherwell Machinery Co
75019	3/52	8/68	G.H. Campbell, Airdrie	75040	8/53	10/67	
75020	11/53	8/68	G.H. Campbell, Airdrie	75041	9/53	1/68	G. Cohen, Kettering

No	Built	Withdrawn	Disposal	No	Built	Withdrawn	Disposal
75042	9/53	10/67		75062	5/57	2/68	T.W. Ward, Inverkeithing
75043	9/53	12/67	Arnott Young, Carmyle	75063	5/57	6/66	Birds, Long Marston
75044	9/53	3/66	T.W. Ward, Beighton	75064	5/57	5/67	J. Cashmore, Newport
75045	9/53	4/66	Birds, Long Marston	75065	8/55	9/66	
75046	10/53	8/67	Birds, Long Marston	75066	9/55	1/66	
75047	10/53	8/67	Birds, Long Marston	75067	9/55	10/64	
75048	10/53	8/68	G.H. Campbell, Airdrie	75068	9/55	7/67	Birds, Risca
75049	10/53	10/66	A. Draper, Hull	75069	9/55	9/66	Woodham Bros
75050	11/56	11/66	Garnham, Harris & Elton, Chesterfield				Preserved—Severn Valley Rly
75051	11/56	11/66	T.W. Ward, Beighton	75070	10/55	9/66	J. Cashmore, Newport
75052	12/56	8/67	Birds, Long Marston	75071	11/55	8/67	Birds, Long Marston
75053	1/57	9/66	A. Draper, Hull	75072	11/55	12/65	T.W. Ward, Ringwood
75054	1/57	8/66		75073	11/55	12/65	T.W. Ward, Ringwood
75055	1/57	6/67	Garnham, Harris & Elton, Chesterfield	75074	11/55	7/67	R.A. King, Norwich
				75075	11/55	7/67	R.A. King, Norwich
75056	3/57	6/66	Birds, Long Marston	75076	12/55	7/67	Birds, Risca
75057	3/57	2/66	T.W. Ward, Beighton	75077	12/55	7/67	R.A. King, Norwich
75058	4/57	12/67	Arnott Young, Carmyle	75078	1/56	7/67	Woodham Bros
75059	4/57	7/67	G.H. Campbell, Airdrie				Preserved by Std Class 4 Pres. Society
75060	5/57	4/67	H. Bolckow, Blyth				
75061	5/57	2/67	T.W. Ward, Killamarsh	75079	1/56	11/66	Woodham Bros, Barry

All locomotives were built at Swindon

Technical Data—The Standard 4-6-0 Classes

Cylinders and valve gear		Class 5MT	Class 4MT
Cylinders—diameter × stroke	....	19in × 28in	18in × 28in
Piston swept volume—one cylinder	....	7935cu in	7125cu in
Clearance volume as % of piston swept volume	....	11.3%	10.8%
Maximum piston thrust	....	63794lb	57256lb
Steam chests—volume between valve heads	....	4056cu in	3895cu in
—volume as % of piston swept volume	....	51.1%	54.6%
Piston valves—diameter	....	11in	10in
—steam lap	....	$1^{11}/_{16}$in	$1^{11}/_{16}$in
—lead	....	¼in	¼in
—exhaust clearance	....	NIL	NIL
Maximum travel of valves	....	7.73in	7.34in
Maximum cut-off %	....	78.0%	75.0/
Travel at 20% cut-off	....	4.05in	4.05in

Balancing data			
Revolving masses—weight per cylinder	....	1419lb	1415lb
Reciprocating masses—total weight per cylinder	....	826lb	760lb
—percentage balanced	....	50%	50%
—unbalanced weight per cylinder	....	413lb	380lb
Ratio—unbalanced reciprocating weight per cylinder to total weight of locomotive	....	1/422	1/400
Hammer-blow at 5 revolutions per second—per wheel	....	2.61 tons	2.40 tons
—per axle	....	3.11 tons	2.86 tons
—per rail	....	6.95 tons	6.49 tons
—whole locomotive	....	8.28 tons	7.73 tons

Boiler proportions			
Free area through tubes—large	....	2.33sq ft	1.74sq ft
—small	....	2.22sq ft	2.04sq ft
—total	....	4.55sq ft	3.78sq ft
Area through large tubes as % of total	....	51.1%	46.0%
Total free area as % of grate area	....	15.9%	14.2%

A/S ratio—large tubes	....	1/383	1/368
—small tubes	....	1/392	1/405
Steam pipe in boiler—bore	....	6in	5½in
—cross-sectional area	....	28.3sq in	23.8sq in
Regulator fully open—area	....	26.3sq in	24.3sq in
Superheater elements—total area	....	27.5sq in	20.6sq in
Steampipes to cylinders—total area	....	39.3sq in	31.8sq in
Blastpipe cap—diameter	....	5⅛in	4¾in
—area	....	20.6sq in	17.7sq in
Chimney throat—diameter	....	1ft 2¼in	1ft 1½in
—area	....	1.11sq ft	1.00sq ft
Throat area as % of grate area	....	3.88%	3.75%
Height—blastpipe cap to chimney throat	....	2ft 9⅝in	2ft 7in
Taper of chimney	....	1 in 14	1 in 14

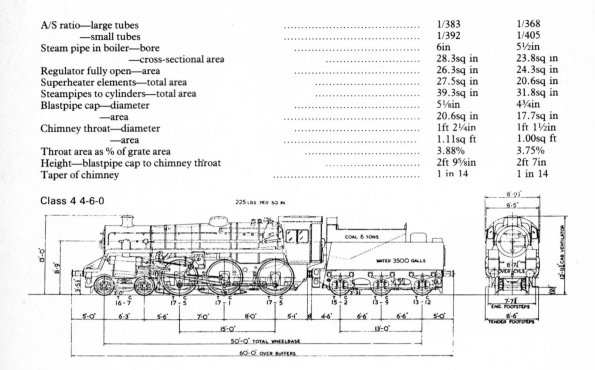

Class 4 4-6-0

8. The 2-6-0s

British Railways Mogul classes provided three different designs of locomotive, though two of these were basically developments of former LMS designs, the Class 3 locomotive coming perhaps the closest to a new Standard design. All three types were designed to pass the smaller L1 loading gauge, rendering them almost universally available.

First to appear were the Class 4MT 2-6-0s, from Horwich in December 1952, followed closely by the Class 2s from Darlington. As with other Standard types, curtailment of production was directly attributable to the steel shortage, with construction reported as very slow even as late as September 1952. These 115 locomotives were based on the LMS Ivatt design of 1947, numbered in the 43XXX series by BR and affectionately known as 'Doodlebugs'. The Standard Class 4 development was confined mainly to alterations to boiler mountings, to accept Standard fittings. In addition, as a result of tests carried out on the Ivatt 2-6-0s, improvements were made to the blastpipe and chimney proportions. The parent office selected for design work was Doncaster, with construction at Doncaster, Derby and Horwich. The selection of Doncaster as the principal design office for what was largely an ex-LMS design may not have been the

break with tradition that it first seems. In fact, during the first four years after nationalisation Doncaster and Darlington in the North East built no fewer than 82 of the Ivatt Class 4 2-6-0s so they were already familiar there. The use of this type and the smaller 2-6-0s of Class 2 in the North Eastern and Eastern Regions was brought to fruition as a result of the need to replace ageing 0-6-0 tender types for mineral work.

The Class 3 2-6-0 was first conceived as the mixed-traffic Type 78, with a 16-ton axle load, and intended for use on the small number of lines where the Class 4 2-6-0s were precluded for reasons of weight. The class as it eventually appeared was suitable for fitting the same LMS boiler design as the Class 4, but in order to meet the axle load restrictions, it was necessary to save around two tons in boiler weight. This was achieved by using the GWR Swindon No 2 boiler, as fitted to GWR 51XX, 56XX and 81XX tank engines. The remaining design details followed closely the Standard pattern with 5ft 3in coupled wheels, slightly less than 20½sq ft of grate area, and a working pressure of 200lb/sq in. Considering the use of a Swindon boiler design, it is not surprising that the parent office for the overall design was also Swindon, with construction carried out there during 1954. Other details, as

The BR Standard equivalent of the Ivatt Class 4MT 2-6-0, seen here on Southern metals is No 76017, built at Horwich in June 1953. The disc headcode carried on the Southern Region differed from the BR standard code. (*Lens of Sutton*)

with all Standard series, were worked out at the Locomotive Drawing Offices of Brighton, Doncaster and Derby.

The last of the three 2-6-0s, and smallest of the Standard tender locomotives was the Class 2, which first appeared in 1953. These were all constructed at Darlington with Derby as the parent office for design. Despite being built in the North East, the first of the BR Standard Class 2s were allocated to the Western Region. Darlington had already built 18 of the Ivatt LMS 2-6-0s, and since alterations were made only to boiler mountings to accept the Standard fittings the type was already familiar. The Standard Class 2 had the same physical details: maximum 13¾ tons axle-load, 5ft 0in coupled wheels, 200lb/sq in boiler pressure and 17½sq ft grate area. The intention of the operating department was that the locomotives would be used not only on freight, but on light main line and cross-country passenger workings. On the WR they were seen as replacements for various 0-6-0 types, including Dean 2301 and Collett 2259 classes.

Mechanical Details

Boilers, Firebox and Smokebox

The three boiler designs developed for the 2-6-0 classes were designated types BR7, BR8 and BR9, for the Class 4, 3 and 2 locomotives respectively. The BR7 and BR9 designs were quite simply former LMS boilers adopted as BR Standard, while the third was the Swindon No 2 with one or two minor dimensional adjustments. All three boilers were built in two rings, the second of which was tapered.

The BR7 boiler for the Class 4s was 10ft 10½in between tubeplates, and used the same flangeing plates as the Ivatt Class 4s. The outside diameter varied from 4ft 9½in at the front to 5ft 3in at the firebox end. Plate thickness was ⅝in mild steel. Within the barrel, there were 156 small tubes of 1⅝in outside diameter, and 24 large 5in diameter superheater flues housing standard 1⅜in diameter elements. This basic LMS boiler had already proved satisfactory in service performance, and was economic in operation and maintenance. A very satisfactory figure for

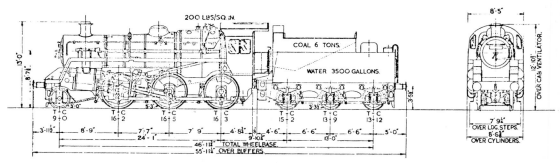

Class 3 2-6-0

One of the Doncaster-built 2-6-0s allocated to the Scottish Region, No 76106, amid a very wintry scene in February 1963. Only three years later this locomotive had been withdrawn and transported to Staffordshire for scrapping. The secondary duties for which the class was intended, had by the early 1960s become the virtual monopoly of Type 2 diesels. Even the menial shunting duties were better suited to the 0-6-0 diesel type seen in this view as No 76106's companion. (*Don Rowland*)

the free gas area as a percentage of grate area was achieved, being no less than 16.5%. The dome-mounted regulator was of the vertical-slide type and operated by the standard arrangement of external rodding and a transverse shaft through a stuffing box in the boiler shell. The boiler feed was taken from the injectors to twin delivery clacks mounted one on each side of the front boiler ring, water being directed away from the tube bank by deflector plates. Total evaporative heating surface of the BR7 boiler was 1075sq ft, with the superheater providing another 247sq ft of heating surface.

Next in line was the BR8 boiler, fitted to the Swindon-built Class 3 locomotives of the 77XXX series. Use was made of the flangeing blocks of the Swindon No 2 boiler, though there were one or two detail alterations to this design as adopted by BR. The overall length of the two rings was shortened by $5^{13}/_{16}$in to give a between-tubeplates length of 10ft 10½in, and to save further weight ½in thick high-tensile steel plates were used in place of the previous mild steel ⅝in plate. Since the GWR boiler was domeless it was necessary to incorporate this feature to house the regulator, and conform with the standard arrangements.

The outside diameter of the boiler tapered from 4ft 5in at the smokebox to 5ft 0½in at the firebox end. Modifications to the tubeplates provided for 145 small tubes of 1⅝in diameter, and 18 large flues of 5⅛in diameter. Originally the Swindon No 2 boiler had been fitted with only seven element superheaters, the new BR8 design having 18, with standard 1⅜in diameter elements. A total heating surface of 924sq ft was available, with 184sq ft from the superheaters.

The last and smallest of the BR Standard boiler designs, type BR9, was identical in almost every respect with the Ivatt Class 2. The two rings of mild-steel plate housed 12 5⅛in diameter superheater flues, and 162 small tubes 1⅝in diameter. Plate thickness varied from ½in for the front ring to $^{17}/_{32}$in for the rear, with the diameter increasing from 4ft 3in at the smokebox to 4ft 8in at the rear. The length between tubeplates of 10ft 10½in was identical with all the other boilers carried by the BR 2-6-0s. Total evaporative heating surface of the boiler was exactly the same as for the BR8 type, ie 724sq ft, with the smaller 12-element superheater contributing 124sq ft of additional heating surface. The actual free gas area of 2¾sq ft through the tubes was 15.9% of grate area. The standard vertical-grid type regulator was mounted in the dome, with the boiler feed clacks mounted on the front ring, approximately 30° on either side of the centre line.

The fireboxes fitted to each of these boilers were constructed with inner boxes of copper, and steel outer plates, although as with all Standard designs consideration had been given at an early stage to the use of steel throughout. The Class 4 firebox provided 131sq ft of heating surface from dimensions of 7ft 6in length and 4ft 0½in width. The grate area was exactly 23sq ft. With the Class 3 design a reduction in length of 7ft 0in was made, and with a width of exactly 4ft 0in over the outside of the wrapper plates provided a heating surface of 118sq ft. The grate area was reduced to 20.35sq ft. The copper inner firebox comprised a ⁹/₁₆in thick wrapper plate and vertical back plate, whilst the throat plate, also vertical, was ⅝in thick. The steel outer wrapper plate was ⁹/₁₆in thick.

The smallest of the three fireboxes provided a heating surface of 101sq ft in its 5ft 11in length, and width of 4ft 0⁷/₁₆in. Again, the outer wrapper plate was steel, ¹⁷/₃₂in thick, with the inner copper wrapper plate ⁹/₁₆in thick, as in the other types. Vertical throat and back plates were ⅝in and ¹⁷/₃₂in thick respectively. The grate area, identical with the Ivatt Class 2, was 17½sq ft.

The basic firebox design was of the Belpaire type, waisted-in to fit between the frames, with the standard rocking grates and self-emptying hopper-type ashpans. All water space stays were monel metal with steel nuts fitted to the end terminating inside the firebox. Roof, transverse, and longitudinal stays were steel. Mounted on the firebox roof, in front of the cab, were two Ross 'Pop' pattern safety-valves, set to blow-off at 225lb/sq in for the Class 4, and 200lb/sq in for the Class 3 and Class 2. A standard feature just to the rear of the safety-valves was the main steam manifold, with separate shut-off valves to each auxiliary steam supply, and a main shut-off valve located in the cab. Although this arrangement had been standardised and generally accepted as a good idea, there were a number of important points of criticism. Not least among them was the fact that in the event of an emergency, it may have proved impossible to reach the main shut-off valve, when in particular, the cab was filled with steam. Curiously, too, it was not until some six years after the first allocations of the Standards were made that a drawing was issued showing the functions of the various manifold shut-off valves. Before that, since none of the valves was individually marked, it was necessary to trace the pipework to determine the function of a particular valve.

Boiler and firebox lagging was accomplished with asbestos mattresses for the Class 4 and Class 3 designs, while the Class 2 was lagged with fibreglass. It is interesting to note that a number of the Standard types were provided with lagging of a combination of the two, hence it was possible to find fibreglass around the firebox wrappers and asbestos mats on the backplate.

At the opposite end of the boiler, the smokebox was a cylindrical rivetted assembly in all three designs, incorporating full self-cleaning equipment. All were supported on cast-steel saddles which in turn acted as frame stays. The single blastpipe with plain circular cap was provided in three separate sizes; 4⅜in diameter for the Class 4, 4½in in the Class 3, and 4⅛in for the Class 2. The standard Cardew pattern blower ring was fitted around the neck of the blastpipe, with four nozzles. None of the 2-6-0 designs was fitted with

a double chimney arrangement, though it may have been considered in the case of the Class 4, which owed its parentage to the LMS Ivatt 2-6-0s which originally had double chimneys. Presumably the poor performance of this latter when compared with single-chimney versions had some influence on the BR Standard design. In fact, the improvement in maximum continuous steam production of the Ivatt Class 4 by a reduction in the chimney choke diameter from 1ft 2¼in to 1ft 0¾in was dramatic, output going up by 89%. Much research had been undertaken by S.O. Ell at Swindon at the time the Standard designs were under development, hence it was possible to incorporate such improvements into the types adapted from former LMSR locomotives.

Cylinders, Wheels and Motion

The main frames were 1in thick mild-steel plate, stayed vertically and horizontally by fabricated plate stretchers, and with a spacing of 4ft 1½in. All coupled wheel axleboxes were plain bearing types, and in all three designs, were steel castings with pressed-on white metal brasses of horseshoe pattern. The use of manganese-steel liners fitted to the wearing faces of the axlebox guides had already been shown to provide greater length of service, freedom from wear and reduced maintenance costs, consequently they were again fitted as standard. The method of attachment was to weld the liners and strips to a backplate which in turn was bolted to the hornguides. Lubrication was effected through a worsted pad fitted into a removable tray in the underkeep and supplied with oil from a mechanical lubricator.

The pony truck for these three locomotives was a bar-framed design, and followed closely that which Ivatt had developed in the last years of the LMSR. It was light in construction and weight, and featured coil springs for load bearing and side control. Two pairs of springs were arranged, one on each side of the axlebox, transmitting the load through a yoke-and-shoe arrangement. Each pair of springs was arranged with one inside the other, providing four to each axlebox. The axleboxes themselves were bronze castings fitted with horseshoe-pattern brasses. The wheels were the standard 3ft 0in diameter with ten spokes and 3in thick tyres shrunk onto a cast-steel centre.

Coupled wheels were of two sizes, 5ft 3in for the Class 4 and Class 3, and 5ft 0in for the Class 2. The introduction of the 5ft 3in diameter wheel was not a planned standard feature; rather it was included because they were fitted to a design to be incorporated in the Standard range. Underhung leaf springs were again a standard feature of the locomotive's suspension and on the coupled wheels were in all three designs of 4ft 0in span, with 16 plates 5in × ½in section.

Steam brakes were provided for these locomotives, the arrangement of the rigging being standardised from the appearance of the first Standard type. Single larger cast-iron shoes were placed ahead of the coupled wheels, with the steam brake cylinder and brake shaft brackets carried in the cast-steel dragbox under the cab floor.

Standard Walschaerts valve gear was used with the former LMS method of carrying the crosshead in two slidebars, as compared with the three-bar underhung arrangement. Both the Class 4 and Class 3 designs incorporated the same cylinder and valve sizes. The castings for the cylinders were steel, with cast-iron liners to provide a diameter of 17½in, with 10in diameter valve liners above. The whole assemblies were bolted to the outer faces of the mainframes, and had a maximum stroke length of 26in. The choice of steel castings for the cylinders was a relatively new idea, and first introduced in this country with Ivatt's Class 2 locomotives for the LMS. Although a number of LMS Compounds were provided with steel castings as replacements for the previous cast-iron, the practice was not common. The BR Standard Class 2 2-6-0 also used this arrangement, with cylinders and valves lined to 16½in and 8in diameter respectively, the stroke being 24in.

The reason for the use of two slidebars was to allow clearance for the coupling rods behind, which was not possible with the three-bar arrangement, within the L1 loading gauge. The cylinders were very close to the leading coupled wheels, and although initially it was proposed to adapt the Laird twin-slidebar design as on the WD 2-8-0s, this proved impracticable, hence the final design was a straightforward adaption of former LMS practice.

In full gear, the valve travel of the Class 4 and Class 3 was 6¼in, with a steam lap of 1½in and giving a maximum cut-off of 75%. The little Class 2, with a travel of just under 6in and 1⁵⁄₁₆in steam lap had a maximum cut-off of 78%. Lubrication of the cylinders was the standardised system with atomised oil control being linked to the operation of the cylinder drain cocks. Valve gear pins were all grease-lubricated, with two exceptions. The return crank

was fitted as standard with a Skefco self-aligning ball bearing, and the expansion link and radius rod die pins and paths were oil-lubricated. Connecting and coupling rods were fluted I-section steel on Class 4 and Class 2 locomotives, whereas the Swindon built Class 3s were provided with plain section coupling rods from new. All revolving masses were balanced, and in common with their larger brethren, the 4-6-0s, 50% of the reciprocating masses of all three designs were balanced. The weights were carried in the conventional manner on the coupled wheels, involving the rivetting of steel plates over a number of spokes, and filled with lead.

Cab, Platework and Details

In keeping with the principal objectives of the overall design policy of accessibility for maintenance and repair, the three 2-6-0s incorporated various features which were not traditional practice, but which came to be standard features. Amongst the most obvious of these was the disposition of only two sets of valve gear, outside the frames, and the anchoring of the running boards to the boiler rather than the frames. Although the position of the running boards eliminated the need for splashers in all three types, the Class 2 locomotives had their running boards attached to the frames. This was essentially due to the almost complete adoption of the Ivatt design from the LMS as it existed, the platework only modified to provide a sloping fall plate between the upper and lower levels at the smokebox end. In the other two designs, the difference in levels was more pronounced, but the overall effect was a pleasing family likeness. The Class 3 in particular seemed a happy compromise of GWR, LMS and BR Standard styles.

The cab layouts were of course the standard pattern with the cantilevered mounting arrangement for the two larger classes. To comply with loading gauge requirements, the side sheets tapered inwards from just below the windows to the gutter. The roof profile was almost pure LMS. The provision of fall plates and

Class 2 2-6-0

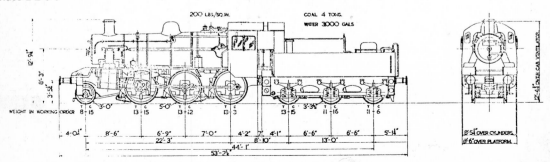

gangway doors was not at first a standard feature, but was re-introduced on the Class 4s on later batches, and from new on the Class 2 and Class 3 locomotives. Controls were grouped according to whether used by either driver or fireman, on the left- and right-hand sides of the footplate respectively. In all cases, the live and exhaust steam injectors were attached to the firebox foundation ring on the fireman's side. It is interesting to note that the fire door itself had come in for some attention, and although the trend seemed to be towards straightforward adoption of the LMS sliding type, the power-operated 'butterfly' door of the Southern received some attention. On all the Standard locomotives in the end there were two types, even of the sliding design. The basic LMS development had large ports in the doors for the admission of secondary air over the fire, and was designed for burning hard coals, while the former GWR arrangement provided a smaller opening for secondary air since that door was designed for fireboxes burning soft coals.

The use of speedometers in locomotive cabs was perhaps rather surprisingly even on the BR standards not considered an essential feature—consequently some locomotives were fitted and some were not. A small generator mounted on a light return crank on the rear coupled wheels provided the source of speed measurement, with the Smiths Instruments gauge recorder mounted on the driver's side of the cab.

The sanding arrangements differed between the three classes. On the Class 4 locomotives front sanding for leading and driving coupled wheels was fitted, with back sanding on the latter. The same arrange-

ments were made for the Class 3 2-6-0s but the Class 2s had front sandpipes to the leading coupled wheels, and rear sandpipes only to the driving wheels. The sandboxes themselves were attached to the mainframes in the two larger classes, while the Class 2 had a large sandbox on the running boards immediately in front of the cab, to supply the driving wheels. In true LMS style the front sandbox was provided with a filler pipe extending out over the running boards. The difficulties with the Downs sanding system referred to in an earlier chapter were not to trouble the 2-6-0 classes to as great a degree, although there were examples of Class 4 and Class 3 locomotives fitted with this system.

The characteristic deep valances were perpetuated on the Class 4 and Class 3 locomotives, though the Class 2 incorporated the LMS/Ivatt style of very thin valance, resulting in the non-appearance of lining on this component during painting. In fact the Class 2 locomotives were the only Standard type not to have valances scheduled to carry lining in the mixed-traffic style.

Last but not least must be mentioned the handrails insofar as this external visible feature was also characteristic of Standard design. From the point of entry of the regulator operating shaft through the boiler shell, the handrails were continuous to the front of the smokebox, curving down towards the running boards but stopping just below the boiler centre line. Some criticism had been offered of the lack of continuity of this feature presenting a safety hazard, but overall it appears to have been more carefully thought out and applied than on most steam locomotives.

Tenders

Of the four types of tender used with the 2-6-0s, three were new designs, with the type BR1B being already in service with the larger Standard locomotives. The other designs were designated types BR2, BR2A and BR3 and were allocated to the locomotives as below:

The Class 2 2-6-0 type was a straightforward adoption of the Ivatt design for the LMS, with only minor alterations to boiler mountings to bring them into line with the Standard series. No 78022 is seen here at Sheffield Millhouses in September 1955. (*J.A. Fleming*)

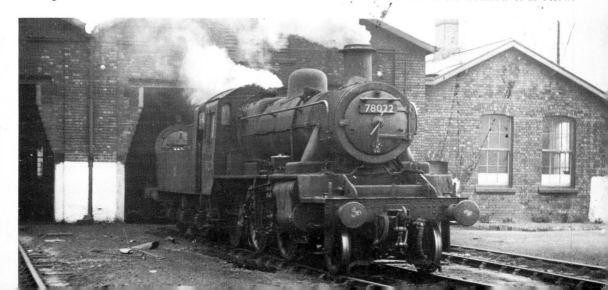

BR1B   Class 4 2-6-0 Nos 76053–69
BR2   Class 4 2-6-0 Nos 76000–44
BR2A   Class 3 2-6-0 Nos 77000–19
BR2A   Class 4 2-6-0 Nos 76045-52, 76070–114
BR3   Class 2 2-6-0 Nos 78000–64

Both the Type 2 and 3 tenders introduced the second and final standard underframe size, with a wheelbase of 13ft 0in, equally divided. Construction followed the same pattern as for the larger sizes, with standard 3ft 2½in diameter wheel pairs running in outside roller-bearing axleboxes, and carried by overhung leaf springs. These latter were the standard span of 3ft 6in and for the type 2, 2A and 3 tenders consisted of 15 leaves of 5in × 7/16in section. The larger tender differed only by having an extra leaf fitted. Brake shoes carried in single hangers were a standard fitting, operating on the rear of the wheels, with all joints grease-lubricated.

The distinguishing feature between the Type 2 and 2A tenders was the fitting of a fall plate and gangway doors. On the Type 2—the original design—there had been no fall plate, and gangway doors were attached only to the cab. In all other respects, these two types of tender were identical, having the tall inset sides to the bunker. The capacity was the same, at six tons of coal and 3,500 gallons of water. The smallest tender in the Standard series, the BR3, was broadly similar, having inset sides to the coal space, but carrying only four tons of coal and 3,000 gallons of water.

In adopting the LMS arrangement for the tender fronts, bunker doors and shovelling plates, some criticism was made of the general design of the latter, though being at the same height above floor level as the firehole was considered satisfactory. The dimensions of the bunker doors were reduced in the BR Standard designs to provide an opening only 2ft 0in wide, and within 1ft 0in of the shovelling plate. Having got this latter feature at the right height it is curious that the fireman's job should then be made more arduous by inadequate allowance for coal feeding. Similarly, the replacement of the *on-off* tap handles for coal sprinkler valves with brass handwheels also found little favour.

The Class 2 2-6-0s fitted with type BR3 tenders were provided with what were referred to as back cabs, much larger in relation to the tender size than the other two classes. The design afforded greater protection for the crew, especially when running tender-first. The type BR1B tender used on a number of the Class 4 locomotives on the Southern Region was of the flush-sided type, and raised the capacity to seven tons of coal and 4,725 gallons of water. The increase in the latter was necessary for some workings, as there were no water troughs on Southern metals. Fittings for water pick-up gear were provided internally on every Standard tender, though external equipment was an optional extra. The feeds from the tank to the injectors were taken through a valve and removable

filter assembly, mounted on the outside of each tender frame between the leading and centre axles.

Construction and Operation

In the building of these three locomotive types, no fewer than five separate works were involved. The Class 4 locomotives were built at Doncaster, Derby and Horwich, the Class 3s at Swindon, with Darlington building the Class 2 locomotives. The original programmes called for the construction of all three classes over a four-year period between 1952 and 1956, equivalent to 50 locomotives per year. Unfortunately things did not go according to plan, for the same reasons which followed the building of other Standard classes, and it was not until late 1957 when the last of the two hundred 2-6-0s appeared. The originally planned construction programmes are listed below:

Class 2 2-6-0

Batch	No	Year	Built at	Allocation
1	78000–9	1952	Darlington	WR
2	78010–9	1953	Darlington	NER
3	78020–44	1953	Darlington	LMR
4	78045–54	1954	Darlington	ScR
5	78055–64	1956	Darlington	LMR

Class 3 2-6-0

Batch	No	Year	Built at	Allocation
1	77000–4	1953	Swindon	NER
2	77005–9	1953	Swindon	ScR
3	77010–4	1953	Swindon	NER
4	77015–9	1953	Swindon	ScR
5	77020–4	—	(Not proceeded with)	—

From the tables, construction of the Class 3 and Class 2 designs followed a more-or-less straightforward pattern, but a number of the Class 4s were planned to be built out of sequence to take account of available workshop capacity. A comparison with the tables of actual building and withdrawal dates shows just how delayed these classes were. Not included in any programmes were the five additional Class 3 locomotives the order for which was cancelled before any construction was undertaken.

Delivery of the two smaller classes was regular and relatively consistent, but the 115 Class 4 locomotives suffered badly from erratic production. Despite the overall picture in late 1952 of very slow progress with the class, particularly at Horwich, no fewer than ten were put to stock in December of that year, four of which (Nos 76020–3) almost completed Doncaster's scheduled commitment of five. Delivery from Horwich was consistent throughout the first six months of 1953, although at both Derby and Doncaster the picture was the very opposite. After the initial batch of four in December 1952, six months elapsed before the fifth Class 4 emerged from Doncaster, followed by one in September, two in October and one each in November and December 1953. Both Derby and Doncaster were building Class 5 4-6-0s also at this time, though the latter's examples were built in 1956, when production of the 2-6-0 Class 4s was stepped-up slightly. The last member of the class to be built was No 76099 turned out from Horwich in November 1957. The highest numbered of the class, No 76114, completed at Doncaster in October 1957, was also the last steam locomotive to be built at those works.

It was intended that the Class 4s would operate many of the secondary services for stopping passenger, and light to medium freight workings. They were distributed throughout all regions except the Western, with most of the passenger duties encountered on the Southern and Scottish Regions. Among their first duties on the Southern were London-bound trains from Brighton over the Oxted line, and by all reports they gave a mixed to favourable account of themselves. On the Eastern Region Nos 76030-4 allocated to Stratford for working the Midland & Great Northern Joint line had large recesses in both lower cabsides, to accommodate table-catching apparatus, and retained the feature when in later years they were transferred away.

As with most Standard types the response to their introduction varied between regions. The Southern, for instance, although showing considerable variety in the rosters, allocating Class 4s to anything from coal trains on the Central Section to Western Section expresses into Waterloo, seemed to demonstrate a certain amount of unpopularity. At least that seemed to be the case initially, reports indicating that they were indifferent steamers, and seemed to be requiring frequent mechanical adjustments by shed staff. Running-in from Doncaster demonstrated, if not the opposite view, then certainly not one of condemnation. At the time, though, the ER seemed short of suitable motive power for local and excursion traffic, at both Northern and Southern extremities of its territory, and the varied nature of Class 4 workings was much apparent.

The Class 3 and Class 2 2-6-0s seemed to find almost immediate success and popularity. The latter were particularly liked in the North-East, and preferred even to the LMR Class 2s which were already in operation. Some of this popularity was explained by their having independent steam brake equipment. The Class 3 locomotives were used on the WR on a variety of duties before their despatch to the North-East and Scotland, with some working as far west as Exeter and Bristol. Initially, the Darlington-based locomotives were used on local goods turns, eventual-

A major compromise between LMS and GWR practice were the Class 3 2-6-0 tender and 2-6-2 tank locomotives. Both types were built at Swindon, with the Class 3 tender types finding their way to the North East, and seeing much service on cross-country lines, including the trans-Pennine Stainmore route. No 77014 emphasises in this view, the clean, uncluttered appearance of all the Standard classes. (*Lens of Sutton*)

ly penetrating the Pennines over the Stainmore route to Kirkby Stephen and beyond. Perhaps unfortunately and surprisingly, they were first given the same route availability as the Class 4, effectively preventing their replacement of older 0-6-0 types on this line, and restricting their use to goods turns and occasional passenger workings to York.

In Scotland, the Class 3s were first seen on the Highland line for banking duties at Blair Atholl, though they were soon noted on passenger workings into Perth. They were reported to have been well

The almost completely dismantled mainframes of No 78022, undergoing restoration at Haworth on the Keighley & Worth Valley Railway, demonstrate characteristic LMS design features adapted to Standard form. The reversing gear consisted of reach rod, from reversing screw in cab, to weighshaft and lifting link, connected with a rearward, slotted extension of the radius rod. The radius link and die block are mounted on the outside motion brackets in true LMS style. (*R. France/Standard 4 Locomotive Preservation Society*)

No 78051 is passing Hurlford with a class K mineral working in June 1966, shortly before its withdrawal in November of that year. (*Don Rowland*)

liked on both passenger and goods duties and were frequently seen at Bonnybridge, Cadder, Robroyston, Perth North and Perth South. Again, the duties were varied, from coal and minerals, to local passenger.

Overall, the class was most popular in the North-East, and following a solution of the route restriction difficulty were passed to work over the Stainmore line. This was one of the most regular duties for the locomotives, which could be found at work on the line up to the beginning of withdrawals in 1966, and similarly on the Darlington to Scarborough duties. Particularly noteworthy were the reports of their economic water consumption over what were difficult routes, and the popularity with footplate crews.

The smaller Class 2s proved just as popular, but were rather more widely distributed, between Western, Scottish, North Eastern and London Midland Regions. The first, allocated to the WR, did indeed find themselves as replacements for older 0-6-0 types, with a number being allocated to Worcester in the West Midlands, and used in the Vale of Evesham. From the outset they occupied all passenger duties

between Worcester and Leamington. Among the early freight workings were included a number of Salisbury to Southampton Docks turns. Perhaps the most well-known duty of the Class 2s was on the Cambrian Coast Express, and despite some unfavourable comments from staff, they seemed well suited to the summer loadings of that steeply-graded coast line.

None of the three Standard designs was ever tested, though the LMS versions of the Class 4 and Class 2 were the subjects of stationary and controlled road trials. The latter was tested in 1950, well before the Standard version appeared, and proved a quite capable performer, though on the BR type a slight reduction was made in the chimney choke diameter.

By the 1960s, the majority of the locomotives had been transferred to the LMR, and were widely scattered from places as far apart as Lostock Hall to Willesden. The Scottish Region retained its allocation to the end also, with the addition of two from other areas. Three examples remain as preserved, Nos 78018 and 78019 at the Market Bosworth and Severn Valley Railways, and No 78022 on the Keighley & Worth Valley line. Similarly, there are two Class 4 2-6-0s in varying states of preservation, No 76079 at Steamport, No 76017 on the Mid-Hants Railway. Sadly perhaps, no Class 3 2-6-0s were saved, more so since the design was an interesting compromise of GWR and LMS construction practice—if not as successful operationally as was hoped.

Class 4 2-6-0

Batch	No		Year	Built at	Allocation
1	76	000–4	1952	Horwich	SR
2	76	005–19	1952	Horwich	SR
3	76	020–24	1952	Doncaster	NER
4	76	025–29	1953	Doncaster	SR
5	76	030–44	1953	Derby	ER
6	76	070–74	1953	Derby	ScR
7	76	045–52	1954	Doncaster	NER
8	76	053–69	1954	Doncaster	SR
9	76	075–89	1956	Horwich	LMR
10	76	090–89	1956	Horwich	ScR
11	76	100–114	1956	Doncaster	ScR

Summary Table—Standard Class 4MT 2-6-0s Nos 76000–76114

No	Built	Withdrawn	Disposal	No	Built	Withdrawn	Disposal
76000	12/52	5/67		76058	6/55	3/67	J. Buttigieg, Newport
76001	12/52	8/66	W. of Scotland Shipbreaking	76059	6/55	11/66	J. Cashmore, Newport
76002	12/52	1/67	Motherwell Machinery Co	76060	7/55	12/65	J. Buttigieg, Newport
76003	12/52	3/66	Motherwell Machinery Co	76061	7/55	12/66	J. Cashmore, Newport
76004	12/52	10/66	G.H. Campbell, Airdrie	76062	7/55	10/65	J. Buttigieg, Newport
76005	12/52	7/67	Birds, Morriston	76063	7/56	4/67	J. Buttigieg, Newport
76006	1/53	7/67	Birds, Morriston	76064	7/56	7/67	Birds, Morriston
76007	1/53	7/67	Birds, Morriston	76065	7/56	10/65	G. Cohen, Morriston
76008	2/53	6/67	G. Cohen, Kettering	76066	7/56	7/67	
76009	2/53	7/67	J. Cashmore, Newport	76067	8/56	7/67	
76010	3/53	9/66	J. Buttigieg, Newport	76068	8/56	9/68	J. Buttigieg, Newport
76011	3/53	9/66	Birds, Morriston	76069	8/56	6/67	
76012	3/53	9/66	J. Buttigieg, Newport	76070	9/56	8/66	Motherwell Machinery Co
76013	4/53	9/66	J. Buttigieg, Newport	76071	10/56	1/66	Motherwell Machinery Co
76014	4/53	9/66	J. Buttigieg, Newport	76072	10/56	10/64	Shipbreaking Industries, Faslane
76015	5/53	10/65	G. Cohen, Morriston	76073	10/56	6/66	Shipbreaking Industries, Faslane
76016	5/53	11/66	J. Cashmore, Newport	76074	11/56	10/66	G.H. Campbell, Airdrie
76017	6/53	8/65	Woodham Bros/Preserved	76075	12/56	10/67	J. Buttigieg, Newport
76018	6/53	11/66	J. Cashmore, Newport	76076	12/56	11/66	T.W. Ward, Killamarsh
76019	7/53	4/66	G. Cohen, Morriston	76077	12/56	11/67	Woodham Bros, Barry
76020	12/52	12/66	Birds, Long Marston	76078	12/56	12/66	T.W. Ward, Beighton
76021	12/52	9/66		76079	1/57	11/67	Woodham Bros/Preserved
76022	12/52	9/66	J. Cashmore, Great Bridge				at Steamport, Southport
76023	12/52	10/65	J. Cashmore, Great Bridge	76080	2/57	11/67	Woodham Bros, Barry
76024	6/53	12/66	Shipbreaking Industries, Faslane	76081	2/57	7/67	J. Buttigieg, Newport
76025	10/53	11/65	J. Buttigieg, Newport	76082	3/57	10/66	A. Draper, Hull
76026	12/53	7/67		76083	3/57	11/66	J. Cashmore, Great Bridge
76027	9/53	10/65	G. Cohen, Morriston	76084	3/57	11/67	Woodham Bros
76028	10/53	5/64	R.A. King, Norwich	76085	4/57	8/66	J. Cashmore, Great Bridge
76029	11/53	10/64	G. Cohen, Morriston	76086	4/57	10/66	J. Cashmore, Newport
76030	11/53	4/65	J. Cashmore, Newport	76087	5/57	1/67	J. Cashmore, Newport
76031	11/53	7/67	Birds, Morriston	76088	5/57	6/67	J. Cashmore, Newport
76032	12/53	8/64	J. Cashmore, Newport	76089	5/57	10/66	A. Draper, Hull
76033	12/53	2/67	J. Cashmore, Newport	76090	6/57	12/66	Shipbreaking Industries, Faslane
76034	12/53	9/64	P. Wood, Queenborough, Kent	76091	6/57	12/66	Shipbreaking Industries, Faslane
76035	5/54	5/66	J. Cashmore, Great Bridge	76092	6/57	8/66	G.H. Campbell, Airdrie
76036	6/54	1/67		76093	7/57	2/67	
76037	6/54	6/67	J. Cashmore, Newport	76094	8/57	5/67	
76038	7/54	8/66	J. Cashmore, Newport	76095	8/57	3/67	G. Cohen, Kettering
76039	7/54	6/67	J. Cashmore, Newport	76096	9/57	12/66	Shipbreaking Industries, Faslane
76040	7/54	4/67	G. Cohen, Morriston	76097	9/57	7/64	Motherwell Machinery Co
76041	7/54	4/67	G. Cohen, Kettering	76098	10/57	5/67	T.W. Ward, Inverkeithing
76042	8/54	7/66		76099	11/57	8/66	J. Cashmore, Great Bridge
76043	8/54	9/66	J. Cashmore, Newport	76100	5/57	8/66	W. of Scotland Shipbreaking
76044	9/54	10/66	G. Cohen, Morriston	76101	6/57	12/66	Shipbreaking Industries, Faslane
76045	3/55	2/66	Motherwell Machinery Co	76102	6/57	12/66	Shipbreaking Industries, Faslane
76046	3/55	5/67	G.H. Campbell, Airdrie	76103	6/57	7/66	W. of Scotland Shipbreaking
76047	3/55	11/66	J. Cashmore, Newport	76104	7/57	5/67	
76048	3/55	2/67	J. Cashmore, Newport	76105	7/57	2/66	Motherwell Machinery Co
76049	4/55	1/66	Motherwell Machinery Co	76106	7/57	10/66	J. Cashmore, Great Bridge
76050	8/56	9/65		76107	8/57	10/65	
76051	8/56	6/67	J. Cashmore, Great Bridge	76108	8/57	7/66	
76052	9/56	12/66	J. Cashmore, Newport	76109	8/57	9/66	Motherwell Machinery Co
76053	4/55	12/66		76110	8/57	12/66	Shipbreaking Industries, Faslane
76054	4/55	11/64	R & S Hayes, Bridgend	76111	8/57	1/66	Motherwell Machinery Co
76055	4/55	10/65	J. Buttigieg, Newport	76112	9/57	10/65	Shipbreaking Industries, Faslane
76056	5/55	11/65		76113	10/57	12/66	Shipbreaking Industries, Faslane
76057	5/55	11/66	J. Cashmore, Newport	76114	10/57	12/66	Shipbreaking Industries, Faslane

Notes: Nos 76000–76019, 76075–76099 were built at Horwich
Nos 76020–76029, 76045–76069, 76100–76114 were built at Doncaster
Nos 76030–76044, 76070–76074 were built at Derby

Summary Table—Standard Class 2MT 2-6-0s Nos 78000–78064

No	Built	Withdrawn	Disposal	No	Built	Withdrawn	Disposal
78000	12/52	6/65	J. Cashmore, Great Bridge	78032	10/54	9/65	J. Cashmore, Great Bridge
78001	12/52	12/65	Birds, Morriston	78033	10/54	9/65	J. Cashmore, Great Bridge
78002	12/52	6/66	Central Wagon Co., Wigan	78034	10/54	1/66	T.W. Ward, Killamarsh
78003	12/52	12/66	J. Cashmore, Newport	78035	10/54	12/65	J. Cashmore, Great Bridge
78004	12/52	11/65	J. Cashmore, Newport	78036	11/54	12/66	J. Cashmore, Newport
78005	2/53	9/64		78037	11/54	5/67	Motherwell Machinery Co
78006	3/53	12/65	Birds, Morriston	78038	11/54	8/66	J. Cashmore, Great Bridge
78007	3/53	5/67	A. Draper, Hull	78039	11/54	9/66	J. Cashmore, Newport
78008	3/53	11/66		78040	1/55	1/66	T.W. Ward, Beighton
78009	4/53	2/64	Swindon Works	78041	1/55	5/67	Motherwell Machinery Co
78010	12/53	9/66	J. Cashmore, Newport	78042	1/55	9/65	T.W. Ward, Killamarsh
78011	12/53	9/65	T.W. Ward, Killamarsh	78043	1/55	9/65	J. Cashmore, Great Bridge
78012	1/54	5/67	A. Draper, Hull	78044	1/55	5/67	A. Draper, Hull
78013	1/54	5/67	A. Draper, Hull	78045	10/55	1/66	Motherwell Machinery Co
78014	2/54	9/65	T.W. Ward, Killamarsh	78046	10/55	11/66	Arnott Young, Old Kilpatrick
78015	2/54	11/63	Darlington Works	78047	10/55	9/66	Shipbreaking Industries, Faslane
78016	3/54	8/66	W. of Scotland Shipbreaking	78048	10/55	7/64	Motherwell Machinery Co
78017	3/54	12/66	J. Cashmore, Newport	78049	11/55	8/66	Motherwell Machinery Co
78018	3/54	11/66	Woodham Bros/Preserved: Market Bosworth	78050	11/55	1/66	Motherwell Machinery Co
				78051	11/55	11/66	Motherwell Machinery Co
78019	3/54	11/66	Woodham Bros/Preserved: Severn Valley Railway	78052	11/55	1/66	Motherwell Machinery Co
				78053	11/55	7/64	P&W McLellan, Bo'ness, Linlithgow
78020	4/54	5/67	Motherwell Machinery Co				
78021	5/54	5/67	Motherwell Machinery Co	78054	12/55	12/65	Shipbreaking Industries, Faslane
78022	5/54	9/66	Woodham Bros./Preserved: K & WVR	78055	8/56	2/67	J. Cashmore, Great Bridge
				78056	8/56	7/66	Birds, Long Marston
78023	5/54	5/67	A. Draper, Hull	78057	9/56	5/66	Motherwell Machinery Co
78024	5/54	2/65	Birds, Long Marston	78058	9/56	12/66	J. Cashmore, Newport
78025	6/54	2/65	Birds, Long Marston	78059	9/56	11/66	Woodham Bros, Barry
78026	6/54	8/67	Arnott Young, Old Kilpatrick	78060	10/56	10/66	J. Cashmore, Newport
78027	6/54	9/65	J. Cashmore, Great Bridge	78061	10/56	11/66	T.W. Ward, Killamarsh
78028	7/54	2/67	J. Cashmore, Great Bridge	78062	10/56	5/67	A. Draper, Hull
78029	7/54	9/65	J. Cashmore, Great Bridge	78063	11/56	12/66	J. Cashmore, Newport
78030	9/54	10/65	J. Cashmore, Great Bridge	78064	11/56	11/66	T.W. Ward, Killamarsh
78031	10/54	10/66	J. Cashmore, Newport				

All were built at Darlington

Summary Table—Standard Class 3MT 2-6-0s Nos 77000–77019

No	Built	Withdrawn	Disposal	No	Built	Withdrawn	Disposal
77000	2/54	12/66	T.W. Ward, Beighton	77010	6/54	11/65	Arnott Young, Parkgate
77001	2/54	1/66		77011	6/54	2/66	Central Wagon Co., Wigan
77002	3/54	6/67	Garnham, Harris & Elton, Chesterfield	77012	6/54	6/67	Garnham, Harris & Elton, Chesterfield
77003	2/54	12/66	T.W. Ward, Beighton	77013	7/54	3/66	T.W. Ward, Beighton
77004	3/54	12/66	T.W. Ward, Beighton	77014	6/54	7/67	Birds, Risca
77005	3/54	11/66	Motherwell Machinery Co	77015	6/54	7/66	G.H. Campbell, Airdrie
77006	3/54	3/66		77016	8/54	3/66	Motherwell Machinery Co
77007	3/54	11/66	T.W. Ward, Wishaw	77017	8/54	11/66	T.W. Ward, Wishaw
77008	4/54	8/66	Motherwell Machinery Co	77019	8/54	11/66	T.W. Ward, Wishaw
77009	6/54	5/66	Motherwell Machinery Co	77019	9/54	11/66	T.W. Ward, Wishaw

All were built at Swindon

Technical Data—The Standard 2-6-0 Classes

Note: The information relates to locomotives in original or 'as built' condition

Cylinders and valve gear		*Class 4MT*	*Class 3MT*	*Class 2MT*
Cylinders—diameter × stroke	....	17½in × 26in	17½in × 26in	16½in × 24in
Piston swept volume—one cylinder	....	6254cu in	6254cu in	5134cu in
Clearance volume as % of piston swept volume	....	11.6%	11.6%	n/a
Maximum piston thrust	....	54119lb	48106lb	42765lb
Steam chests—volume between valve heads	....	3037cu in	3037cu in	n/a
—volume as % of piston swept volume	....	48.5%	48.5%	n/a
Piston valves—diameter	....	10in	10in	8in
—steam lap	....	1½in	1½in	1⁵⁄₁₆in
—lead	....	¼in	¼in	¼in
—exhaust clearance	....	NIL	NIL	NIL
Maximum travel of valves	....	6.25in	6.25in	5.92in
Maximum cut-off %	....	75.0%	75.0%	78.0%
Travel at 20% cut-off	....	3.62in	3.62in	3.23in

Balancing data		*Class 4MT*	*Class 3MT*	*Class 2MT*
Revolving masses—weight per cylinder	....	1316lb	1189lb	1172lb
Reciprocating masses—total weight per cylinder	....	737lb	737lb	564lb
—percentage balanced	....	50%	50%	50%
—unbalanced weight per cylinder	....	369lb	368lb	282lb
Ratio—unbalanced reciprocating weight per cylinder to total weight of locomotive	....	1/363	1.350	1/391
Hammer-blow at 5 revolutions per second—per wheel	....	2.17 tons	2.17 tons	1.53 tons
—per axle	....	2.58 tons	2.58 tons	1.82 tons
—per rail	....	5.93 tons	5.93 tons	4.29 tons
—whole locomotive	......	7.05 tons	7.05 tons	5.11 tons

Boiler proportions		*Class 4MT*	*Class 3MT*	*Class 2MT*
Free area through tubes—large	....	1.96sq ft	1.49sq ft	0.98sq ft
—small	....	1.70sq ft	1.59sq ft	1.76sq ft
—total	....	3.66sq ft	3.08sq ft	2.74sq ft
Area through large tubes as % of total		53.6%	48.4%	36.5%
Total free area as % of grate area		16.5%	15.2%	15.9%
A/S ratio—large tubes	....	1/334	1/302	1/343
—small tubes	....	1/368	1/374	1/369
Steam pipe in boiler—bore	....	5½in	5½in	5in
—cross-sectional area	....	23.8sq in	23.8sq in	19.6sq in
Regulator fully open—area	....	22.2sq in	24.3sq in	21.5sq in
Superheater elements—total area	....	31.8sq in	31.8sq in	22.1sq in
Blastpipe cap—diameter	....	4⅜in	4½in	4⅛in
—area	....	15.0sq in	15.9sq in	13.4sq in
Chimney throat—diameter	....	1ft 0¹¹⁄₁₆in	1ft 0¾in	1ft 0in
—area	....	0.88sq ft	0.89sq ft	0.79sq ft
Throat area as % of grate area	....	3.82%	4.35%	4.40%
Height—blastpipe cap to chimney throat	....	2ft 7¾in	2ft 7in	2ft 5½in
Taper of chimney	....	1 in 14	1 in 14	1 in 14

9. Standard Tank Locomotives

It may seem on the face of it that there was no need for a new design of tank locomotive for British Railways, considering the existing varieties and sizes in traffic in the early 1950s, a number of which were of quite recent design and construction. On the other hand, there were many considerably older types, some of which were composite, rebuilt designs dating from the 19th century. The newer designs of H.G. Ivatt on the LMS were in reality the only locomotives that adequately met the requirements of BR locomotive policy, though having said that, some existing regional types had been developed to complying, at least in part, with the standardisation ideology. Included in this might well be the LNER L1 2-6-4T of Thompson's design, although its route availability was restricted considerably more than was desirable for a Standard tank type. Later classes of GWR Prairie tank would have filled the operationl requirements, but having inside motion and right-hand drive was a great disadvantage. Detail improvements in component design on all regions had resulted in increased availability and mileages between repairs, but only the LMS seemed able to provide a synthesis of these developments in one locomotive type.

Like the 2-6-0 tender locomotives detailed in the previous chapter, the Class 4 and Class 2 tank engines of Fairburn and Ivatt design were already accepted and used outside their home regions. Also like the tender locomotives, examples had been built at both Brighton and Darlington. It was a relatively logical step to base the eventual Standard classes on these LMS types, which had demonstrated within their respective power classes their wide route availability.

Of the three Standard types, the Class 4 2-6-4T and Class 2 2-6-2T were essentially adaptations of existing LMS locomotives, with the third, the Class 3 2-6-2T, coming from a need for a tank locomotive with an axle load of 16 tons. This axle load restriction prevented the use of a Class 4 and resulted in a new design, which like the equivalent tender locomotive was a compromise of GWR and LMS features. Operationally they were intended for branch line, and short- and medium-distance stopping passenger duties. Suburban and outer suburban services also came into this category, which was where most of the Class 4s in particular found their early careers.

Mechanical Details

Boilers, Smokeboxes, Fireboxes and Ashpans

Two of the boilers, designated types BR5 and BR8, were more-or-less straightforward adaptions of the LMS type. Type BR6 was entirely different, and based on the Swindon No 2 boiler, as fitted to GWR 51XX class locomotives. The same flangeing plates were used in the BR design, but the barrel length was slightly reduced, as in the tender locomotive version. The Class 4 locomotives with the BR5 boiler, taken from the Fairburn series of tank engines, had the pressure increased to 225lb/sq in. Originally, the Fairburn tanks had boilers pressed to 200lb/sq in, and needing 19⅝in × 26in cylinders for Class 4 use, would have fouled the L1 loading gauge. It was found possible to increase the working pressure using the same materials and fastenings, to keep the cylinder diameter down to 18in, thus enabling the design to squeeze through BR's universal loading gauge. The smallest of the boilers, fitted as BR8 to the Class 2 2-6-2 tanks, was the Ivatt 412XX boiler, the only modifications being to accept Standard fittings.

All three boiler types were constructed from two rings, with the second ring tapered. The material used

Class 4 2-6-4T

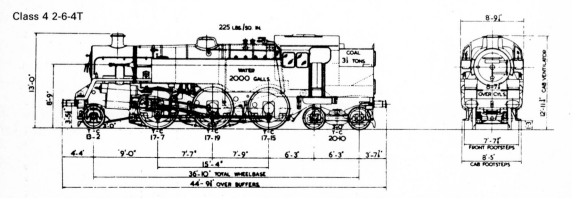

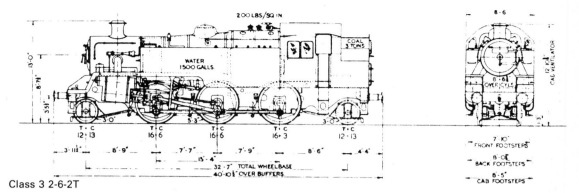

Class 3 2-6-2T

was ½in thick high-tensile steel plate, another feature inherited from LMS practice. The intermediate size boiler had to be provided with a dome, since the Swindon No 2 design was domeless. In the Class 4, the outside diameter tapered from 4ft 9in at the smokebox tubeplate, to 5ft 3in at the firebox end. For the Class 3 and Class 2, these dimensions were 4ft 5in to 5ft 0½in, and 4ft 3in to 4ft 8in respectively. The drumhead-pattern smokebox tubeplates were ⅝in thick, with the length between tubeplates varying from 12ft 3in in the Class 4, to 10ft 10½in in the Class 2. This dimension in the Class 3 was also 10ft 10½in, showing a reduction of 5¹³/₁₆in on the original GWR design.

The superheater flues were the conventional 5⅛in diameter, with the Superheater Co's 1⅜in diameter elements. These numbered 21 in the Class 4, eighteen in the Class 3, and twelve in the Class 2. The small tubes were also a standard fitting at 1⅝in outside diameter, and numbering 145 and 162 for the Class 3 and Class 2 locomotives respectively. The slight increase in the number of small tubes in the Class 2 resulted in their having a slightly greater tube heating surface than the Class 3, though in the latter design, this was more than compensated for in a much larger superheater and firebox heating surface. The Class 4 boiler housed 157 small tubes of 1¾in diameter, and was more-or-less identical with the Class 4 4-6-0 tender locomotives, albeit with a 9in shorter tube length.

The fireboxes were constructed along the established standard pattern, of Belpaire design, to fit between the frames. The inner firebox was constructed of copper, with a steel outer wrapper. For the Class 4 locomotives the overall dimensions were 8ft 6in long by 4ft 0½in wide, with a grate area of 26.7sq ft. The Class 3 and Class 2 designs were 7ft 0in by 4ft 0in, and 5ft 11in by 4ft 0⁷/₁₆in respectively. All were fitted with the standard rocking grate, the front and rear portions of which could be rocked independently. The throatplates were vertical, with sloping backplates on the Class 4, and vertical backplates on the two smaller classes. The copper tubeplates were of 1in thick material in the largest, to ⅞in thick for the

two smaller designs. Water-space stays were of monel metal, with steel nuts on the inside of the firebox. In the Class 4 design there was some re-arrangement of stays in the roof and sides, to take account of the increased working pressure to which the BR5 boiler was subject compared with its Fairburn ancestor. All roof, longitudinal and transverse stays were of steel.

Ashpans of the hopper type, with bottom flap doors, were again a standard feature. They could be operated from the side of the locomotive by a separate handle, which was locked in the closed position when running to prevent the contents being discharged onto the track. Front and rear damper doors were provided, operated by screw-down handwheels in the cab.

The smokebox arrangement followed the standard pattern used on tender types, dimensions only being altered. These were rivetted, cylindrical assemblies, attached to the locomotive frame via a fabricated saddle, and standard self-cleaning apparatus was fitted. To suggest that the self-cleaning smokebox was an advance may with hindsight seem to be something of a rash statement. It was with this system likely to be hurling out more ash than a conventional smokebox, though admittedly fewer of the particles would be incandescent.

Results of research into locomotive draughting carried out at the time of development of the Standard series was incorporated in the design stage. All locomotives were fitted with single blastpipes having a plain, circular cap, including the Cardew blower nozzles. Blastpipe diameters were 4¾in for Class 4, 4½in for Class 3, and 4⅛in for Class 2.

Boiler Fittings

Because Swindon was given overall responsibility for boiler design, there was a natural tendency to recommend Swindon practice, unless there were some overriding objection. The principal fittings on the boiler assembly were regulator, injectors, top-feed clacks, and steam manifold, with the various fittings and controls located on the firebox backplate in the cab. All three Standard designs incorporated a two-valve vertical-slide type regulator mounted in the dome. Operation of the regulator was through the transverse shaft mounted immediately behind the dome, and connected at its outer end through a stuffing gland in the boiler ring to an external reach rod on the left-hand side of the boiler.

The two injectors were fitted on the fireman's side, just to the rear of the trailing coupled wheels, as standard practice, on a bracket fixed to the firebox foundation ring. The design of the live steam injector was a standard GWR type, adopted for all the BR locomotives. The examples fitted to the tank engines were capable of a maximum delivery of 18,500lb of water per hour each, through the two top-feed clacks mounted on the front cab boiler ring.

In front of the cab spectacle plate on the firebox roof was fitted the main steam manifold, and twin Ross 'Pop' safety-valves. These latter were set to blow-off at 225lb/sq in on the Class 4, and 200lb/sq in on the two smaller types. The manifold supplied steam for such auxiliary functions as cylinder drain cock operation, and cylinder lubricating oil atomisers.

Frames, Wheels, Motion and Cylinders

There was never any firm proposal that the BR tank engine designs would have bar frames, unlike the early ideas for the tender types. It is interesting to speculate on the possibility—the initial costs of fabrication and machining may well have proved greater even than the proposals for tender locomotives. A complete break with traditional practices was less warranted with these classes.

The main frames finally decided upon were conventional mild-steel plates, and varied in thickness from 1in in the Class 2, to 1¼in for the Class 4 locomotives. All were provided with fabricated and cast stays, in both horizontal and vertical arrangement. The main horn guides were steel castings, rivetted to the frames and fitted with manganese-steel liners on their wearing faces. Axleboxes were steel castings for the coupled wheels, and in all cases were of the plain bearing type with pressed in white metal brasses. Lubrication was provided in the manner adopted on other Standard locomotives, with a worsted pad fitted to a sliding underkeep and supplied with oil from the mechanical lubricator. The manganese-steel liners fitted to the axlebox wearing faces were grease-lubricated. In the original designs, only the driving axleboxes were fitted with traditional horn blocks; for the leading and trailing wheels it was deemed sufficient to provide only the welded-in guides.

The leading pony truck was a standardised design, and common to the 2-6-0 tender locomotives, though including additional friction dampers arranged in front and to the rear of the axle. The axleboxes were bronze castings with pressed-in brasses, as before. Both load-bearing and side control was effected through helical springs, with four springs to each box, arranged in two pairs, to transmit the load to the

axlebox through the standard yoke-and-shoe assembly. The trailing pony truck in the 2-6-2s was of identical design, and although the same method of coil springing was used for side control in the trailing bogie of the Class 4 locomotives, the main suspension was of laminated springs. The load on the trailing bogie was transmitted to the axleboxes through bolsters and compensating beams.

The coupled wheels themselves were of three diameters, 5ft 8in for the Class 4, 5ft 3in for the Class 3, with 5ft 0in fitted to the Class 2 locomotives. The carrying wheels were 10-spoke 3ft 0in diameter, assembly being identical with the larger coupled wheels, having the tyre shrunk on to a cast-steel centre. Balance weights, carried in the coupled wheels, accounted for 40% of the reciprocating masses in the Class 4 design, and 50% in the two smaller classes. The lead weights were carried between two steel plates rivetted to the spokes. The proportion of the masses balanced in the Class 4 locomotives was the same as that of the Class 7 and Class 6 Pacifics, and Class 9F 2-10-0s, whereas all other types had 50% of these masses balanced. Although the values selected were a compromise, and resulted in modifications to the tender locomotives drawbar spring, no other alterations were found to be necessary in the balancing of the Standard types.

The locomotives' main suspension was through underhung leaf springs, and in the first designs to appear fitted with the cotter fastening system, to provide quick release of the wheel pairs for maintenance or repair. Modifications to the hanger brackets carried out on other Standard types were not continued to the tank locomotives.

Common to all three tank designs were the two outside cylinders, with inside admission piston valves operated by Walschaerts valve gear. Whereas the LMS-based designs of Class 4 and Class 2 had cylinders wholly of cast-iron, including the liners, for the Class 3 design the Swindon practice of a cast-steel body with cast-iron liners was preferred. Two sizes of piston valve were used, with 10in diameter for the Class 4 and Class 3, and 8in diameter for the Class 2. The box-type cast-iron piston head was fitted to all three classes, incorporating the spring-loaded piston head carrier, or slipper, fitted to the underside. In keeping with the basic parameters for the design of the BR Standard locomotives, the steam ports and passages were as large as possible, consistent with limitations imposed by loading and structure gauges. The long-lap travel valves provided a maximum cut-off of 75% in forward gear for the Class 4 and Class 3 designs, with a 78% maximum in the Class 2.

The difficulties arising from the adaptation of the Fairburn Class 4 2-6-4T were not wholly overcome by increasing the boiler pressure to achieve a reduction in cylinder dimensions. Some physical pruning was needed to enable the Class 4 with 18in diameter cylinders to pass the L1 loading gauge, and this is

The Southern Region's allocation of Class 4MT tanks was regularly employed on suburban duties over LB & SCR and SE & C lines. No 80153 seen here at Oxted, carries the additional headcode brackets on the smokebox door to allow the display of SR route codes. (*G.M. Kichenside*)

seen in the slight flattening of the cylinder sides to give a maximum width of 8ft 7⅜in. In all three Standard types the proximity of the rear of the cylinders to the leading coupled wheels demanded the use of the LMS-pattern double slidebar arrangement, to give clearance for the coupling rod.

The motion was constructed from high-tensile steel, and for all rods was originally deep-fluted I-section, with the object of keeping the weight down. From January 1954 all new locomotives were provided with plain, rectangular-section coupling rods. This affected Class 4 tank engines from No 80076 onwards, Class 3 from No 82020, and the final ten Class 2 locomotives, Nos 84020–84029. The decision to adopt slab-sided coupling rods may have been based both on the difficulties of straightening over-stressed fluted rods, and the less reliable quality of steel being achieved at that time. All the smaller rods, and the connecting rods, retained the fluting.

The reversing arrangement adopted in the tender locomotives with the reversing screw placed forward, and acting directly on the weighshaft, was not used for the tank engines. The main reason for this was the more restricted space available on tank locomotives, and consequently the reversing screw was placed in the more traditional position in the cab.

The braking arrangement was common to all Stan-

dard designs, and provided for steam brakes on the locomotive, and vacuum on the train. The cast-iron shoes were carried on single hanger brackets ahead of the wheels.

Sanding arrangements were based on the Downs system for the earliest examples but later modified as described earlier, with the sandboxes fixed to the frames. The sand pipes were arranged to deliver in front and behind the driving wheels of the Class 4, and in front of the leading coupled wheels. The two smaller classes were altered to provide sand ahead of the leading coupled wheels and to the rear of the trailing wheels only.

Superstructure and General Constructional Features

The upper works of tank locomotives often show several constructional points of interest. The design and layout of the superstructure as a whole also has a marked effect on the overall appearance and impression. Viewed in this way, the degree of similarity between the three Standard types provided an excellent example of co-ordinated design, considering their quite varied ancestry.

The tanks and bunkers were built-up by welding alone in the case of the two largest designs, while the Class 2 perpetuated the rivetting and welding combination used on the LMS Ivatt version. The capacities varied from 2,000 gallons of water and 3½ tons of coal carried by the Class 4 locomotives, to 1,500 and 1,350 gallons of water and three tons of coal in the Class 3 and Class 2 types. The Class 3 locomotives Nos 82030 and 82036–82044 were provided with a slightly larger bunker, having a capacity of 3¾ tons of

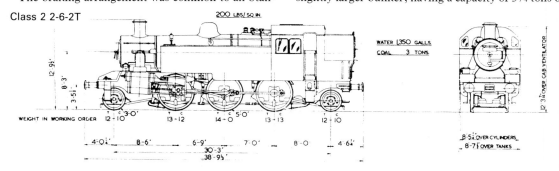

Class 2 2-6-2T

In addition to the fact that it carried an essentially GWR boiler, the Class 3 tank engine showed a number of other, interesting features. No 82004, allocated to the WR's Wellington shed in the West Midlands, is painted in lined green livery, as were a number of other Standard locomotives on the Western Region. A curious addition to the boiler was the fitting of short handrails just in front of the steam dome, as on the GWR Prairie tanks. (*Lens of Sutton*)

coal. No water was carried under the bunker on the Class 3 locomotives. Each of the side tanks on all locomotives had a pressed U-shaped bottom, and was supported at the leading end on the outside slidebar brackets, and at the rear on brackets attached to the locomotive frame. The front corners of the tanks were radiused on the Class 3 locomotives, which on the other two types were quite sharp angles—perhaps retained as a feature of their LMS ancestors.

Flat sides to the tanks were seen only on the two smaller designs; on the Class 4 locomotives a curved profile was adopted for tanks and bunker. The reason for this was primarily to pass the L1 loading gauge, and the shape was made to conform as near as was practicable to that of the standard coaching stock. The result of which was undoubtedly one of the most attractive British tank locomotive designs.

In all cases the cab was satisfactorily incorporated into the lines of the superstructure, and internally was of the same layout so far as controls and basic arrangements were concerned as the Standard tender locomotives. The most noticeable external differences between the two classes was that the spectacle plate of the two smaller designs was flat throughout its width, whereas in the Class 4 locomotives the cab front windows were set at an angle of 37° to the spectacle plate, the idea being to improve the forward visibility and maintain the family characteristics with other Standard types.

The front portion of the running boards was carried on brackets fixed to the boiler and smokebox sides,

with the large gap between the upper and lower levels joined by a sloping plate, as before. The difference between these two levels was markedly less on the Class 2 locomotives, and the running boards were actually fixed to the frames, as in the tender version. Noteworthy too was that the short section of handrail from the front of the tanks to the smoke box door was essentially the same as on the larger locomotives and curved downwards at the front end, following the smokebox wrapper. The Class 2 tanks were, however, provided with very short, straight handrails along the smokebox side, exactly as in the Ivatt LMS design. A number of the Class 2 locomotives were fitted for push-pull working, with the auxiliary regulator valves mounted on the left-hand side of the smokebox, above the mechanical lubricators.

The cab layout was standard for all locomotives, whether tender or tank. A shortcoming of Standard locomotives was the draughty nature of the cab, this being particularly evident on the Class 4 tanks when running bunker-first. A glazed screen behind the driver's upholstered seat gave him some protection, though no such facility was provided for the fireman. Storm sheets or draught screens were available though were not really to be considered as compensation for a bad design.

Grouping of the controls into both fireman and driver's positions was carried out for accessibility, and the inclusion of such controls as vacuum brake, blower and sanding valves in a pedestal also served as a firehole screen for the driver. Having said that, the suitability of having clusters of pipes in close proximity to the enginemen's working positions was in some case questionable. It was said that health problems could arise due to the localised heating effects from these pipes. The regulator arm was duplicated on the fireman's side, and actuated by fore-and-aft movement as standard practice.

On the fireman's side, below the footplate, were the two injectors and the water sieve boxes. These on tender locomotives were fixed to the outside of the tender frames. The feed pipe to the valves mounted on the front boiler ring was visible below the lower edges of the side tanks, passing beneath the front portion of the tank and upwards around the boiler barrel. Some members of all three classes were fitted with speedometers, the drive for which was taken from a light return crank assembly mounted on the rear coupled axle. Rather surprisingly, even on the tank engine designs this was not a standard feature.

Construction and Operation

Responsibility for overall design of each of the three tank locomotives was distributed between three different drawing offices. For the Class 4 locomotives, Brighton was selected as the parent office, with the work proceeding at the same time as the Class 4 4-6-0 tender locomotives. The Class 3 tanks were like the tender equivalent a product of Swindon, largely as the Swindon No 2 boiler was to be used for these locomotives. The diminutive Class 2 became the responsibility of Derby, perhaps not surprisingly since the Ivatt version emanated from the Locomotive Drawing Office there only a few years previously. The distribution of component and detail design for such items as boiler fittings, suspension and brake gear were as outlined in Chapter 3, with that responsibility delegated throughout five of the six BR regions.

The construction of the three classes, totalling 230 locomotives, showed a similar distribution, with six works being involved in the building. Of the Class 4 locomotives, 130 were constructed at Brighton, fifteen at Derby and ten at Doncaster. Even within the region responsible for overall construction, certain production work was carried out at Ashford and Eastleigh. All the Class 3 2-6-2s were built at Swindon, with eighteen further locomotives planned for inclusion in the 1954 building programme, but subsequently cancelled. Construction of the Class 2 tanks was carried out at Crewe and Darlington, with the former works having the distinction of building examples of both the largest and smallest locomotives in the Standard series. It must be said, however, that the tank locomotives were beset with the same production delays that affected the entire range, though it does appear curious that the first ten running numbers of Class 4 were allocated to Derby-built locomotives, rather than those produced by Brighton. The upshot of this was that almost all of batches Nos 2–5 in the Class 4 category were in service before the first-numbered locomotives in the class appeared from Derby.

Delivery of the Class 4 locomotives was particularly erratic throughout 1951 and 1952, with the first two emerging from Brighton in July 1951, followed by a third two months later, then a batch of six in October, one in November and six more in December. During the first ten months of 1952, production was still at a very low level, averaging just two locomotives per

month, and demonstrating the quite damaging effects of the steel shortage. The Class 3 locomotives built at Swindon were also to have appeared in 1951, but for the same reasons production was delayed until April 1952, though delivery was more consistent. Again, there were some quite large gaps between scheduled and actual appearance, including individual locomotives built out of sequence, as with the Class 4s. Of the fourth batch of Class 3s, intended to be supplied to the Western Region in 1952, none was built until late 1954 and early 1955. Least affected were the Class 2 locomotives, which in the case of those constructed at Derby were put back by only six or seven months. The ten Darlington-built locomotives were delayed by four years; with their introduction on the Southern Region planned for 1953, they were not first seen until March 1957.

All three classes were intended for use on suburban, cross-country and stopping passenger, and short-haul freight workings. Of the Class 4 locomotives, examples were delivered to opposite ends of the BR network, with Nos 80010–9 allocated to Tunbridge Wells West on the Southern, and No 80020 onwards going to Aberdeen. Initially all the Brighton-built locomotives worked running-in turns from Tunbridge Wells, and were noted on a variety of trains, working as far west as Salisbury. Regular workings for the Southern's allocation included most Central Section duties, operating additionally from Eastbourne over the former SER line. It is interesting to note that the Fairburn equivalents were barred from these duties on clearance grounds. Use of the locomotives fast became widespread, with examples being sent to Exmouth Junction on the Southern, and the newer constructions being despatched to Watford on the London Midland, and various lines in Scotland. Brighton-built locomotives for other areas were provided with water pick-up apparatus, and some had tablet-catchers for single-line working.

The first Scottish Region locomotives were sent to Aberdeen, Kittybrewster and Ferryhill, though for a short time they were employed on local workings in the Glasgow area. In 1952, the first-numbered locomotive in the class, No 80000, arrived at Corkerhill from Derby, and in company with other members of the class began work between Glasgow (St Enoch) and various routes and stations in Ayrshire and Renfrewshire.

The London Midland's initial allocations were soon put to work on suburban services into Euston and Broad Street. Locomotives of the same class built in the following year (1953) had the driver's side tank vent altered in size, and placed further forward. The earlier arrangement, with the vent well up to the driver's front look-out tended to obscure forward visibility. In all, the locomotives were scattered far and wide throughout the regions, and were recognised by-and-large as capable performers on the duties for which they were intended. The main concentrations were on the LMR suburban lines, in Scotland, and non-electrified routes for the Southern. In later years, many of the Southern locomotives were fitted with TIA water-treatment equipment, and carried a small triangular mark under the running number.

Almost all the class was withdrawn between mid-1964 and the end of 1966. Although 23 remained until 1967, none survived to the end of steam, and six have been preserved. These are to be found, almost like their distribution in steam days, in various parts of the country, from Falkirk in Scotland, to the Keighley & Worth Valley Railway, the Bluebell Railway in the South of England—and even on the Torbay & Dartmouth line in GWR territory.

The Class 3 locomotives were built for use on the Western and Southern Regions, with the first ten going to the WR and working in the Birmingham and Bristol areas. The first Southern locomotives, from No 82010, were put to work in and around Exeter, with later ones from the same batch going to Eastleigh for branch line and stopping passenger duties. In 1954, a number were transferred to Cardiff, and were employed initially on Taff Vale services, with the introduction of a fixed-interval timetable. Later some found their way to the Cambrian Coast Line, and were based at Machynlleth. Bristol, Bath and Exmouth Junction all retained an allocation until withdrawals began in 1964/5. Similarly the Southern Region kept thirteen of the original 20 allocated, though in later years they were to be found at Nine Elms employed almost exclusively on suburban workings. At least three examples found themselves in the North-West, working over LMR metals from Birkenhead.

No extensive modifications were carried out to the original design, though as with the Class 4 tanks a number were provided with the TIA water-treatment apparatus.

Finally, there were the Class 2 locomotives built at Crewe and Darlington for the London Midland and Southern Regions. With one exception, these locomotives were first put to use in the North-West at various depots, with the majority at Plodder Lane, Low Moor and Bury, insofar as the 20 locomotives built in 1953 and destined for the London Midland Region were concerned. The Darlington-built locomotives were sent in 1957 to the Southern, though none was fitted with water-treatment apparatus.

The LMR locomotives in the main were employed on local passenger workings, although shortly after their arrival at Plodder Lane, passenger services were withdrawn from the Bolton to Manchester Exchange and Kenyon lines, and the Standard Class 2 tanks were transferred to Wrexham. There they were employed essentially on branch line work between Wrexham and Seacombe.

The first use of the push-pull equipment was on what were referred to as motor-fitted trains from Fleetwood, the locomotives being Nos 84016/7/8. The locomotives themselves were first used on non-motor-fitted trains, as there were not enough motor sets to go around! At Fleetwood, they were replacements for the Ivatt Class 2 2-6-2Ts Nos 41260/1/2.

As with most Standard locomotives, withdrawal followed a short working life in comparison with the age of most steam locomotives. In fact, barely seven years had elapsed before members of the class built in 1957 were scrapped. Most of the Darlington-built locomotives disappearing in 1964. By that time all the Class 2 tanks were operated by the London Midland Region, but being rather more scattered than when new. Most of those which remained were in the North West, at Llandudno Junction, Croes Newydd and Fleetwood, with a number at Crewe Works, and on the Midland Lines, working from Leicester.

Unfortunately, no examples of the Standard Class 3 or Class 2 tank locomotives were saved for preservation, since most had been withdrawn and scrapped a number of years before the inevitable end of steam traction.

Summary Table—The Standard Class 4MT 2-6-4T Nos 80000–80154

No	Built	Withdrawn	Disposal	No	Built	Withdrawn	Disposal
80000	10/52	12/66	Shipbreaking Industries, Faslane	80011	7/51	7/67	Birds Commercial Motors, Risca
80001	11/52	7/66	Metal Industries, Faslane	80012	9/51	3/67	J. Buttigieg, Newport
80002	11/52	3/67	Preserved	80013	10/51	6/66	R.A. King, Norwich
80003	11/52	4/65	Shipbreaking Industries, Faslane	80014	10/51	5/65	
80004	11/52	5/67	G.H. Campbell, Airdrie	80015	10/51	7/67	
80005	11/52	8/66	Motherwell Machinery Co, Wishaw	80016	10/51	7/67	Birds Commercial Motors, Risca
				80017	10/51	9/64	
80006	11/52	9/66	Shipbreaking Industries, Faslane	80018	10/51	5/65	G. Cohen, Morriston
80007	12/52	7/66	Metal Industries, Faslane	80019	12/51	3/67	J. Buttigieg, Newport
80008	12/52	7/64	Motherwell Machinery Co, Wishaw	80020	11/51	6/65	
				80021	12/51	7/64	Motherwell Machinery Co, Wishaw
80009	12/52	9/64	Motherwell Machinery Co, Wishaw				
				80022	1/52	6/65	
80010	7/51	6/64	J. Cashmore, Newport	80023	12/51	11/65	Shipbreaking Industries, Faslane

No	Built	Withdrawn	Disposal	No	Built	Withdrawn	Disposal
80024	12/51	9/66	Metal Industries, Faslane	80074	12/53	9/64	Motherwell Machinery Co, Wishaw
80025	12/51	9/66	Metal Industries, Faslane				
80026	12/51	9/66	Shipbreaking Industries, Faslane	80075	12/53	9/64	Motherwell Machinery Co, Wishaw
80027	1/52	12/66	Motherwell Machinery Co, Wishaw	80076	1/54	9/64	Motherwell Machinery Co, Wishaw
80028	1/52	10/66	G.H. Campbell, Airdrie				
80029	1/52	12/65		80077	1/54	10/64	Motherwell Machinery Co, Wishaw
80030	2/52	6/64	Arnott Young, Troon				
80031	3/52	9/64	Steel Supply Co, West Drayton	80078	2/54	9/65	Woodham Bros, Barry
80032	3/52	1/67	J. Cashmore, Newport	80079	3/54	9/65	Woodham Bros, Barry
80033	3/52	10/66	J. Cashmore, Newport	80080	3/54	9/65	Woodham Bros, Barry
80034	4/52	1/66	Cox & Danks, Park Royal	80081	4/54	6/65	
80035	6/52	4/65	Birds Commercial Motors, Bynea	80082	4/54	9/66	J. Cashmore, Newport
80036	6/52	11/64	J. Cashmore, Newport	80083	6/54	8/66	
80037	6/52	3/66	J. Cashmore, Newport	80084	6/54	6/65	
80038	6/52	10/64		80085	6/54	7/67	Birds Commercial Motors, Risca
80039	7/52	2/66	J. Cashmore, Newport	80086	6/54	5/67	
80040	7/52	7/64		80087	7/54	6/64	J. Cashmore, Newport
80041	7/52	3/66	J. Cashmore, Newport	80088	7/54	6/65	
80042	8/52	2/65	R.S. Hayes, Bridgend	80089	8/54	12/66	
80043	8/52	3/66	J. Cashmore, Newport	80090	8/54	4/65	
80044	9/52	11/64		80091	9/54	12/66	Motherwell Machinery Co, Wishaw
80045	9/52	5/67	G.H. Campbell, Airdrie				
80046	10/52	5/67	G.H. Campbell, Airdrie	80092	10/54	10/66	G.H. Campbell, Airdrie
80047	10/52	9/66	Metal Industries, Faslane	80093	11/54	10/66	G.H. Campbell, Airdrie
80048	11/52	6/65	Birds Commercial Motors, Morriston	80094	11/54	8/66	
				80095	12/54	12/66	
80049	11/52	6/64	Arnott Young, Troon	80096	12/54	1/66	T.W. Ward, Ringwood
80050	11/52	11/64	Central Wagon Co, Wigan	80097	12/54	9/65	Woodham Bros, Barry
80051	11/52	8/66	Metal Industries, Faslane	80098	12/54	9/65	Woodham Bros, Barry
80052	1/53	7/64	Motherwell Machinery Co, Wishaw	80099	1/55	6/65	
				80100	2/55	9/65	Woodham Bros, Barry
80053	1/53	7/64	Motherwell Machinery Co, Wishaw	80101	2/55	7/65	Birds Commercial Motors, Morriston
80054	11/54	7/66	Motherwell Machinery Co, Wishaw	80102	3/55	12/65	T.W. Ward, Ringwood
				80103	3/55	7/62	Stratford Works
80055	12/54	9/66	Shipbreaking Industries, Faslane	80104	4/55	9/65	Woodham Bros, Barry
				80105	4/55	9/65	Woodham Bros, Barry
80056	12/54	10/64		80106	10/54	10/64	Motherwell Machinery Co, Wishaw
80057	12/54	12/66	Shipbreaking Industries, Faslane	80107	10/54	9/64	Motherwell Machinery Co, Wishaw
80058	1/55	7/66	Metal Industries, Faslane				
80059	3/53	1/66	J. Buttigieg, Newport	80108	11/54	5/65	Motherwell Machinery Co, Wishaw
80060	3/53	3/66	Motherwell Machinery Co, Wishaw	80109	11/54	11/65	
80061	4/53	12/66	Shipbreaking Industries, Faslane	80110	11/54	5/65	Motherwell Machinery Co, Wishaw
80062	5/53	10/64	Motherwell Machinery Co, Wishaw	80111	11/54	12/66	Motherwell Machinery Co, Wishaw
80063	7/53	9/66	Metal Industries, Faslane	80112	12/54	9/66	Metal Industries, Faslane
80064	7/53	9/65	Woodham Bros, Barry	80113	12/54	9/66	Shipbreaking Industries, Faslane
80065	7/53	9/66	J. Cashmore, Newport				
80066	8/53	6/65		80114	1/55	12/66	Shipbreaking Industries, Faslane
80067	8/53	6/65	Woodham Bros, Barry	80115	1/55	10/64	Motherwell Machinery Co, Wishaw
80068	9/53	12/66	J. Cashmore, Newport				
80069	10/53	2/66		80116	5/55	5/67	G.H. Campbell, Airdrie
80070	10/53	7/65	Cox & Danks, Park Royal	80117	6/55	3/66	Motherwell Machinery Co, Wishaw
80071	10/53	8/64	Motherwell Machinery Co, Wishaw	80118	6/55	12/66	Motherwell Machinery Co, Wishaw
80072	11/53	9/65	Woodham Bros, Barry				
80073	11/53	9/64	Motherwell Machinery Co, Wishaw				

No	Built	Withdrawn	Disposal	No	Built	Withdrawn	Disposal
80119	7/55	5/65	Motherwell Machinery Co, Wishaw	80136	5/56	9/65	Woodham Bros, Barry
80120	7/55	5/67	G.H. Campbell, Airdrie	80137	6/56	11/65	Cox & Danks, Park Royal
80121	8/55	6/66		80138	6/56	12/66	
80122	9/55	12/66	Shipbreaking Industries, Faslane	80139	7/56	7/67	
80123	10/55	8/66	Metal Industries, Faslane	80140	7/56	7/67	Birds Commercial Motors, Risca
80124	10/55	12/66	Shipbreaking Industries, Faslane	80141	8/56	2/66	Cox & Danks, Park Royal
80125	10/55	10/64	Maden & McKee, Stanley, Liverpool	80142	8/56	5/66	Birds Commercial Motors, Bridgend
80126	10/55	11/66	G.H. Campbell, Airdrie	80143	9/56	7/67	Birds Commercial Motors, Risca
80127	11/55	9/64		80144	10/56	6/66	Birds Commercial Motors, Bridgend
80128	11/55	4/67	P. & W. McLellan, Langloan, Coatbridge	80145	10/56	6/67	J. Cashmore, Newport
80129	12/55	10/64		80146	11/56	7/67	
80130	12/55	8/66	Metal Industries, Faslane	80147	11/56	6/65	Birds Commercial Motors, Morriston
80131	3/56	6/65		80148	11/56	6/64	Steel Supply Co, West Drayton
80132	3/56	1/66	Eastleigh Works (By G. Cohen)	80149	11/56	4/65	Cox & Danks, Park Royal
80133	4/56	7/67	Birds Commercial Motors, Risca	80150	11/56	10/65	Woodham Bros, Barry
80134	4/56	7/67	Birds Commercial Motors, Risca	80151	11/56	5/67	Woodham Bros, Barry
80135	5/56	9/65	Woodham Bros, Barry	80152	11/56	7/67	Birds Commercial Motors, Risca
				80153	11/56	4/65	Cox & Danks, Park Royal
				80154	11/56	4/67	J. Buttigieg, Newport

Note: Nos 80000–80009, 80054–80058, were built at Derby.
Nos 80010–80053, 80059–80105, 80116–80154 were built at Brighton.
Nos 80106–80115 were built at Doncaster.

Summary Table—The Standard Class 3MT 2-6-2T Nos 82000–82044

No	Built	Withdrawn	Disposal	No	Built	Withdrawn	Disposal
82000	4/52	12/66	J. Cashmore, Newport	82024	8/54	2/66	
82001	4/52	1/66	J. Cashmore, Newport	82025	8/54	8/64	G. Cohen, Kettering
82002	4/52	2/64	Eastleigh Works	82026	11/54	8/66	J. Buttigieg, Newport
82003	5/52	12/66	J. Cashmore, Newport	82027	12/54	1/66	Cox & Danks, Park Royal
82004	5/52	11/65	Birds Commercial Motors, Bridgend	82028	12/54	9/66	J. Cashmore, Newport
82005	5/52	9/65	Birds Commercial Motors, Bridgend	82029	12/54	7/67	Birds Commercial Motors, Risca
				83030	12/54	1/66	J. Cashmore, Newport
82006	5/52	10/66	J. Buttigieg, Newport	82031	12/54	12/66	J. Cashmore, Newport
82007	5/52	7/64	J. Cashmore, Newport	82032	1/55	6/65	Birds Commercial Motors, Morriston
82008	6/52	2/64	Eastleigh Works				
82009	6/52	12/66	J. Cashmore, Great Bridge	82033	1/55	9/65	Birds Commercial Motors, Risca
82010	7/52	5/65	Woodham Bros, Barry	82034	1/55	12/66	J. Cashmore, Newport
82011	8/52	9/64	G. Cohen, Kettering	82035	3/55	8/65	J. Cashmore, Newport
82012	8/52	6/64	G. Cohen, Kettering	82036	4/55	8/65	J. Cashmore, Newport
82013	8/52	6/64	G. Cohen, Kettering	82037	4/55	9/65	J. Cashmore, Newport
82014	9/52	6/64	G. Cohen, Kettering	82038	5/55	8/65	Birds Commercial Motors, Bridgend
82015	9/52	12/64	J. Cashmore, Newport				
82016	9/52	5/65		82039	5/55	7/65	Birds Commercial Motors, Long Marston
82017	9/52	5/65					
82018	10/52	8/66	J. Buttigieg, Newport	82040	5/55	7/65	Birds Commercial Motors, Long Marston
82019	10/52	7/67	Birds Commercial Motors, Risca	82041	6/55	1/66	J. Cashmore, Newport
82020	8/54	9/65	Birds Commercial Motors, Risca	82042	7/55	7/65	Birds Commercial Motors, Bridgend
82021	8/54	10/65	J. Buttigieg, Newport				
82022	11/54	10/65	J. Buttigieg, Newport	82043	7/55	2/64	Eastleigh Works
82023	11/54	12/66	J. Cashmore, Newport	82044	8/55	1/66	J. Buttigieg, Newport

All locomotives were built at Swindon.

Summary Table—The Standard Class 2MT 2-6-2T Nos 84000–84029

No	Built	Withdrawn	Disposal	No	Built	Withdrawn	Disposal
84000	7/53	11/65		84015	10/53	1/66	Central Wagon Co, Wigan
84001	7/53	10/64	H. Bolckow, Blyth	84016	10/53	1/66	Central Wagon Co, Wigan
84002	8/53	4/65	J. Buttigieg, Newport	84017	10/53	1/66	Arnott Young, Parkgate
84003	9/53	10/65	J. Cashmore, Great Bridge	84018	10/53	6/65	H. Bolckow, Blyth
84004	9/53	11/65	J. Buttigieg, Newport	84019	10/53	1/66	Arnott Young, Parkgate
84005	9/53	11/65	J. Buttigieg, Newport	84020	3/57	10/64	H. Bolckow, Blyth
84006	9/53	11/65	J. Buttigieg, Newport	84021	3/57	9/64	Crewe Works
84007	9/53	1/64	A. Loom, Spondon	84022	3/57	9/64	Crewe Works
84008	9/53	11/65	J. Buttigieg, Newport	84023	4/57	9/64	Crewe Works
84009	9/53	12/65	J. Cashmore, Great Bridge	84024	4/57	9/64	Crewe Works
84010	10/53	1/66	Central Wagon Co, Wigan	84025	4/57	1/66	Arnott Young, Parkgate
84011	10/53	4/65	H. Bolckow, Blyth	84026	4/57	1/66	Arnott Young, Parkgate
84012	10/53	11/63		84027	5/57	5/64	
84013	10/53	1/66	Arnott Young, Parkgate	84028	5/57	1/66	Central Wagon Co, Wigan
84014	10/53	1/66	J. Cashmore, Newport	84029	6/57	7/64	J. Cashmore, Great Bridge

Note: Nos 84000–84019 were built at Crewe, Nos 84020–84029 at Darlington.

Technical Data—The Standard Tank Locomotives

Note: This information relates to locomotives in original or 'as built' condition

Cylinders and valve gear		*Class 4MT*	*Class 3MT*	*Class 2MT*
Cylinders—diameter × stroke		18in × 28in	17½in × 26in	16½in × 24in
Piston swept volume—one cylinder		7125cu in	6254cu in	5134cu in
Clearance volume as % of piston swept volume		10.8%	11.6%	n/a
Maximum piston thrust		57256lb	48106lb	42765lb
Steam chests—volume between valve heads		3912cu in	3037cu in	n/a
—volume as % of piston swept volume		54.9%	48.5%	n/a
Piston valves—diameter		10in	10in	8in
—steam lap		1½in	1½in	1⁵⁄₁₆in
—lead		¼in	¼in	¼in
—exhaust clearance		NIL	NIL	NIL
Maximum travel of valves		6.58in	6.25in	5.92in
Maximum cut-off %		75.0%	75.0%	78.0%
Travel at 20% cut-off		3.62in	3.62in	3.23in

Balancing data		*Class 4MT*	*Class 3MT*	*Class 2MT*
Revolving masses—weight per cylinder		1396lb	1189lb	1172lb
Reciprocating masses—total weight per cylinder		757lb	737lb	564lb
—percentage balanced		40%	50%	50%
—unbalanced weight per cylinder		454lb	368lb	282lb
Ratio—unbalanced reciprocating weight per cylinder to total weight of locomotive		1/427	1/451	1/526
Hammer-blow at 5 revolutions per second—per wheel		1.91 tons	2.17 tons	1.53 tons
—per axle		2.28 tons	2.58 tons	1.82 tons
—per rail		5.10 tons	5.93 tons	4.29 tons
—whole locomotive		6.08 tons	7.05 tons	5.11 tons

Boiler proportions		Class 4MT	Class 3MT	Class 2MT
Free area through tubes—large	................:.......	1.74sqft	1.49sqft	0.98sqft
—small	....	2.04sqft	1.59sqft	1.76sqft
—total	....	3.78sqft	3.08sqft	2.74sqft
Area through large tubes as % of total	....	46.0%	48.4%	36.5%
Total free area as % of grate area	....	14.2%	15.2%	15.9%
A/S ratio—large tubes	....	1/345	1/302	1/343
—small tubes	....	1/382	1/374	1/369
Steam pipe in boiler—bore	....	5½in	5½in	5in
—cross-sectional area	....	23.8sq in	23.8sq in	19.5sq in
Regulator fully open—area	....	24.3sq in	24.3sq in	21.5sq in
Superheater elements—total area	....	20.6sq in	17.7sq in	11.1sq in
Steampipes to cylinders—total area	....	31.8sq in	31.8sq in	22.1sq in
Blastpipe cap—diameter	....	4¾in	4½in	4⅛in
—area	....	17.7sq in	15.9sq in	13.4sq in
Chimney throat—diameter	....	1ft 1½in	1ft 0¾in	1ft 0in
—area	....	1.0sqft	0.89sqft	0.79sqft
Throat area as % of grate area	....	3.75%	4.35%	4.40%
Height—blastpipe cap to chimney throat	....	2ft 7in	2ft 7in	2ft 5½in
Taper of chimney	....	1 in 14	1 in 14	1 in 14

10. Some Details of Performance and Testing

The testing of steam locomotives in BR days was carried out under the auspices of the Locomotive Testing Joint Sub-Committee of the British Transport Commission. During the 1950s, five Standard designs were put through their paces, including the Class 7 and the Class 8 Pacifics, Class 5 and Class 4 4-6-0s, and Class 9 2-10-0. In addition, former LMS Class 4 and Class 2 2-6-0s were examined, since the BR Standard versions were developments of these two types.

A very considerable amount of data was available from the various stationary tests, carried out at the Swindon and Rugby testing establishments, and from controlled road trials on the Western and London Midland Regions. The Railway Executive had also instigated a practice of publishing much of this information in the form of *Test Bulletins*, offered for sale to the general public. Such a step by-and-large would show the not so good as well as the successful aspects of a locomotive design. Fortunately the various Standard classes showed up well on the tests, and in comparison with other locomotives of similar size and capacity.

The Britannia design was the first of the Standards to be put to the test with No 70005 *John Bunyan* going to Rugby soon after its construction in 1951. As a check in the autumn of 1952 No 70025 was sent to the Testing Plant for a further series of stationary trials, though the controlled road tests were not repeated. No 70005 provided results that showed the locomotives' capabilities under ideal conditions, with hard South Kirkby coals and the softer Blidworth variety.

The design of the boiler proved an outstanding success, and showed itself capable of a maximum evaporation of over 31,000lb of steam per hour. Curiously though, this figure was exceeded on the road tests between Settle and Carlisle when no less than 37,560lb/hr was sustained for almost 45 minutes. The efficiency was recorded at 75% with a firing rate of 2,000lb/hr, reducing to 66% at the front end limit, with a coal rate of 5,066lb/hr, using Blidworth coal. It is worth noting that the maximum continuous firing rate with one fireman was taken as 3,000lb coal/h, and at that rate the Britannia boiler was supplying 21,060lb of steam to the cylinders. Using the lower quality coals—with which the wide firebox types were designed to operate—the maximum efficiency of the cylinders was recorded at 14%. This figure was achieved at powers of 1,300ihp to 1,600ihp, and speeds of 60mph to 70mph. At the maximum steam rate of 30,000lb per hour, cylinder ihp was 2,200, with 35% cut-off. At the drawbar, 1,800dbhp was the maximum achieved with 40% cut-off at 45mph, while the maximum thermal efficiency recorded was 8.3%.

Overall, the large boiler provided on the Britannias in relation to the cylinder size, offered a number of advantages in operation. Included in these was a boiler efficiency sustainable over the range of working which could be achieved by one fireman, and did not fall away markedly at the higher firing rates. The wide grate, in being able to support a greater quantity of ash and clinker, showed itself capable of more efficient combustion of poorer quality coals. However, such characteristics would be negated through

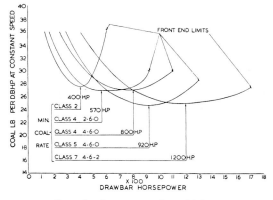

MINIMUM COAL CONSUMPTIONS WITH VARIOUS B.R. ENGINES
AT 60 M.P.H.

inadequate utilisation, where rostering allowed much waiting time.

The Class 8 Pacific sought to employ characteristics of the Britannia boiler design, though with an increased grate area of 48.6sq ft, and produced some curious and surprising results. In this case the locomotive was sent to Swindon for testing, again using South Kirkby and Blidworth coals. The controlled road tests were carried out between Marston Yard, Swindon and Westbury, running over the Bristol main line to Reading, and then along the Berks & Hants line through Newbury. Maximum evaporation was determined in this locomotive not by the front end limit, but by the grate limit, achieved in this

design at the quite low figure of only 34,000lb of steam per hour, supplied to the cylinders. The coal rate at the grate limit was 6850lb/hr, and with the same quantity of the poorer quality Blidworth coal, only 30,250lb of steam per hour was attainable. On the road, the maximum steam rate of 30,000lb per hour demanded a firing rate of no less than 4,850lb of coal. Comparison of the boiler efficiency with the Britannia, shows the Class 8 to be markedly inferior at the higher firing rates, falling-off rapidly towards the point at which the grate limit was reached. Using 2,000lb of coal per hour, the Class 8 achieved 76.7%, whilst at the grate limit of 6,850lb, this had fallen rapidly to only 44.6%.

The Class 8 Pacific was provided with British Caprotti valve gear, which proved highly successful in operation. Under test, the cylinder efficiency was found to be 15.7%, 86% of that which was theoretically achievable; this figure was recorded at a steam rate of 22,800lb/hr, and a road speed of 90mph. Maximum ihp at 30,000lb/hr steam rate was 2,440 at 65mph. At the drawbar, 2,100dbhp was achieved at 40% cut-off, and 40mph. In the Britannia design, the ihp at constant steam rates reached a maximum at around 65mph, while in *Duke of Gloucester* design, the value was still increasing at 90mph. Per unit of steam rate the ihp figures for the Class 8 locomotive were the highest recorded for a Standard type.

Overall, the Class 8 was provided with the best cylinders and valve gear available, while the steam producer fell a long way short from what could reasonably be expected from a locomotive of this type.

British Railways Class '7' Locomotive Tests

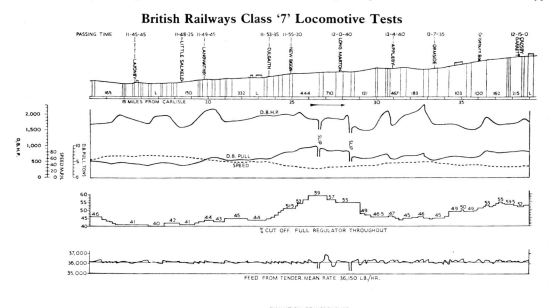

– Dynamometer car test, South Kirkby coal at 14,000 B.Th.U /lb. as fired, exhaust steam injector, supplemented by live steam. Example of run at constant evaporation, maximum power, at high steaming rate

POWER OUTPUT AND CUT-OFF AT 24,000 lb. STEAM/HOUR

(BR Standard Britannia, W.R. King, and V2 2-6-2)

——————— Standard C1.7 4-6-2
— — — — W.R. King C1 4-6-0
— - - — - - E. NER V2 2-6-2

Figures represent cut-off %

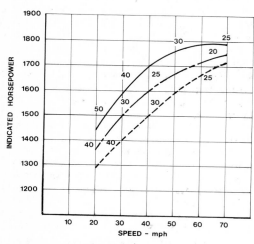

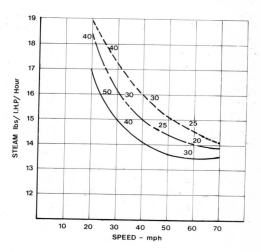

The reasons for this were never fully investigated, and hence not satisfactorily explained. The increased size of grate in relation to the boiler proportions resulted in a free gas area as a percentage of grate area much lower than on the Britannia design. However, even at 14% this was still greater than the Class 9F 2-10-0, which over the range through which it was tested proved an excellent steamer. Similarly it was shown that the high-frequency vibrations set up at the back end of the firegrate, from the undamped coil springs on the trailing truck, caused disintegration of the fire at high power outputs. Having said that, the Britan-

Of the 27 Standard locomotives in varying states of preservation, no fewer than nine Class 4MT 2-6-4 tank engines are either restored, or as in this case, about to be. This rarely-seen view of the frames, cylinders, and parts of the motion of No 80002 before work had commenced in the yard at Haworth shows interesting detail. On the lower edge of the frame, between the leading and driving wheels, is a group of grease nipples, for lubrication of the leading and driving hornguides. (*R. France/Standard 4 Locomotive Preservation Society*)

nias and Merchant Navy Pacifics—from where the trailing truck design was taken—showed no such characteristics.

The Class 9F 2-10-0 locomotives were the subject of the BTC *Test Bulletin* No 13, published in 1959, and referred to the standard locomotive of the class with single blastpipe and chimney. Partial tests were carried out with the mechanical stoker fitted locomotives, the Crosti-boilered versions and the solitary Giesel ejector fitted locomotive No 92250. In the main the tests on these later variations concentrated on the results of the performance of these modifications. One of the double-chimney Class 9Fs was subjected to tests in 1958.

The stationary tests were performed at Rugby, with road tests on the former Glasgow & South Western line between Carlisle and Hurlford, and also over the Settle & Carlisle route from Skipton. A minor alteration to the blastpipe nozzle was made prior to the tests, it being reduced in diameter from 5⅜in to 5¼in, to improve the draught. Maximum evaporation of 29,000lb of water per hour was attained with this arrangement, and determined by the front end limit at

a firing rate of 4,655lb of coal per hour. At the 3,000lb/coal/hr, 22,000lb of steam were supplied to the cylinders which, considering their close similarity, yielded results almost identical with the Britannia design. At this same firing rate on a test run over the Settle & Carlisle line, with a trailing load of almost 650 tons, the 2-10-0 maintained a speed of 30mph almost throughout the 16½-mile climb from Appleby to Ais Gill. The drawbar horsepower of 1,100 was sustained, with no correction for gradient.

Of the 4-6-0 types tested the results from Class 5 No 73008, in addition to demonstrating characteristic features of Standard design, served as an interesting comparison with the former LMS Class 5. Initially, under test at Rugby, the 5⅛in diameter blastpipe was able to provide maximum evaporation rates of only 26,310lb of steam, and this with good quality South Kirkby coal. Subsequent reduction of the nozzle diameter to 4⅞in, with modifications to the grate and firebars, increasing the air space, improved evaporation rates, particularly with poorer quality coals. The front end limit was raised by a maximum of 26%, and the alterations were carried through to the remaining locomotives in the class.

In comparison with Stanier's Class 5 design, the Standard locomotives offered no advantage with their increased valve travel, cylinder diameter or wheel size, and in fact were marginally inferior in terms of cylinder efficiency and steam consumption. However, in view of the improvement to the front end design with the Standard locomotives, and considering that the capacity and abilities of the two designs were identical, the Stanier locomotives could well have benefitted with improvements to their draughting.

The Class 4 4-6-0 No 75006 was tested at Swindon and, curiously perhaps, showed greater cylinder efficiency and steam consumption figures than the Class 5 design. Also demonstrated under test conditions with the Class 4 locomotive was that the only advantage of Welsh Grade 2 coals over the Midlands variety was at maximum output, when 13% less fuel was consumed per hour. No more water was evaporated, and no improvement in either cylinder efficiency or steam consumption was achieved.

With a single blastpipe and chimney the Class 4's maximum evaporation rate was 19,600lb of steam per hour. In order to provide a greater margin of performance on the Class 5 duties for which some Class 4 locomotives were rostered, double chimneys were fitted to a number of locomotives, giving maximum evaporation rates of 22,400lb of steam per hour. At the maximum firing rate for one fireman of 3,000lb of coal per hour, it would have been possible to attain an evaporation rate of 19,800lb per hour, although this was not determined under test. Overall, boiler efficiency ranged from just over 82% at the lowest rates of firing, to 65.5% and 62% at the front end limit, for Bedwas and Blidworth coals, respectively.

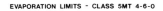

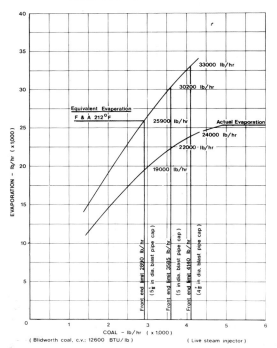

EVAPORATION LIMITS - CLASS 5MT 4-6-0

At the maximum evaporation rate of 19,600lb of steam per hour, 1,100dbhp was developed at 45mph.

The 2-6-0 classes tested at Swindon were the former LMS designs. Both were identical, as outlined in previous chapters, in all aspects affecting performance, with the BR Standard developments. The Class 2 locomotive was tested in 1950, and involved minor modifications to the draughting, resulting in a degree of tuning-up of the front end. On the road trials this diminutive locomotive was able to haul over 450 tons up an adverse 1 in 300 gradient, at a maximum speed of 40mph.

The picture that was presented by the various tests on the Standard types displayed a successful range of locomotive designs, which were the equal of, and in a number of instances, superior to, their regional counterparts.

Considering that the Standard classes were intended to effect improvements in maintenance costs, by being economical in operation and in running greater mileages between repairs, their comparison with regional types was a measure of this achievement. Maintenance of the Standard classes was assigned to various works, not necessarily those of either the operating region or the building works. Minimum repair periods were laid down for each class, which it was intended would elapse before a locomotive could be considered for shopping, and these are listed below:

```
Class 7 4-6-2.....................................15 months
Class 6 4-6-2.....................................18 months
Class 5 4-6-0.....................................24 months
Class 4 4-6-0.....................................28 months
Class 4 2-6-0.....................................30 months
Class 3 2-6-0.....................................33 months
Class 2 2-6-0.....................................36 months
Class 4 2-6-4T....................................28 months
Class 3 2-6-2T....................................33 months
Class 2 2-6-2T....................................36 months
```

In the early 1950s an overall average mileage between general repairs of 101,130 miles, was achieved for the entire locomotive stock. From general to intermediate repairs, this figure was 64,268 miles. These mileages represented a length of time in service of 47 and 28 months respectively. In the case of specific regional types, comparison with similar Standard designs showed an increase in the mileages run between periodical repairs (see next column).

The table shows how far the trend of increasing mileages between periodical repairs had been developed in the Standard series. The figures for regional types are for 1951, while those for the Standard locomotives are for 1957. It is worth noting, too, that the use of manganese-steel liners to the hornguides had very considerably improved the service life of London Midland locomotives. With this single modification, the Stanier Class 5 4-6-0 mileage was almost

doubled, while that of the Class 4 tank type had increased by around 50%. The high mileages achieved by the Standard locomotives were not exceptional, but generally speaking were an improvement on previous levels.

Region	Class of locomotive	Average mileage between repairs
LMR	Cl.7P Royal Scot 4-6-0	70,495
LMR	Cl.5 4-6-0	56,969
LMR	Cl.5 4-6-0★	97,291
LMR	Cl.4 2-6-0	90,663
LMR	Cl.4 2-6-4T	55,579
LMR	Cl.4 2-6-4T★	79,361
E/NER	V2 2-6-2	77,892
E/NER	B1 4-6-0	78,396
E/NER	L1 2-6-4T	67,213
WR	Castle 4-6-0	87,424
WR	Hall 4-6-0	87,942
WR	81XX 2-6-2T	71,720
SR	Merchant Navy 4-6-2	75,687
SR	West Country 4-6-2	74,650
SR	U 2-6-0	68,941
SR	N 2-6-0	58,852

Standard Classes

LMR	7MT 4-6-2	136,582
LMR	5MT 4-6-0	95,052
SR	4MT 2-6-0	92,111
SR	4MT 2-6-4T	86,551

★These locomotives fitted with manganese-steel liners to hornguides.

Repair costs per mile were also showing improvements over regional types, if only marginally in most cases, since many of the more modern types incorporated cost-saving features in their design. Overall repair costs for the Britannias in the mid-1950s averaged 8.7d per mile, while WR Castle Class 4-6-0s of power class 7 were costing 9.37d per mile. ER A1 Pacifics averaged 8.53d, and the LMR Royal Scots almost 10d per mile. Further down the scale the comparison of Class 5 locomotives with their LMR equivalent at the same period reveals identical figures of 8.02d per mile. The WR Hall Class 4-6-0s were costing around 8.28d per mile to repair, with the poor old West Country Pacifics almost as expensive to repair as the LMR Duchess Class locomotives.

In considering the quality of the BR Standard locomotive designs from an engineering viewpoint there were many improvements on what had gone before. Unfortunately the decision to standardise on a few types of locomotive could never be considered wholly successful or unsuccessful. Soon after their introduction, it was decided that the future of motive power lay in a massive programme of dieselisation and electrification. The objective of considerably reducing stocks of spares through use of fewer locomotive designs was never to be realised. Labour and cost-saving features included in these locomotives were of only temporary value to BR, and in a comparatively short space of time some of these features were required to show their worth, though many did not.

Even as the writing was appearing on the wall for steam traction, modifications and experiments were still being carried out. A number of these have already been discussed, particularly in connection with the 2-10-0 freight locomotives—mechanical stokers, double chimneys and Crosti boilers, with Caprotti valve gear on the Class 8 Pacific and a number of Class 5 4-6-0s. These large and dramatic modifications were supplemented by more modest experiments and alterations. On the Southern Region, for example, many of the Class 4 and Class 2 tank locomotives were fitted with TIA (*Traitment Intégral Armand*) water-softening apparatus.

While the provision of AWS equipment was not an experiment, most of the tender types acquired this during their working lives. The AWS equipment was fitted to Standard classes in the late 1950s, at a cost of between £300 and £400. As developed from 1952, the system was known as ATC (Automatic Train Control). However, the more precise Audible Warning System (AWS) was quickly adopted, giving a clearer indication of the function. Electromagnets fitted between the rails in advance of a distant signal actuated a

Standard Class 5 4-6-0 No 73030 on its first day's testing at Rugby on 23 July 1953. Following reductions in blastpipe diameter from the original 5⅛in to 4⅞in, the front-end limit was raised by more than 25%, from 19000 to 24000lb/hr of steam produced. Note the pipework trailing over the locomotive, for monitoring such details as blastpipe pressure, steam temperature, etc. (*R. Shenton*)

receiver mounted at the front of the locomotive, a few inches above rail level, to give an audible and visual indication to the footplate crew on a cab instrument, of the aspect of the signal. In an emergency, should the warning not be acknowledged by the driver or fireman by depressing a lever on the cab instrument the brakes were automatically applied, after a short time interval.

Much criticism was levelled at these locomotives in their early years, perhaps occasioned by the amalgamation of so many ideas in one design, perhaps by the numerous breaks with established traditions. Following their withdrawal and the end of steam traction, it was all too easy to write them off as unnecessary. Yet in the short space of time they had to establish themselves, they were successful and popular locomotives when properly worked. Even in the mid-1950s, their designers could still forsee a time when the Standard classes would comprise the majority of steam locomotive types on British Railways.

Liveries

Although with the exception of the Class 9F 2-10-0 all the Standard classes, tender and tank, were mixed-traffic locomotives, three separate colour schemes were used. For the three Pacific types, lined-green livery was selected; with all other classes, excluding the Class 9Fs, lined-black was applied. The 2-10-0s were unlined black except for No 92220 *Evening Star*, which was given a special lined-green livery, and the ultimate Swindon accolade of a copper-capped chimney.

All surfaces, excluding wheels and brakework, footplate, undersides of tenders, coal bunkers and side tanks, and the interior surfaces of tender and side tanks, were given a coat of red oxide primer. This was

Almost the end of the line, this close-up view of BR1B tender No 1042 at Haworth on the Keighley & Worth Valley Railway shows some similarity with LMS-style tenders in the general appearance of the upper works. The underframe was one of two standard sizes adopted for the BR locomotives, either 13ft 6in or 14ft 0in wheelbase, and 3ft 3½in diameter wheels. The list of original tender pairings given in Appendix II, notes that it was attached to Class 4MT 4-6-0 No 75078, with which it now remains, as preserved. The wheels had been removed for re-tyring. (*R. France/Standard 4 Locomotive Preservation Society*)

of two types, the BR mixtures 161 and 101, with the latter used on the exterior surfaces of the boiler, sides and back of tender and coal bunker, inner sides, outsides, ends and tops of side tanks. The exceptions mentioned as not receiving a coat of primer were given instead a coat of General Purpose Black paint to BR Spec 30, item 5.

Following preparatory work, knife-stopping and rubbing-down of surface blemishes on livery areas was the next stage of the process. Finishing of livery areas was carried out as follows:

Green Livery (Britannia, Clan, *Duke of Gloucester, Evening Star* and examples from Class 5 and Class 4 4-6-0, and Class 3 2-6-2T)

One coat of green sealer/undercoat to either BR Spec 30 item 33 or item 6, covering boiler barrel, firebox, cab front, sides, footplate valance, tender sides and rear. This was followed by a single coat of green enamel to Spec 30 item 34 or item 7, and one coat of varnish. Lining was orange and black, and applied to all boiler, front and rear firebox lagging bands, cab and tender sides, and in the case of the Pacifics, the deep footplate/running board valances also had orange lines and black border at their upper

and lower edges. Cylinders were lined with twin orange lines at front and rear. The lining, together with running numbers and totems were applied before the final coat of varnish.

Black Livery

Using synthetic resin paints, a first coat of sealer/undercoat to BR Spec 30, item 35, was applied to the same livery areas as for green-painted locomotives, followed by a coat of black enamel to BR Spec 30 item 36, and varnish. The oleo-resin process consisted of a single coat of black, airdrying enamel to BR Spec 30 item 8, which was also used for the unlined Class 9F locomotives. The lined-black tender and tank locomotives were lined red, cream and grey, with running numbers and transfers applied before the final coat of varnish.

The non-livery areas, including the cab roof (above the weather strip), inside of cab (including boiler/firebox backplate and tender/bunker fronts), cylinder cleading and smoke deflector plates were also black. The smokebox, chimney, and outside steampipes were given a coat of heat resisting black enamel to BR Spec 30, item 39. The buffer beams and stocks were given a single coat of red enamel to BR Spec 30, item 9. No lining was applied to the rear of either bunkers or tenders, and even on the green-liveried locomotives the upper surfaces of footplates and tender tops were black.

Most of the locomotives followed the standard schemes laid down, although there were a number of exceptions, including the application of lined-green livery to Class 5 and Class 4 4-6-0 locomotives, and a number of Class 3 2-6-2 tank types. These latter variations mostly appeared on the Western Region. Some locomotives had a yellow disc applied below the running number, when working on the Southern

Region. The purpose of this was to show that they were fitted with the TIA water-treatment apparatus, though its shape was later changed to a triangle to avoid any confusion with the WR route restriction discs. The Britannia Pacific No 70004 *William Shakespeare*, which for a long time was regularly rostered to work the Golden Arrow, had received a very special finish for the Festival of Britain Exhibition in 1951. In addition to highly-polished motion, handrails, cylinder end covers and buffing/drawgear, even the upper edges of the front mainframe extensions were polished!

Two different designs of crest were carried by these locomotives, the first of these, which appeared with the first standard livery schemes for BR in 1949, was not a true heraldic device. It was a symbol devised by the Railway Executive, consisting of a lion astride a locomotive wheel, with the words *British Railways* in a rectangular box across its centre. Application of this totem was such that the lion faced forward on both sides of the locomotive tender or tank, the transfers being either right- or left-handed.

The second style of crest was a true heraldic device, and registered with the College of Arms in England, and the Lyon Court in Scotland. The design was prepared by Dr C.A.H. Franklyn, and comprised a demi-lion rampant, the British lion, holding a silver locomotive wheel between its paws. The lion was issuant from a heraldic crown of gold, with the rose (for England), thistle (for Scotland), leek (for Wales), and the oak leaf for all Great Britain, arranged around the base. This was enclosed in a gold circle, flanked

by the words *British Railways*, and was first seen on No 70016 *Ariel* at Marylebone Station on 21 June 1956. For the lion to be heraldically correct, when any part of the achievement was used, it needed to face left only. Despite this, there were numerous incorrect applications with lion facing forward on the right-hand side of the locomotive.

Running numbers carried on the cab sides were in pale straw, of either 8in or 10in size, with the power classification in 2in numerals above. Style was Gill Sans, and on green-liveried locomotives a thin black border was applied. The same style of numbering was provided for the smokebox door numberplates, with the numbers raised from a flat background. At the lower edge of the smokebox door, the traditional cast-iron shed allocation plate was fitted, below which were added the letters SC to denote the provision of self-cleaning apparatus. Similarly, works/builders' plates were fixed to the front frame extensions, giving year and place of building, while on the rear of the tender tanks and bunkers could be found similar cast plates showing tender numbers and capacities.

In the closing years of steam on BR all Standard types and many others were fitted with small plastic plates warning of overhead electrified wires. These were fixed to various points on the locomotive, though unlike many London Midland locomotives none of the Standards was barred from working south of Crewe following completion of electrification, since being lower than some of the LMS express types did not infringe the clearances required beneath the overhead catenary to prevent flashovers of the high voltage electrification system.

Boiler Data...Blidworth Grade 2B Coal

	At front end limit						Under maximum sustained condition					
Locomotive	Steam rate lb/hr	Coal rate lb/hr	Boiler efficiency %	Steam temp. °F	Smoke-box draught water (in)	Blast-pipe pressure	Steam rate lb/hr	Coal rate lb/hr	Boiler efficiency %	Steam temp. °F	Smoke-box draught water (in)	Blast-pipe pressure
BR Cl 7 (1)	31,410	5066	67	737	7.3	9.3	24,000	3600	72	715	5.0	5.3
King (2)	30,780	5300	57	711	7.3	10.0	24,000	3250	72	679	5.3	5.6
V2 2-6-2 (1)	31,000	5670	58	736	7.0	9.0	24,000	3540	70	700	4.8	5.5
Merchant Navy (3)	35,000	6000	60	685	6.2	7.8	24,000	3600	68	630	3.2	3.4
							26,000	4000	66	640	3.6	3.9
BR Cl 5 (1)	24,000	4100	62	706	9.2	9.3	18,000	2700	70	672	5.6	4.6
WR Hall (2),(4)	21,690	4260	49	590	505	3.2	16,000	2045	74	570	3.6	1.8
BR Cl 4 4-6-0 (1)	19,600	3250	62	643	7.0	6.0	14,700	2200	71	623	4.0	3.5
WR Manor (2),(4)	20,750	4186	48	520	7.5	7.0	15,500	2100	71	510	4.0	4.0

(1) Self-cleaning smokebox.
(2) Non self-cleaning deflector plates.
(3) Multiple-jet blastpipe. No self-cleaning plates. 35,000lb steam/hour was maximum reached on test, but front end and grate limits were not established.
(4) Front end limit coincides with grate limit.

Overall Efficiency...Blidworth Grade 2B Coal...60 mph

		At front end limit					Under maximum sustained conditions			
		Efficiencies %					Efficiencies %			
Locomotive type	Steam rate lb/hr	Maximum cylinder	Boiler	Estimated mechanical	Overall	Steam rate lb/hr	Maximum cylinder	Boiler	Estimated mechanical	Overall
BR Cl 7 4-6-2	31,410	12.75	67	90	7.7	24,000	13.75	72	90	8.9
WR King 4-6-0	30,780	12.75	57	90	6.5	24,000	13.75	72	90	8.9
ER V2 2-6-2	31,000	12.50	58	90	6.5	24,000	13.75	72	90	8.9
SR Merchant Navy 4-6-2	35,000	11.60	50	90	6.3	24,000	12.00	68	90	7.4
						26,000	12.00	66	90	7.1
BR Cl 5 4-6-0	24,000	14.00	62	90	7.8	18,000	14.00	70	90	8.8
WR Hall 4-6-0	21,690	13.25	49	90	5.8	16,000	13.50	74	90	9.0
BR Cl 4 4-6-0	19,600	14.00	62	90	7.8	14,700	14.00	71	90	8.9
WR Manor 4-6-0	20,750	12.40	48	90	5.4	15,500	13.30	71	90	8.5

This table is reproduced by permission of the Council of the Institution of Mechanical Engineers from the *Journal of the Institution of Locomotive Engineers* Vol 44 (1954).

Appendix I

Leading Dimensions

Standard Class 9F 2-10-0

Class: 9F   Running numbers: 92000–92250
Wheel arrangement: 2-10-0
Wheel diameter (coupled):   5ft 0in
Axle load (coupled):

Tons Cwt	Tons Cwt	Tons Cwt	Tons Cwt	Tons Cwt
15 19	15 12	16 17	15 7	16 11

Bogie wheel diameter: 3ft 0in
Trailing wheel diameter: —
Bogie axle load:

Tons	Cwt
8	4

Trailing wheel axle load: —

Tender types(s):   BR1K (BR1B, BR1C, BR1F, BR1G)

Tender wheel diameter: 3ft 3½in
Tender axle load:

Tons Cwt	Tons Cwt	Tons Cwt
16 6	17 19	18 2

Cylinders: number – 2,
                        size 20in × 28in
Boiler type: BR9: Working pressure: 250lb/sq in
Boiler barrel diameter (o/s):   5ft 9in increasing to 6ft 1in
Boiler tubes: small: 138 (2in o/d × 11swg)
              large: 35 (5¼in o/d × 7swg)
Superheater elements: 1⅜in o/d × 9swg
Length between tubeplates: 15ft 3in
Heating surface:

tubes:	1836 sq ft
firebox:	179 sq ft
Total evaporative:	2015 sq ft

Superheater: 535 sq ft
Free flue area: 5.49 sq ft
Firebox (o/s): 7ft 5½in long × 7ft 0⅛in to 6ft 6^{7}/₁₆in wide
Grate area: 40.2 sq ft
Tractive effort: 39,667lb
Adhesion factory: 4.56
Brake % locomotive and tender: 69.5

Fuel Capacities: coal: 9 tons
                          water: 4,325 gallons

Weights:

	Full Tons Cwt		Empty Tons Cwt	
Locomotive:	88	10	79	16
Tender:	52	7	24	13
Total:	140	17	104	9

N.B.: These details are based on type BR1K tender; for details of axle loads and weights with alternative tenders see following data.

Additional data for alternative tender pairings

BR1B TENDER:

Axle loads:

Tons Cwt	Tons Cwt	Tons Cwt
17 2	17 1	17 2
(in working order)		

Total weights:

Full Tons Cwt		Empty Tons Cwt	
51	5	23	3

	Capacities	
	Coal	Water
	7 tons	4,725 gallons

BR1C TENDER:

	Tons Cwt	Tons Cwt	Tons Cwt
Axle loads:	17 18	17 15	17 12
	(in working order)		

Total weights:	*Full*	*Empty*
	Tons Cwt	Tons Cwt
	53 5	23 3

	Capacities	
	Coal	Water
	9 tons	4,725 gallons

BR1F TENDER:

	Tons Cwt	Tons Cwt	Tons Cwt
Axle loads:	18 1	18 8	18 8
	(in working order)		

Total weights:	*Full*	*Empty*
	Tons Cwt	Ton Cwt
	54 17	23 3

	Capacities	
	Coal	Water
	7 tons	5,625 gallons

BR1G TENDER:

	Tons Cwt	Tons Cwt	Tons Cwt
Axle loads:	16 10	17 10	18 10
	(in working order)		

Total weights:	*Full*	*Empty*
	Tons Cwt	Tons Cwt
	52 10	23 3

	Capacities	
	Coal	Water
	7 tons	5,000 gallons

NB: This last tender type was fitted with fall plate and gangway doors, these being the only differences between it and the BR1A type.

Standard Class 8P 4-6-2

Class: 8P   Running number and name:
  71000 *Duke of Gloucester*
Wheel arrangement: 4-6-2
Wheel diameter (coupled):   6ft 2in
Axle load (coupled):

Tons Cwt	*Tons Cwt*	*Tons Cwt*
22 0	22 0	22 0

Bogie wheel diameter: 3ft 0in
Trailing wheel diameter: 3ft 3½in
Bogie axle load:

Tons Cwt
19 2

Trailing wheel axle load:

Tons Cwt
16 3

Tender type(s):   BR1J (BR1E)
Tender wheel diameter: 3ft 3½in
Tender axle load:

Tons Cwt	*Tons Cwt*	*Tons Cwt*
17 18	17 18	17 18

Cylinders: number: 3
                                          size: 18in × 28in

Boiler type: BR13; Working pressure: 250lb/sq in
Boiler barrel diameter (o/s): 5ft 9in increasing to 6ft 5½in

Boiler tubes:	small:	136 (2⅛in o/d × 11swg)
	large:	40 (5½in o/d × 7swg)
Superheater elements:		1⅜in o/d × 9swg)

Length between tubeplates: 17ft 0in

Heating surface:	tubes:	2264 sq ft
	firebox:	226 sq ft
	Total evaporative:	2490 sq ft
	Superheater:	677 sq ft

Free flue area: 6.80 sq ft
Firebox (o/s): 8ft 0⅛in long × 7ft 9in to 7ft 4in wide
Grate area: 48.60 sq ft
Tractive effort: 39,080lb
Adhesion factor: 3.78
Brake % locomotive and tender: 51.17
Fuel capacities: coal: 10 tons
                             water: 4,325 gallons

Weights:		*Full*	*Empty*
		Tons Cwt	*Tons Cwt*
Locomotive:		101 5	92 0
Tender:		53 14	24 8
		154 19	116 8

NB: These details are based on type BR1J tender; for details of axle loads and weights with alternative type BR1E tender, see following data.

Additional data for alternative tender pairing

BR1E TENDER:

	Tons Cwt	*Tons Cwt*	*Tons Cwt*
Axle loads:	18 10	18 10	18 10
	(in working order)		

★Total weights:	*Full*	*Empty*
	Tons Cwt	*Tons Cwt*
	55 10	24 8

	Capacities	
	Coal	Water
	10 tons	4,725 gallons

★Includes weight of coal pusher fitted to this tender.

Standard Class 7MT 4-6-2

Class: 7MT   Running numbers 70000–70054
Wheel arrangement: 4-6-2
Wheel diameter (coupled):   6ft 2in
Axle load (coupled):

Tons Cwt	*Tons Cwt*	*Tons Cwt*
20 5	20 5	20 5

Bogie wheel diameter: 3ft 0in
Trailing wheel diameter: 3ft 3½in

Bogie axle load:

Tons Cwt
17 2

Trailing wheel axle load:

Tons Cwt
16 3

Tender type(s):   BR1 (BR1A, BR1D)
Tender wheel diameter: 3ft 3½in

Tender axle load:

Tons	Cwt	Tons	Cwt	Tons	Cwt
16	10	17	10	18	10

Cylinders: number: 2
size: 20in × 28in

Boiler type: BR1; Working pressure: 250lb/sq in
Boiler barrel diameter (o/s): 5ft 9in increasing to 6ft 5½in
Boiler tubes: small: 136 (2⅛in o/d × 11swg)
large: 40 (5¼in o/d × × 7swg)
Superheater elements: 1⅜in o/d × 10swg
Length between tubeplates: 17ft 0in

Heating surface: tubes: 2264 sq ft
firebox: 210 sq ft

Total evaporative: 2474 sq ft

Superheater: 718 sq ft

Free flue area: 6.8 sq ft
Firebox (o/s): 7ft 0in long × 7ft 9in to 7ft 4in wide
Grate area: 42 sq ft
Tractive effort: 32,150lb
Adhesion factor: 4.23
Brake % locomotive and tender: 53.4
Capacities: coal: 7 tons
water: 4,250 gallons

Weights:	Full Tons Cwt		Empty Tons Cwt	
Locomotive:	94	00	85	03
Tender	49	03	23	03
Total	143	03	108	06

NB: These details are based on type BR1 tender; for details of axle loads and weights with alternative tenders, see following data.

Additional data for alternative tender pairings

BR1A TENDER:

	Tons	Cwt	Tons	Cwt	Tons	Cwt
Axle loads:	16	10	17	10	18	10

(in working order)

Total weights:	Full Tons Cwt		Empty Tons Cwt	
	52	10	23	03

Capacities	
Coal	Water
7 tons	5,000 gallons

BR1D TENDER:

	Tons	Cwt	Tons	Cwt	Tons	Cwt
Axle loads:	17	10	18	10	18	10

Total weights:	Full Tons Cwt		Empty Tons Cwt	
	54	10	24	08

Capacities	
Coal	Water
9 tons	4,725 gallons

Standard Class 6MT 4-6-2

Class: 6MT Running numbers: 72000–72009
Wheel arrangement: 4-6-2
Wheel diameter (coupled): 6ft 2in

Axle load (coupled):

Tons	Cwt	Tons	Cwt	Tons	Cwt
18	18	19	00	19	00

Bogie wheel diameter: 3ft 0in
Trailing wheel diameter: 3ft 3½in
Bogie axle load:

Tons	Cwt
16	04

Trailing wheel axle load:

Tons	Cwt
15	08

Tender type: BR1
Tender wheel diameter: 3ft 3½in
Tender axle load:

Tons	Cwt	Tons	Cwt	Tons	Cwt
16	08	16	12	16	03

Cylinders: number: 2
size: 19½in × 28in

Boiler type: BR1; Working pressure 225lb/sq in
Boiler barrel diameter(o/s): 5ft 4in increasing to 6ft 1in
Boiler tubes: small: 108 (2⅛in o/d × 11swg)
large: 35 (5½in o/d × 7swg)
Superheater elements: 1⅜in × 9swg
Length between tubeplates: 17ft 0in

Heating surface: tubes: 1878 sq ft
firebox: 195 sq ft

Total evaporative: 2073 sq ft

Superheater: 592 sq ft

Free flue area: 5.73 sq ft
Firebox (o/s): 6ft 9in long × 7ft 0in to 6ft 8in wide
Grate area: 36 sq ft
Tractive effort: 27,520lb
Adhesion factor: 4.63
Brake % locomotive and tender: 49.9
Fuel capacities: coal: 7 tons
water: 4,250 gallons

Weights:	Full Tons Cwt		Empty Tons Cwt	
Locomotive:	88	10	79	16
Tender:	49	03	23	03
Total:	137	13	104	01

Standard Class 5MT 4-6-0

Class: 5MT Running numbers: 73000–73171
Wheel arrangement: 4-6-0
Wheel diameter (coupled): 6ft 2in
Axle load (coupled):

Tons	Cwt	Tons	Cwt	Tons	Cwt
18	16	19	14	19	11

Bogie wheel diameter: 3ft 0in
Trailing wheel diameter: —
Bogie axle load:

Tons	Cwt
17	19

Trailing wheel axle load: —

Tender type(s): BR1 (BR1B, BR1C, BR1F, BR1G, BR1H)
Tender wheel diameter: 3ft 3½in

Tender axle load:

Tons	Cwt	Tons	Cwt	Tons	Cwt
16	08	16	12	16	03

Cylinders: number: 2
                                              size: 19in × 28in
Boiler type: BR3; Working pressure: 225lb/sq in
Boiler barrel diameter (o/s):
    4ft 11¹¹⁄₁₆in increasing to 5ft 8½in
Boiler tubes: small: 151 (1⅞in o/d × 11swg)
                       large: 28 (5⅛in o/d × 7swg)
Superheater elements: 1⅜in o/d × 9swg
Length between tubeplates: 13ft 2⅞in
Heating surfaces: tubes: 1479 sq ft
                       firebox: 171 sq ft

                       Total evaporative: 1650 sq ft

                       Superheater: 358 sq ft

Free flue area: 4.5 sq ft
Firebox (o/s):   9ft 2¹³⁄₁₆in long × 3ft 11⅞in wide
Grate area: 28.7 sq ft
Tractive effort: 26,120lb
Adhesion factor: 4.97
Brake % locomotive and tender: 60.7
Fuel capacities: coal: 7 tons
                           water: 4,250 gallons

Weights:	Full		Empty	
	Tons	Cwt	Tons	Cwt
Locomotive:	76	00	69	05
Tender:	49	03	23	03
Total:	125	03	92	08

NB: These details are based on the type BR1 tender; for
details of axle loads and weights with alternative
tenders; see following data.

Additional data for alternative tender pairings

BR1B TENDER:	Tons	Cwt	Tons	Cwt	Tons	Cwt
Axle loads:	17	02	17	01	17	02
(in working order)						

Total weights:	Full		Empty	
	Tons	Cwt	Tons	Cwt
	51	05	23	03

	Capacities	
Coal		Water
7 tons		4,725 gallons

BR1C TENDER:	Tons	Cwt	Tons	Cwt	Tons	Cwt
Axle loads:	17	18	17	15	17	12
(in working order)						

Total weights:	Full		Empty	
	Tons	Cwt	Tons	Cwt
	53	05	23	03

	Capacities	
Coal		Water
9 tons		4,725 gallons

BR1F TENDER:	Tons	Cwt	Tons	Cwt	Tons	Cwt
Axle loads:	18	01	18	08	18	08
(in working order)						

Total weights	Full		Empty	
	Tons	Cwt	Tons	Cwt
	54	17	23	03

	Capacities	
Coal		Water
7 tons		5,625 gallons

BR1G TENDER:	Tons	Cwt	Tons	Cwt	Tons	Cwt
Axle loads:	16	10	17	10	18	10
(in working order)						

Total weights:	Full		Empty	
	Tons	Cwt	Tons	Cwt
	52	10	23	03

	Capacities	
Coal		Water
7 tons		5,000 gallons

BR1H TENDER:	Tons	Cwt	Tons	Cwt	Tons	Cwt
Axle loads:	16	08	16	12	16	03
(in working order)						

Total weights:	Full		Empty	
	Tons	Cwt	Tons	Cwt
	49	03	23	03

	Capacities	
Coal		Water
7 tons		4,250 gallons

Standard Class 4MT 4-6-0

Class: 4MT   Running numbers: 75000–75079
Wheel arrangement: 4-6-0
Wheel diameter (coupled): 5ft 8in
Axle load (coupled):

Tons	Cwt	Tons	Cwt	Tons	Cwt
17	05	17	01	17	05

Bogie wheel diameter: 3ft 0in
Bogie axle load:

Tons	Cwt
16	07

Trailing wheel diameter: —
Tender type(s):   BR2 (BR2A, BR1B)
Tender wheel diameter: 3ft 3½in
Tender axle load:

Tons	Cwt	Tons	Cwt	Tons	Cwt
15	02	13	09	13	12

Cylinders: number: 2
                              size: 18in × 28in
Boiler type: BR4; Working pressure: 225lb/sq in
Boiler barrel diameter (o/s): 4ft 9in increasing to 5ft 3in
Boiler tubes: small: 157 (1¾in o/d × 12swg)
                       large: 21 (5⅛in o/d × 7swg)
Superheater elements: 1⅜in o/d × 9swg
Length between tubeplates: 13ft 0in
Heating surface: tubes: 1301 sq ft
                       firebox: 143 sq ft

                       Total evaporative: 1444 sq ft

                       Superheater: 258 sq ft

Free flue area: 3.78 sq ft
Firebox (o/s):   8ft 6in long × 4ft 0½in wide

Grate area:	26.7 sq ft	
Tractive effort:	25,515lb	
Adhesion factor:	4.52	
Brake % locomotive and tender:	55.1	
Fuel capacities:	coal:	6 tons
	water:	3,500 gallons

Weights:

	Full		Empty	
	Tons	Cwt	Tons	Cwt
Locomotive:	67	18	63	06
Tender:	42	03	20	10
Total:	110	01	83	16

NB: These details are based on type BR2 tender; for details of axle loads and weights with alternative tenders, see following data.

Additional data for alternative tender pairings

BR2A TENDER:

	Tons	Cwt	Tons	Cwt	Tons	Cwt
Axle loads:	15	02	13	09	13	12

(in working order)

Total weights:

Full		Empty	
Tons	Cwt	Tons	Cwt
42	03	20	10

Capacities	
Coal	Water
6 tons	3,500 gallons

BR1B TENDER:

	Tons	Cwt	Tons	Cwt	Tons	Cwt
Axle loads:	17	02	17	01	17	02

(in working order)

Total weights:

Full		Empty	
Tons	Cwt	Tons	Cwt
51	05	23	03

Capacities	
Coal	Water
7 tons	4,725 gallons

Standard Class 4MT 2-6-0

Class: 4MT   Running numbers: 76000–76114
Wheel arrangement: 2-6-0
Wheel diameter (coupled):   5ft 3in
Axle load (coupled):

Tons	Cwt	Tons	Cwt	Tons	Cwt
16	13	16	19	16	17

Bogie wheel diameter: 3ft 0in
Bogie axle load:

Tons	Cwt
9	06

Trailing wheel diameter: —
Trailing wheel axle load: —
Tender type(s):   BR2 (BR2A, BR1B)
Tender wheel diameter: 3ft 3½in
Tender axle load:

Tons	Cwt	Tons	Cwt	Tons	Cwt
15	02	13	09	13	12

Cylinders:	number: 2
	size: 17½in × 26in

Boiler type: BR7;   Working pressure: 225lb/sq in

Boiler barrel diameter (o/s):	4ft 9½in increasing to 5ft 3in	
Boiler tubes:	small:	156 (1⅜in o/d × 12swg)
	large:	24 (5⅛in o/d × 7swg)
Superheater elements:		1⅜in o/d × 9swg)
Length between tubeplates:	10ft 10½in	
Heating surface:	tubes:	1075 sq ft
	firebox:	131 sq ft
Total evaporative:		1206 sq ft
Superheater:		247 sq ft

Free flue area:	3.8 sq ft
Firebox (o/s):	7ft 6in long × 4ft 0½in wide
Grate area:	23 sq ft
Tractive effort:	24,170lb
Adhesion factor:	4.68
Brake % locomotive and tender:	63.75
Fuel capacities:	coal: 6 tons
	water: 3,500 gallons

Weights:

	Full		Empty		
	Tons	Cwt	Tons	Cwt	Qr
Locomotive:	59	15	55	18	02
Tender:	42	03	20	10	02
Total:	101	18	76	09	00

NB: These details are based on type BR2 tender; details of axle loads and weights with alternative tenders, see data following.

Additional data for alternative tender pairings

BR2A TENDER:

	Tons	Cwt	Tons	Cwt	Tons	Cwt
Axle loads:	15	02	13	09	13	12

Total weights:

Full		Empty	
Tons	Cwt	Tons	Cwt
42	03	20	10

Capacities	
Coal	Water
6 tons	3,500 gallons

BR1B TENDER:

	Tons	Cwt	Tons	Cwt	Tons	Cwt
Axle loads:	17	02	17	01	17	02

Total weights:

Full		Empty	
Tons	Cwt	Tons	Cwt
51	05	23	03

Capacities	
Coal	Water
7 tons	4,725 gallons

Standard Class 3MT 2-6-0

Class: 3MT   Running numbers: 77000–77019
Wheel arrangement: 2-6-0
Wheel diameter (coupled):   5ft 3in

Axle load (coupled):

Tons Cwt	Tons Cwt	Tons Cwt
16 2	16 5	16 3

Bogie wheel diameter: 3ft 0in
Trailing wheel diameter: —
Bogie axle load:

	Tons Cwt
	9 0

Trailing wheel axle load: —
Tender type):   BR2A
Tender wheel diameter: 3ft 3½in
Tender axle load:

Tons Cwt	Tons Cwt	Tons Cwt
15 2	13 9	13 12

Cylinders: number: 2
                                 size: 17½in × 26in
Boiler type: BR6; Working pressure: 200lb/sq in
Boiler tubes: small: 143 (1⅜in o/d × 12swg)
                    large: 18 (5⅛in o/d ×   7swg)
Superheater elements: 1⅜in o/d × 9swg
Length between tubeplates: 10ft 10½in
Heating surface: tubes: 923.54 sq ft
                       firebox: 118.42 sq ft

Total evaporative:	1041.96 sq ft
Superheater:	184.50 sq ft

Free flue area: 3.054 sq ft
Firebox (o/s): 7ft 0in long by 4ft 0in wide
Grate area: 20.35 sq ft
Tractive effort: 21,490lb
Adhesion factor: 5.05
Brake % locomotive and tender: 60.7
Fuel capacities: coal: 6 tons
                          water: 3,500 gallons
Weights: Full   Empty
                          Tons Cwt   Tons Cwt
    Locomotive: 57   10   53   00
    Tender: 42   03   20   10

99	13	73	10

Standard Class 2MT 2-6-0

Class: 2MT Running numbers: 78000–78064
Wheel arrangement: 2-6-0
Wheel diameter (coupled):   5ft 0in
Axle load (coupled):

Tons Cwt	Tons Cwt	Tons Cwt
13 15	13 12	13 03

Bogie wheel diameter: 3ft 0in
Trailing wheel diameter: —
Bogie axle load:

	Tons Cwt
	8 15

Trailing wheel axle load: —
Tender type: BR3
Tender wheel diameter: 3ft 3½in
Tender axle load:

Tons Cwt	Tons Cwt	Tons Cwt
13 15	11 16	11 06

Cylinders: number: 2
                                 size: 16½in × 24in
Boiler type: BR8; Working pressure: 200lb/sq in
Boiler barrel diameter (o/s):   4ft 3in increasing to 4ft 8in
Boiler tubes: small: 162 (1⅜in o/d × 12swg)
                    large: 12 (5⅛in o/d ×   7swg)

Superheater elements: 1⅜in o/d × 9swg
Length between tubeplates: 10ft 10½in
Heating surface: tubes: 924 sq ft
                       firebox: 101 sq ft

Total evaporative:	1025 sq ft
Superheater:	124 sq ft

Free flue area: 2.77 sq ft
Firebox (o/s): 5ft 11in long × 4ft 0³/₁₆in
Grate area: 17.5 sq ft
Tractive effort: 18,513lb
Adhesion factor: 4.9
Brake % locomotive and tender: 60.23
Fuel capacities: coal: 4 tons
                          water: 3,000 gallons
Weights: Full   Empty
                          Tons Cwt   Tons Cwt
    Locomotive: 49   05   45   08
    Tender: 36   17   19   09

86	02	64	17

Standard Class 4MT 2-6-4T

Class: 4MT Running numbers: 80000–80154
Wheel arrangement: 2-6-4T
Wheel diameter (coupled): 5ft 8in
Axle load (coupled):

Tons Cwt	Tons Cwt	Tons Cwt
17 07	17 19	17 15

Pony truck wheel diameter: 3ft 0in
Trailing truck wheel diameter: 3ft 0in
Bogie axle load:

	Tons Cwt
	13 02

Trailing truck load:

	Tons Cwt
	20 10

Tender type(s):   —
Tender wheel diameter: —
Tender axle load: —
Cylinders: number: 2
                                 size: 18in × 28in
Boiler type: ABR5; Working pressure: 225lb/sq in
Boiler barrel diameter (o/s):   4ft 9in increasing to 5ft 3in
Boiler tubes: small: 157 (1¾in o/d × 12swg)
                    large: 21 (5⅜in o/d ×   7swg)
Superheater elements: 1⅜in o/d × 9swg
Length between tubeplates: 12ft 3in
Heating surface: tubes: 1223 sq ft
                       firebox: 143 sq ft

Total evaporative.	1366 sq ft
Superheater:	240 sq ft

Free flue area: 3.78 sq ft
Firebox (o/s): 8ft 6in long by 4ft 0½in wide
Grate area: 26.7 sq ft
Tractive effort: 25,515lb
Adhesion factor: 4.65
Brake force % locomotive
    and tender: 44.2
Fuel capacities: coal: 3½ tons
                          water: 2,000 gallons

Weights:	*Full*		*Empty*	
	Tons Cwt		*Tons Cwt*	
Locomotive:	86	13	69	08

Standard Class 3MT 2-6-2T

Class: 3MT Running numbers: 82000–82044
Wheel arrangement: 2-6-2T
Wheel diameter (coupled): 5ft 3in
Axle load (coupled):

Tons Cwt	*Tons Cwt*	*Tons Cwt*
16 06	16 06	16 03

Pony truck wheel diameter: 3ft 0in
Trailing truck wheel diameter: 3ft 0in
Pony truck axle load:

Tons Cwt
12   13

Trailing truck axle load:

Tons Cwt
12   13

Tender type(s):   —
Tender wheel diameter: —
Tender axle load: —
Cylinders: number: 2
                         size: 17½in × 26in
Boiler type: BR6; Working pressure: 200lb/sq in
Boiler barrel diameter (o/s): 4ft 5in increasing to 5ft 0½in
Boiler tubes: small: 143 (1⅝in o/d × 12swg)
                  large: 18 (5⅛in o/d × 7swg)
Superheater elements: 1⅜in o/d × 9swg
Length between tubeplates: 10ft 10½in

Heating surface:	tubes:	923.54 sq ft
	firebox:	118.42 sq ft
	Total evaporative:	1041.96 sq ft
	Superheater:	184.50 sq ft

Free flue area: 3.054 sq ft
Firebox (o/s): 7ft 0in long by 4ft 0in wide
Grate area: 20.35 sq ft
Tractive effort: 21,490lb
Adhesion factor: 5.08
Brake force %:   51.5
Fuel capacities: coal: 3 tons
                          water: 1,500 gallons

Weights:	*Full*		*Empty*	
	Tons Cwt		*Tons Cwt*	
Locomotive:	74	01	60	18

Standard Class 2MT 2-6-2T

Class: 2MT Running numbers: 84000–84029
Wheel arrangement: 2-6-2T
Wheel diameter (coupled): 5ft 0in
Axle load (coupled):

Tons Cwt	*Tons Cwt*	*Tons Cwt*
13 12	14 00	13 13

Pony truck wheel diameter: 3ft 0in
Trailing truck wheel diameter: 3ft 0in
Pony truck axle load:

Tons Cwt
12   10

Trailing truck axle load:

Tons Cwt
12   10

Tender type(s):   —
Tender wheel diameter: —
Tender axle load: —
Cylinders: number: 2
                         size: 16½in × 24in
Boiler type: BR8; Working pressure: 200lb/sq in
Boiler barrel diameter (o/s): 4ft 3in increasing to 4ft 8in
Boiler tubes: small: 162 (1⅝in o/d × 12swg)
                  large: 12 (5⅛in o/d × 7swg)
Superheater elements: 1⅜in o/d × 9swg
Length between tubeplates: 10ft 10½in

Heating surface:	tubes:	924 sq ft
	firebox:	101 sq ft
	Total evaporative:	1025 sq ft
	Superheater:	124 sq ft

Free flue area: 2.77 sq ft
Firebox (o/s): 5ft 11in long by 4ft 0⁷/₁₆in wide
Grate area: 17.5 sq ft
Tractive effort: 18,513lb
Adhesion factor: 5.0
Brake force %:   47
Fuel capacities: coal: 3 tons
                          water: 1,350 gallons

Weights:	*Full*		*Empty*	
	Tons Cwt		*Tons Cwt*	
Locomotive:	66	05	53	12

British Railways Standard Locomotive Tenders

Tender Nos	Type	Locomotives to which allocated Class	Running Nos	Tender Nos	Type	Locomotives to which allocated Class	Running Nos
759– 783	BR1	7MT 4-6-0	70000–70024	1156–1165	BR1F	9F 2-10-0	92067–92076
784– 793	BR1	6MT 4-6-2	72000–72009	1166–1175	BR1C	9F 2-10-0	92077–92086
794– 823	BR1	5MT 4-6-0	73000–73029	1176–1185	BR1F	9F 2-10-0	92087–92096
824– 843	BR2	4MT 4-6-0	75000–75019	1206–1215	BR1B	5MT 4-6-0	73080–73089
844– 848	BR1A	7MT 4-6-2	70025–70029	1226–1233	BR2A	4MT 2-6-0	76045–76052
849– 863	BR1	7MT 4-6-2	70030–70044	1234–1250	BR1B	4MT 2-6-0	76053–76069
864– 883	BR1	5MT 4-6-0	73030–73049	1251–1255	BR2A	4MT 2-6-0	76070–76074
884– 913	BR2	4MT 4-6-0	75020–75049	1261–1270	BR3	2MT 2-6-0	78045–78054
914– 933	BR2	4MT 2-6-0	76000–76019	1271	BR1E	8P 4-6-2	71000
934– 938	BR2	4MT 2-6-0	76020–76024	1272–1281	BR1C	5MT 4-6-0	73090–73099
939– 948	BR3	2MT 2-6-0	78000–78009	1282–1291	BR1B	5MT 4-6-0	73100–73109
949– 958	BR1G	9F 2-10-0	92000–92009	1292–1301	BR1F	5MT 4-6-0	73110–73119
959– 963	BR1F	9F 2-10-0	92010–92014	1302–1306	BR1B	5MT 4-6-0	73120–73124
964– 968	BR1C	9F 2-10-0	92015–92019	1307–1309	BR1B	9F 2-10-0	92097–92099
969– 978	BR1B	9F 2-10-0	92020–92029	1310–1349	BR1C	9F 2-10-0	92100–92139
979– 988	BR1D	7MT 4-6-2	70045–70054	1350–1359	BR1F	9F 2-10-0	92140–92149
989– 991	BR1G	5MT 4-6-0	73050–73052	1360–1377	BR1C	9F 2-10-0	92150–92167
992–1003	BR1H	5MT 4-6-0	73053–73064	1378–1412	BR1F	9F 2-10-0	92168–92202
1004–1013	BR1C	5MT 4-6-0	73065–73079	1413–1422	BR1B	5MT 4-6-0	73125–73134
1014–1028	BR2A	4MT 4-6-0	75050–75064	1423–1432	BR1C	5MT 4-6-0	73135–73144
1029–1043	BR1B	4MT 4-6-0	75065–75079	1433–1459	BR1B	5MT 4-6-0	73145–73171
1044–1063	BR2A	4MT 2-6-0	76025–76044	1460–1499	BR2A	4MT 2-6-0	76075–76114
1064–1083	BR2A	3MT 2-6-0	77000–77019	1500–1509	BR3	2MT 2-6-0	78055–78064
1084–1118	BR3	2MT 2-6-0	78010–78044	1510–1527	BR1G	9F 2-10-0	92203–92220
1119–1133	BR1F	9F 2-10-0	92030–92044	1532–1561	BR1G	9F 2-10-0	92221–92250
1134–1148	BR1C	9F 2-10-0	92045–92059	1528	BR1J	8P 4-6-2	71000
1149–1155	BR1B	9F 2-10-0	92060–92066				

Notes:

1. In addition to the tenders listed, with their original locomotive pairings, the following were allocated to locomotives which were subsequently cancelled from building programmes:

   BR1 No 1186–1200, for Class 6MT 4-6-2s Nos 72010–72024

   BR2A Nos 1216–1225, for Class 4MT 4-6-0s Nos 75080–75089

   BR2A Nos 1256–1260, for Class 3MT 2-6-0s Nos 77020–77024

2. In November 1957 the BR1E tender No 1271, paired with the solitary Class 8P Pacific No 71000, was replaced by BR1J tender No 1528, then newly built. The earlier tender No 1271 was modified to BR1C and fitted to Class 9F 2-10-0 No 92150.

Index